UNBREAKABLE

A Navy SEAL's Way of Life

Thom Shea

Clovercroft Publishing

ENDORSEMENTS
The Masters of the Five Pyramids of Human Performance

PHYSICAL MASTERY

"Thom Shea is a real hero, who delved deeply into himself to dedicate himself to the most noble of goals: Human Performance. Valor is the right term for his service, courage, and true bravery."

—Dr. Wayne Andersen, author of *Habits of Health*

INTELLECTUAL MASTERY

"*Unbreakable* is the raw inside story of what it is like to thrive and excel in the Margin of war. The parallels are clear in the corporate world, especially as an entrepreneur. Internal Dialogue does drive all human performance. If you want to learn what it is to succeed in the Margin while maintaining balance with a wife or significant other and family, read *Unbreakable*."

—Carl Stecker, CEO of Net Profit Advisors and Benefits In A Card

WEALTH MASTERY

"*Unbreakable* is a treasure. Navy Seals are Americans who lead us from the front. They are the best in the world. Thom Shea and his wife, Stacy, unveil a riveting insight into exactly how they not only survived unimaginable challenges, but prospered. Their book is a riveting lesson from their hearts to their children and to all of us. Initially, people will want to read this book out of curiosity, but then they will be knocked out by its message that builds success in every category. Personally, I am so thankful for the Sheas' clear message for all Americans and our free enterprise system."

—Leighton M. Cubbage, Chairman, Serrus Capital Partners, Greenville, SC

Spiritual Mastery

"I'm a raving fan of *Unbreakable.* It not only is a powerful story of an amazing human being and his 25 years as a Navy SEAL, but it also provides a powerful self-development tool. Let Thom Shea teach you about Internal Dialogue—what you say to yourself about who you are—and how managing that dialogue can increase your goal achievement and effectiveness in life."

—Ken Blanchard, coauthor of *The One Minute Manager*® and *Leading at a Higher Level*

Relationship Mastery

"Thom Shea captures the key to communication in his book *Unbreakable.* He introduces the power of Internal Dialogue and its exceptional effectiveness in creating and maintaining healthy relationships. Thom Shea provides real insight and clarity with the use of his personal experiences as a Navy SEAL on the battlefield, as an athlete in extreme adventure racing, and in the privacy of his home with his wife and children. This book will be proven invaluable to anyone who wants to better themselves and the relationships in their lives."

—Tamara Johnson, MS, MFT/PhD

CONTENTS

INTRODUCTION

UNBREAKABLE: A NAVY SEAL'S WAY OF LIFE

In each word and section of this book, I have been tasked with telling my story, so should I die in combat, my children will get a sense of their father. Actually, my wife, Stacy, pleaded with me for two years to put to words *who* I am and *how* I am. Therefore, this project is not simply a day-to-day recount of all I've done, but rather a retelling of what I faced and what I learned in order to teach my children (and anyone interested) how to *be* the men and women who live the fullest possibilities they create for themselves. Simply put, being "Unbreakable" is creating and finding a language in yourself that will give you access to your own possibilities. Above all else, this project is a way to make up for being gone 220 days per year for twenty-five years as a Navy SEAL.

This book contains no hidden secrets. It is a painstaking study of my experiences in striving for excellence, which I share with you. I have learned what traits and habits are effective and efficient in pursuit of personal transformation in order to perform above and beyond what humans think possible.

My children . . . when you are ready to read *Unbreakable* and put it to use, you will recognize a pattern in each section. I wish I could tell you how to know when you are ready; however, that would truly deny you the benefit you receive by making the discovery in your own way.

When you get discouraged, when you have difficulty overcoming the obstacles draining your soul, when you try and fail, or when you feel reduced by injuries, use this book as a light to guide you through the forest. A strange thing will happen when you acquire and apply the lessons shared in this text . . . you will be propelled to unfathomable success.

We cannot achieve success without first enduring countless hours of practice. While reading *Unbreakable*, you'll learn about something I call "Internal Dialogue." Internal Dialogue is a trait common to all successful people, whether they know it or not. In fact, the practice of Internal Dialogue is the single-most important factor in bridging your genetic gifts, passions, and dreams. I will show you how to consciously use Internal Dialogue to your advantage . . . even if I do not return.

It's important to remember that Internal Dialogue is available only to those who are actively pursuing their passions. In other words, you must have something you are wildly committed to *being* or *doing* with your life. The gift of mastering your Internal Dialogue cannot be given away for free, nor can it be bought. The most dangerous or useless gift is one bought or given without being earned.

An Internal Dialogue to create an unbreakable condition will serve each of you equally well—when you are ready. Trust me on this—education has nothing to do with it.

Who am I to say that in reading this book you will know, grasp solidly, the use of Internal Dialogue? I have spent twenty-five years living and researching what it takes to overcome any obstacle in the way of success. I have survived countless overwhelming combat engagements and failures that tested and validated the use of my own Internal Dialogue to live an "Unbreakable Life." I have personally taught 330 basic SEAL students, and 112 SEAL sniper students, testing the use of an unbreakable Internal Dialogue to perform beyond what I thought possible.

I have never known a single person who used Internal Dialogue who did not achieve remarkable success. I have never known anyone to distinguish themselves, or to survive overwhelming battles, without possession of an unbreakable Internal Dialogue. For these reasons, I conclude the experience and education gained using an unbreakable Internal Dialogue is more important, as a part of the human paradigm to create a better life, than anything one learns through the standard educational system.

As you read, your own Unbreakable Internal Dialogue will jump from the pages and stand boldly in front of you. When you are ready to use it, you will see it. When your Internal Dialogue pops out, I want you to stop and drink a Guinness for me, because it will signify the most important turning point in your life.

Take note: I will be sharing my life for you—the facts, the failures, the "me," so to speak. Through my eyes and experiences, I hope to convey the *who* to be and *how* to be!

Finally, I offer two suggestions: don't fear the need to achieve anything, and never give up . . . **never**. All great accomplishments, all earned awards, start with an Internal Dialogue that needs to be fulfilled . . . *needs* to be *needed*.

PREFACE

Shortly after we were married in 2005, Thom checked into SEAL Team Seven. Being a new member of the community, I was unsure what to expect. Everyone knows the danger involved in his line of work. I felt strongly he should put to paper the lessons he would want shared with our kids if he didn't survive the war. I'm not talking about a farewell letter, which many of our men write to each of their children and their wives before they leave, in case they don't survive. I'm talking about a guide-book for the rest of their lives if they should have to carry on without the strength and mentoring of a father—*their* father.

From the time I first met Thom, I saw something in him that was clearly unbreakable, somewhat un-tethered, and massively appealing. In all my broken relationships of the past, this was the one quality I had longed for, and here it was in front of me. I wanted to preserve this for our children, knowing all too well they faced the possibility of knowing their father only in stories of who he was to me and to the men he worked with in the Teams. I needed him to translate for us, especially the kids, all the things he thought were important—all the things which made him the man who made me, and our family, whole.

In April of 2009, he deployed again with SEAL Team Seven. This time, he went to Afghanistan. He was part of the first element of SEALs sent to fight in Afghanistan since the tragedy of Operation Red Wings in June of 2005. For a warrior like Thom, this represented the culmination of a career serving his nation spanning nearly twenty years. As his wife and the mother of his children, it represented an opportunity for me to find what was unbreakable in our character.

I asked Thom to chronicle these things because I wanted what every woman wants for her children: for their father to teach them the lessons only a father can teach. The things I wanted to know from my father—like how to get through the tough times in life without giving up on commit-ments or blaming other people. I wanted them to know at their core they have a say in their lives and can create whatever life they want. I wanted them to learn to be powerful in the face of the overwhelming challenges life will inevitably hand them—to be generous in the face of stinginess and to be loving in the face of all the hostilities the world would present to them. I wanted them to be tough.

—*Stacy Shea*

We had corresponded with Thom and Stacy during his deployment in order to reach out and help a family who truly needed our help. We recognized all human beings truly need to be needed, at both the genetic/evolutionary level and during the "real life" times we all have. We were also dramatically impacted by our involvement with Thom and Stacy. After the 2009 deployment, we chaired the SEAL gala in Greenville, South Carolina, so we could give back to the men who keep us all safe and free.

—*Tammy and Jerry Barber*

SECTION ONE

UNBREAKABLE

CHIEF SEATTLE (a fictionalized speech written in 1971)
"And when the last Red Man shall have perished, and the memory of my tribe shall have become a myth among the White Man, these shores will swarm with the invisible dead of my tribe, and when your children's children think themselves alone in the field, the store, the shop, upon the roads, or in the silence of the pathless woods, they will not be alone. In all the earth there is no place dedicated to solitude. At night, when the streets of your cities and villages are silent and you think them deserted, they will throng with the returning hosts that once filled them and still love this beautiful land. The White Man will never be alone."

Adamantine: (ad·a·man·tahyn)
The reason I have settled on the word Adamantine is for the context it creates. Adamantine literally means a thing that is not tangible but when it is consumed makes anything Unbreakable. No more fitting meaning to one single word could capture the power of mastering Internal Dialogue.

As I sit in my study looking at the calligraphy of this quote which my father, a professional calligrapher, made for me, written in the blood of a deer I shot long ago, it occurs to me how fitting the quote is as I leave for war. I realize this may be the last time I will see my wife and kids—not to mention the land I love.

Stacy asked me to write down what I am doing and experiencing, for her and for my kids, to teach essential life lessons. Like Chief Seattle, I must let go of my life here, yet I want my children to be filled forever with the warrior song I am singing, and also that, as Chief Seattle put it, "The

White Man will never be alone." He meant it in a different context, but for me, my writing will ensure my wife and children will never be alone. This is my bequest to them.

I want to explain how distant and stressed I am. My stress is different from the kind you experience. I have been in so many battles and risked my life so many times that stress, while there, it doesn't control my performance. I do regret the toll it's taken on my family these last two days as they prepare to watch me board a plane that may take me away forever. Especially for kids: it is like tearing out part of your soul when your daddy sits next to you that final night around the dinner table, and you try not to cry or even mention your thoughts. I understand.

Looking into their eyes and realizing I might never see them again, or be around when they need me later in life, was the hardest. I tried to let them cry, and I tried to cry myself, but years of leaving for combat makes me distant and often angry. When I am angry, I tend to yell. I think yelling makes leaving easier. I regret my frequent distance and anger.

Here I am, going to what may be my final battle, to the most dangerous place on earth, knowing I may not see my children again. As my three kids, the last of the Shea clan, read this, I want them to know what happened with their mother, Stacy, and me the night before I left. We lay beside each other, silent. I could not bear the thought of never seeing her again, and she must have known what I was thinking.

As I tried to speak, she reached up and put her hands on my face. The light from the window behind her outlined her long flowing hair that covered her body. Our eyes met, and we just looked at each other, not speaking, for ten minutes. Then she said something that will always resonate in my mind:

Thom, I need you to come back to us. Do not fear dying. Fear makes you weak.

Sharing my life with you is only part of my project. Adamantine—tough and hard, the opposite of fear and weakness—is my true gift to you: the gift of quality thinking—the control of your Internal Dialogue. You will have to search and work for it all your life. I will explain how I discovered and realized the power of being unbreakable. I call it "Adamantine." I will teach you how to attain it for yourself.

Reading and understanding this will be tough for you, my children; even harder will be attempting to accomplish many of the things I will ask you to do without me. As Stacy said to me that last night—it also holds true for each you kids individually:

Thom, I need you to come back to us. Do not fear dying. Fear makes you weak.

I need you, my children, to never give up. Do not fear dying. Fear makes you weak. I need you to fight through the obstacles that would stop you from becoming the men and woman you ARE . . . fearless and strong.

You can control fear if you can control the words in your thoughts. Your Internal Dialogue, what you tell yourselves every conscious moment, is the source of power when properly controlled, but it's also the source of weakness if you lose control. You will learn this by reading this book.

As you children grow into adulthood, my dream for you, individually, is to be among the few extraordinary people who master their own Internal Dialogue, so you can perform beyond what is thought possible, and become reliable partners and family. Internal Dialogue controls everyone's actions, but only a few people spend the time essential for mastery—maybe one in five, or one in ten, or even fewer. For those who can master Internal Dialogue, the possibilities are limitless.

So, I have a request of you, my family, in case I do not return. My request will engage your physical bodies and enable you to master your Internal Dialogue, but the task is not simple and is in a place so hard to reach that few have gone there. When you arrive, you'll be in the most beautiful place you've ever seen. This place is not just a metaphor. Between two pristine lakes in Ontario, Canada, lies a waterfall. In the center is a naturally formed bathtub where I want you to strip down, get in, and let the water cascade over you . . . go in the heat of summer. Most importantly, I want you to take my ashes and pour them in the top of Louisa Falls. I will be waiting for you, forever.

§

DESTINATION: HELL

I am seated in a C-5 transport aircraft with the men of SEAL Team Seven, Task Unit Trident, Bravo Platoon, on our way to another Godforsaken country. Our journey is taking us to Dover Air Force Base in Delaware, on to Germany, and finally, to hell. Like all things SEAL, everything about the beginning of this trip is managed chaos. C-5s are notorious for delays. We started with a two-day delay in San Diego. To hell with post-traumatic stress; pre-traumatic stress is far worse.

As I look around at my men, my thoughts are exclusively for them. Only three rules matter to me now, ingrained after twenty years of being a SEAL embarking on countless combat missions:

1. Use every asset at my disposal to bring each man back alive;
2. Overwhelm the enemy and win every battle;
3. Support each other so that rules one and two come true.

Each of my men deals with pre-deployment stress in his own way. Two hours into the first leg of the flight, some are sleeping. Others are talking about what we will see once we hit the ground. I can never sleep on these flights. (A doctor might diagnose an affliction preventing me from further combat.) Yet on any given day, even at home, I only get four hours of sleep. No one in his or her right mind would do what I do, anyway, so I guess all SEALs fit right in.

The stream of thought before a combat deployment can be overwhelming. Each SEAL's control over his thinking is what separates us from everyone else I have met. From the first day of training, we learn to be aware of our own thoughts—to see the effect they have on our physical performance and how they affect the performance of others. For us, in the deadly moment of battle, it is the control of Internal Dialogue that shifts the chaos of battle to the calm of victory.

These men have come a long way since we formed up eighteen months ago. We started out as the "bastard" platoon. Many of the men had suffered through poor leadership on a previous deployment to Iraq. Leaders have such an effect on men, good and bad. I inherited an angry, bitter, dysfunctional bunch of guys. And still we had been selected out of six other platoons to change deployment within a month of leaving to take the battle to the Taliban.

I trained all but four of the men as an instructor in third phase of Basic Underwater Demolitions/SEAL (BUD/S) training. One great thing about SEALs is we all come from the same mold of man and training. Something is familiar about each other, something unique, creating a unity among us all. I hope as you grow up you will feel this way about your family, your team, or your business associates. The greatest gift you can receive is oneness, through countless hours of pain and mutual suffering and success, through a common sharing of goals and life, and, most importantly, a common Internal Dialogue pushing out everything except the moment at hand . . . the NOW.

My point man and lead sniper, Nike, is the most detail-oriented man I have ever known. He is inexhaustible. He was an Olympic-level rower before becoming a SEAL. Typical of our platoon, he doesn't deal well with being told what to do. Nor do I, for that matter. The key to Nike is to give him free rein and make sure he feels like he can win—not always easy in the military—and not always doable in combat.

Next to Nike is Mister All Around—breacher, sniper, my lead assaulter. He smiles often and never has a negative thing to say in any situation. No words are necessary here, and I hope someday you kids have a powerful, positive friend like him, who is always there to help.

Stretched out across from me is KM, our primary assault breacher and primary heavy gunner. He epitomizes everyone's image of a SEAL: built like a fireplug, fitness personified, works out daily. He smiles no matter the climate or condition, and as long as we don't drink and shoot guns, he is the man.

My lieutenant is the only officer I have known whom I admire and see eye to eye with. Paradoxically, after twenty years in the military, I fight my leaders daily. When he and I joined up, we both agreed the primary platoon relationship was the one between the boss (him) and the chief (me). Since then, we have worked toward giving each other room to do our different jobs while always looking out for each other. As the men saw us work toward doing things for each other and the platoon, they, too, worked toward the same simple vision: we win or lose together and live to fight another day together. Everyone makes mistakes, but we grow stronger together.

Each platoon has a man who is comic relief. Ours wears two hats. He is my secondary communications expert and air controller . . . I call him Lawyer. After four years of working with him, I cannot recall a single instance where he has failed to make me laugh so hard I had to wipe the tears from my eyes. I have no idea how he keeps the intricate details of communications and controlling birds (attack aircraft) under control, but he has a knack for making good communications (comms) when no one else can. I just wish he would stop giving me broken radios and laughing when I lose my mind trying to make them work. If I hear him ask me again, "Have you turned the radio on yet?" I will take my radio off and make him carry it.

Next to Lawyer sits Jake, the angriest sniper and corpsman in the Teams—probably why he works so well for this platoon. I think we are all gifted in the "I-hate-everyone" arena, and Jake is Olympic level in the category. But his stability transcends his anger. I laugh as I write this—I think he actually loves the platoon and hates everyone else, but this attitude works for me.

My heavy weapons expert, Carnie—amazing. Early on, when I was with SEAL Team Two, I was invited to a civilian sniper course. Two of us showed up, and lo and behold, here was a fifteen-year-old boy. I thought I was a good shot, but this quiet youngster out-shot me every time. Years passed before I heard from him again. He called me with a simple request: "I want to be a SEAL. What must I do?" At the time, I was racing professionally on the adventure racing circuit, and my answer to him was simple, "Run with me. If you can do it and like the pain, you will be a good SEAL."

As fate would have it, he made it through BUD/S and was assigned, with no help from me, to my platoon at SEAL Team Seven. He is the most reliable man in the platoon. I just hope I don't make a decision that gets him killed. I love this man so much I made him and his wife your godparents.

Then, my leading corpsman and lead breacher, Ground Launch, headphones on, is watching some extreme parachuting video . . . dreaming of ground launching off some mountain in hell with a knife between his teeth, I am sure. To Ground Launch the world is not enough. I think he would shoot a Taliban just to see if he could then keep him alive.

Looking around, I see the youngest man in the platoon, Texas. He is a true short Texan in every sense of the word—happy being angry. I didn't have time to do enough for this man in training with just one specialty skill: breacher. Texas will have to learn fast if he is to survive.

Lying next to Texas is the most gifted communications and tactical air controller in SEAL Team Seven, Snowman. He has a way of acquiring the best and latest communications gear without spending a dime. I have no idea how he does it. Actually, I need to inspect Snowman's gear when we get off this plane to see if he has a nuclear detonator tucked away somewhere.

Finally, since we are going to the fight of the century, we seem to have acquired the best dog handler and dog in the Teams, as well as the highest-ranking explosive ordnance disposal (EOD) warrant officer expert in the Navy. You couldn't pay me to cut wire or manage a dog in the middle of a gunfight. But I am thankful such hombres wanna get some with us.

For some political reason, only half my platoon is authorized to come into hell with us on the first half of the deployment. But as Secretary of Defense Donald Rumsfeld said early in the war on terror, you go to war with the troops and gear you have, and make it work. Nevertheless, our sister platoon is at full strength, and thirty SEALs can do serious damage to the enemy.

The first leg of the journey is ending. If the history of C-5 travel holds true, once this big beast lands, it will be three days before it takes off. I love flying in these things, but the landing must surely beat the systems up every time.

Since we had a one-day delay, we have been put up in a military hotel here in Dover. We are all eager to get to the fight. I want to take this time to tell you more about what I think is important for you to know about my life and about your own. You all have so much to do in your lives. I may not be there to help and show you. So I want to tell you the key things you must learn to lead a full life and be able to face the good and bad times.

§

The first important discovery you must make in accessing, and thus mastering, your bodies is the discovery of your own Internal Dialogue as the core of your physical performance. Since the world in general puts little emphasis on the body and health—only how it looks and feels—physical performance may not seem terribly important for kids. Overweight kids should be a sign that, without any understanding of our own Internal Dialogue and how it impacts our body and health, youth are left to satiate and act on what their Internal Dialogue is saying. I will go into more detail, but for now suffice to realize our actions are directed by our own Internal Dialogue. Yet, you kids have been born with incredible genetic gifts passed down through the Shea bloodlines.

I know of no other way to teach you about your bodies then to tell you about what I have gone through, and show you how you can access your marvelous physical potential. Fathers are supposed to demonstrate and be present to help their kids learn. In light of the situation we face, please take this as the only way left for me to impart to you . . . *me*. Me as athlete.

I have been an athlete all my life. From my earliest memories, I couldn't get enough of being physical. I have always been amazed watching men and women do seemingly impossible things with their bodies. From the age of five until this moment, my thoughts and mind have been filled with dreams of physically doing the impossible. Even now, my thoughts are of running through a hail of bullets while shooting the impossibly long shot to save a trapped or dying teammate.

When I was five, living in Texas, I was the youngest boy on the street. In summertime, the older boys would play street tackle football. I watched them from the safety of my house and begged my father to let me play. He would say, "No way, son. Those boys are too big for you to play—fourteen-year-old boys are too old to play with." I can still recall saying to myself, "When you leave for work I am going out to play. I want to show them I can run faster and harder than any of them."

Of course, he would leave for work, and I would run out and play with the big boys all day long. I hated the fact so many of them were faster and stronger. I still hate it. When dad returned from work, I was bruised, and my lip was cut and still bleeding. He was furious I had disobeyed him. True to form, I was punished and grounded from playing street football. This went on for weeks. Finally, dad sat me down and said, "Son, why do you disobey me and risk getting hurt?"

I can recall, as if it were yesterday, what I yelled back at him: "Dad, they need me to play with them 'cause I love it, and I am fast and strong like you."

This desire has followed me into my adult life. I won't go into detail here, but I couldn't get enough physical tests throughout high school and college. The need to be physical, to be forever fighting my way through something or back to something, like now, is always in me. I know the Internal Dialogue of *need* to *be* and *need* to be *needed* is inside everyone. In some, it gets killed off for some reason; it gets put in a box and hidden.

In high school, I lettered in track, wrestling, and football. I set school records in the 200-meter dash and the long jump. In college, I enjoyed football, track, and judo, though my academic performance lacked, well, everything resembling good grades. I became rooted in the physical.

> Now, to the point of *Unbreakable* and what you are to do after reading this introduction. You are to discover your physical bodies by learning about and listening to your own language in the form of your Internal Dialogue, while pushing beyond what you think you can do. I hope by sharing how I overcame impossible things, and what my own Internal Dialogue was at various times, will provide you the points a good father should deliver to his children. Your bodies are amazing already. Your minds are malleable and will, used properly, help you to greatness.

My greatest physical achievement is the years I spent adventure racing. While I was a third-phase instructor, I had three years to prepare myself to go back to a SEAL platoon to be the man in charge, platoon Chief.

The war on terror had just started, and I knew war was on my horizon. I had to do something to make myself a better leader. I needed to be superior physically and mentally. War is truly one of the only experiences where things either work or do not, and the measure is in bodies. Don't let the press and politicians distort that truth. Success in war is not measured in nation-building or people manipulated to your side. Success in war is measured in who won and who lost, who killed whom, and who survived . . . period. The wars since WWII have been left unresolved by uncommitted politicians. The war I am going to will never be resolved for the same uncommitted reasons, but my victory will be to survive, or kill as many as I can, so I live to see my family again.

I further understood the men would need me to be more than just a guy trying to make rank. I needed to go beyond what other SEALs could do physically, and I *needed* to learn "real" leadership—leadership not driven by having to follow orders. The men had to want to follow me, and I had to want to follow them. For me, wanting to follow was what made up a great team.

Here is the first point: I knew as long as I could control my own Internal Dialogue, I could achieve any physical goal. I did not know this key point until after my racing career. I learned it through hundreds of failures, pain and mistakes, and by continually transforming my Internal Dialogue, and thus, my physical performance. Please read this chapter and understand my failures; assimilate fully what my own Internal Dialogue did to me and my team.

ADVENTURE RACING: WINNING . . . AND LOSING

Initially, I faced daunting obstacles that would have stopped most people. I had never run over fourteen miles. I had never mountain biked. I had never climbed a wall over twenty feet, nor paddled a kayak over ten miles. When I looked at what an adventure race consisted of, my mind nearly stopped thinking. What I said to myself (my Internal Dialogue) was trying to destroy my efforts and tell me I could not do it. Always . . . until I learned to control that Internal Dialogue.

Adventure racing is everything to the extreme. Teams consist of four, one being the opposite sex. The first race I signed up for was 700 miles . . . yes, 700 miles, not 70. Those 700 miles were broken down to 350 miles on a mountain bike, 250 miles on foot, and 100 miles paddling. As I studied, I noticed they had thrown in a 1,100-foot climb and a 300-foot rappel for good measure. After reading the details, I closed my laptop, walked to my bed, and fell asleep—at noon on Saturday. When I finally awoke, it was Sunday noon. My mind was racing out of control with thoughts of *I have never done something like this*, and, *Jeez, Thom, you don't even own a mountain bike*. Eventually, reality overwhelmed me when I realized I didn't have a team or the money to pay for it. The cost of entrance—$8,500—is a lot for a man with, at that time, two kids. Needless to say, the cost in gear and training, after an initial calculation, would be much more—around $30,000.

All I could think of that Sunday night was how stupid I was, what a fool I was to even think about it, and how impossible a task it would be. I think this is what most people go through when they attempt something difficult; maybe it is what we all go through, even on the smallest things. We subconsciously talk ourselves out of everything new, and never realize we actually talked ourselves out of it in the first place. We become resigned and cynical and go to bed each night untransformed and unmoved by how great we all truly are.

Monday I went back to work, exhausted and angry at myself for dreaming big when the reality I lived in screamed so loudly. Yet, as I prepared to lead my class in an eight-mile rucksack run, my courage returned. I looked at those future SEALs and saw in their eyes one unmistakable thing: possibility. To be better than others, not to let obstacles obstruct their dreams and desires. My own Internal Dialogue shifted. What had seemed impossible was becoming possible. When my Internal Dialogue shifted, so did my attitude and the possibility of a new future.

Maybe the endorphins coursing through my veins in the middle of long runs or the hard physical events were affecting me, but I said to myself, "Thom, you need to do this adventure race." When I got back home that night, I opened my computer, went to the website, and paid half the fees to secure my spot. Nothing transforms you more than laying down money toward your goal. A funny thing happened about a millisecond after I closed the computer. My hands started shaking; my own Internal Dialogue went from, *You need this*, to, *You are nuts!* Maybe that is what courage is: staking yourself out in the face of your enemy, as the Sioux Indians would do. They staked themselves in the ground because the urge of the Internal Dialogue to run in the face of the enemy is so powerful.

The first step is the hardest: to act, to commit, to sign on the line so all you have and all you need is engaged—at least that is what I have found in all great efforts in the history of man. A fully engaged Internal Dialogue, controlled by you, screaming into the void of the life you want but has no evidence to support it, serves to put the emotionally-uncommitted rollercoaster to rest for a time.

The next big step was to get a team together on short notice. Only three months remained until the beginning of the race. I had no team, no money, and no gear, yet every single day I said to myself, "I must get all of us through this race, no matter what." Within a week, I manipulated and cajoled three other SEALs to join me. I got a waiver from the race director to allow an all-male team to participate. But none of us had extra money to spend on this harebrained plan to push for ten days—the race duration—and endure unforeseeable mental and physical challenges.

Another great resource you will have to learn is the gift of gab—how to fearlessly engage everyone with your dream and passion. Learn how to ask for what you want and how to hear rejection as only a momentary setback. I must have sent out 200 Internet requests for money and gear, and received 205 no answers, if that is even possible. Hearing no as anything other than a momentary no breaks down your health, your drive, your ambition, everything. The problem is not with being told no, but your belief that the answer will always be no. I began to play with no as if it were a dance. Instead of blindly asking for what I wanted, I danced in the various conversations I had with people and engaged every potential sponsor as if they were already friends who wanted to be a part of the effort.

Within a month, I had secured four top-of-the-line mountain bikes and all the gear we needed. All my sponsors wanted in return was our committed effort to do the best we could to represent their products. Most people want connection to each other and want to feel needed. The excitement of everything coming together, and the exhilaration of being able to cold-call anyone pushed me to call two of the wealthiest men I knew. I was so confident I was not going to embarrass the team or the SEALs with our effort that during these two cold calls, I asked for a specific amount and explained where, how, and why I needed it. Both men said yes, and were happy to help. We were $20,000 on the way. The race fees were paid in full, and travel costs were easily met.

Three days before the start, we found two attractive women as support crew—trust me, pretty women make a man perform better. With the two vehicles packed, we headed out. Four hours into the road trip, we were on the side of the road with three flat tires. Everyone was ticked off and blaming each other—my first real-world leadership experience outside the military. My solution was to say, "We are all in this together. Keep working the problem until it is solved. I think we are in good shape. We have money for tires and time before the start. Two of us can stay here and drink beer while the other four get the tires." I am sure more words were exchanged, but I felt being in the moment and not making people mad was a better solution than pointing out who messed up and how this would affect the time line.

Finally, we came to race day. Everyone handles stress uniquely, and SEALs are already unique. Two of us studied maps and checked gear, one spent the entire night trying to more than engage our race crew, and one went to a bar and drank. My second key leadership lesson came on day one, two hours before the race started. With his two hours of sleep and the smell of booze permeating the air, it occurred to me to laugh and say aloud to my drunken teammate, "How can I help you? Can I carry your pack?" He politely said, "No, I am good. There ain't no way I am going to let you tell everyone you carried me through this race. No way."

With that, we headed to the start line and out on the first leg of the race—twelve miles straight uphill from 8,000 to 11,500 feet, and back down to 9,000 feet. A strange thing occurs to me at the start of any race or situation I have chosen. I feel truly alive. Nothing else matters but that moment. The air was crisp and I could smell the dirt and high mountain air. The ground was exceptionally noisy as the dirt and pebbles gritted under my feet. I recall an odd sound for the entire first hour, like a metronome of step/grind/step/grind. My body felt alive, my legs strong, though my breathing was rapid due to the thin air at that altitude.

By the end of the first leg, all the booze had miraculously worked its way out of my buddy's system, through one end or the other, and we jumped on our bikes for an eight-hour mountain bike ride to Provo and Utah Lake.

During the first twenty hours, we reached thirteenth place out of fifty-eight teams. We made a strategic, dangerous navigational move to chop off ten miles of easy riding for one mile of cliffhanger riding. As we traversed this cliff on a twenty-inch ledge, one foot kicking off the wall for support, the other hanging precariously in space, my buddy turned to me and said, "Falling off the ledge would be easier, wouldn't it?" I smiled and said, "Maybe for you, but I'd have to drag your ass the rest of the way. And if you died, how would I explain that to your wife and daughter?" Then I realized my state of exhaustion, "Brother, I think we need to stop soon. I can't focus at all."

In adventure racing, when you think you need to stop, it is already too late, and you end up stopping right where you are: eating, drinking, and sleeping in that exact spot. We thought stopping on a ledge with bikes made no sense, but stop we did and slept for an hour. When we woke, daylight came, and things were far scarier than they had seemed at night. I had somehow wedged my bike into a crack in the wall, pulled out my sleeping bag, and crawled in. My legs were hanging off the cliff, and my feet were swollen terribly from hanging like that for an hour. I was too scared to move. Looking at the other three, I could tell they, too, were freaked. Finally, I managed to get my body out of the sleeping bag without falling, grabbed it and my bike, and shuffled the next 200 feet to more secure footing. Once we were all off the ledge, we laughed so hard we cried.

The next ten miles were uneventful, and the thought of reprieve from the heat in a long paddle around Utah Lake silenced the demons of our Internal Dialogues for a while. Sometimes, small moments of good thoughts make all the difference. When the sun comes up, especially in an outdoor adventure race, spirits soar and attitudes shift automatically. Millions of years of genetic programming kicks in when you leave the confines and rules of today's society behind. Sun means energy . . . and you can see better.

As we traversed the maze of bike routes and trails mandated by the race committee, we wondered where we would rank when we pulled into the transition area (TA) and met our crew and other racers. We hadn't seen another team in six hours. Since I was navigator, and we had made interesting navigation choices earlier, I wondered if we had made a bad choice. But I didn't reveal my misgivings to the rest of the team. Nothing can crush physical effort faster than a lack of faith in the navigator. After an hour we turned a corner and rode into the transition area.

Checking in, we noticed only two other teams had officially arrived, and none had decided to get on the water. We were third. Here is where it got interesting. We had a choice to make, and our choice could either crush us or put us in the lead: rest and eat slowly, or grab food and paddle gear and get to the water ahead of all the others. My body was screaming for rest and food. My eyes burned from riding all night without protective glasses. Since I was a mountain-biking virgin, I had never considered getting clear eye protection to keep the wind from blasting my eyes. So we all suffered.

My body ached where the saddle had rubbed it raw. The thought of sitting in a kayak made the choice even more difficult. Moving toward our crew and gear, we saw the British team move toward the boats with their paddles in hand. The choice now made, all the exhilaration of the sun and the new day faded. SEALs cannot stand to be near the front and not be first.

The girls on our crew had set breakfast out on the table and were hurt when we said we were grabbing our food and paddle gear and leaving. Looking back, I realize our choice, and how we interacted with the crew, completely shut them down for the next three days. I realized I needed to apologize and thank them for their effort. This is a key element in human performance I will never forget. I want you to learn this point, too: recognize the effect you have on others, and acknowledge others' contributions, no matter how small. Human connection pays dividends in the business of performance and team dynamics.

With paddle gear on and food bags in hand, we moved to the boats and made our way to the shore. The route seemed straightforward, and the mountains around the lake provided easy navigational landmarks. But water is never to be trifled with, a lesson we had all learned in SEAL training.

The first of the four legs was a five-mile, straight-line paddle to the lake's south side, where there was to be a punch-style marker on the bank. As we got into the rhythm of paddling and eating and drinking, we easily pushed through the first leg and found the marker. Each consecutive marker was the same, but as the heat grew, so did the wind and waves. We had a slight tailwind on the first two legs. However, the next three legs were harder. As the wind picked up to 20 mph, we noticed no other teams were on the lake. We were alone and exhausted on a huge lake in the middle of an adventure race with fifty-eight other teams who had paid to do this, and not one other team had ventured forth . . . surreal. But we pressed on and tried to keep each other in sight.

The struggle was overwhelming. We weren't making headway paddling into the wind. The other boat crew dropped a food bag in the water and we had to rescue it—a desperate mission costing us energy and an hour. After recovering the food and pulling into the bank to find the last marker, we were spent. I knew I didn't have the strength to paddle into a crosswind for three more hours. We had a what-are-we-doing-here talk, then rested on the shore for an hour and prayed the wind would die down. It didn't. And the temperature rose to 100 degrees, leaving us even more broken.

Finally, we decided to just do it, and we'd sleep in the air-conditioned van for three hours when we got to the transition area. I knew we'd be blown down the leg by the crosswind, but we had seen a bike path next to the east side of the lake and had agreed that if we were blown south, we would get out and carry the kayak instead of paddling into the wind. Noble thoughts: don't you just love them?

The first mile took one hour. Near the middle of Utah Lake, four jet skis pulled up alongside and said they had been sent to escort us. All the other teams had been held back, so we had been the only team to complete the paddle. The other teams were on an eight-hour race delay. Nice, I recall thinking, we can rest for eight hours and start anew, and we would need to.

The next two miles took three hours. As we pulled into the transition area, the race director met us with a congratulatory handshake and said the teams had been put on an eight-hour delay. For some reason this made sense, but as we dragged the boats up and limped to our support crew, I noticed ten teams were mounted on their bikes, listening to the race director count down . . . 5, 4, 3, 2. "What's happening?" I asked my buddies. "You mean they all got to sleep eight hours, and we took eight hours to complete the paddle? Are you kidding me?"

My protests to the race director must not have been clear. I thought I was speaking English, but after that paddle, maybe I wasn't. He just couldn't understand why I was saying we needed an eight-hour rest, too. I just recall telling him he was an idiot. My remark would come back to haunt us, but the damage was done. He *was* an idiot, and we were exhausted.

We sat and ate the meal the girls had laid out—delicious, but I can't even recall what it was. I sent the rest of the team to bed and got out the maps for the next leg. In trying to plot the points and keep my eyes open, I somehow calculated the next leg to be 125 miles of mountain biking. When I woke, I was still sitting in the front seat of the van, air-conditioning still on, with the maps all over me. My legs were asleep, and I had peed all over myself. That didn't bother me as much as waking up the others and saying, "OK, time to roll. The next leg is 125 miles; pack at least thirty hours of food."

The girls had left in the other car to get us food. It wasn't their fault. No one had told them the plan. I had been the leader. I had fallen asleep and smelled like an outhouse. A great role model.

Just when we mounted and were headed out, the girls rolled in, so we turned around and ate what they had brought us. I asked them to wash our gear and told them we wouldn't see them again for at least a day. They were wearing bikini tops, creating an interesting conversation for the next two hours.

Endurance cross-country mountain biking is no joke, but doing it while exhausted, carrying thirty hours of food and water, and a sleeping bag, is a joke. It is actually funny because it hurts so badly. We had hard-tailed bikes, and every bump felt like it punched the saddle into my stomach. The first three hours took us from the valley floor up 4,500 feet, to some unnamed pass.

We rode until we couldn't any longer, then got off and pushed. We made a valiant effort, laughing at the pain, telling stories about the crew, and joking about life, with a pedal continually catching on the back of my calf and eventually tearing a hole in it. I finally picked up the bike and carried it for the last mile. As we approached the top, we passed the first of the teams who had slept for eight hours. When we passed them, they had questioning looks in their eyes.

Once on top, we stopped where two other teams were resting and joined them in a celebration of Snickers bars and Gatorade. They told us we looked like hell. Finally, a woman on the French team said, "You guys will never complete this course. You are pushing too hard."

In the midst of a beautiful sunset and the flavor of chocolate and Gatorade, the sound of a predator—me—snapped and broke the silence, "Fuck you, Frenchie. Why don't you shave your armpits?" The prey huddled into a herd of four, and the predators—us—moved off.

The rest of the night was a blur of branches, cliffs, rocks, and glancing at my map. We babbled on about women, family, and anything else that came to mind as the night wore on. We crossed several streams and took time to replenish our water, rest, and eat. The sun rose on four guys who no longer cared. My knees were hurting from the lack of mountain bike training . . . and about fifty falls on the trails. I noticed one of my teammates had blood running down his inner thighs. When I asked him what had happened—I didn't recall him falling or crying out in pain—he said, "My ass is bleeding from the seat."

Since I am a SEAL corpsman, I felt as if I should be able to help him. When we stopped, I said, "Let's see the damage." He dropped his shorts, bent over, and spread his cheeks. What I was seeing didn't register. He had a blister the shape of his bike saddle, torn open and bleeding. He turned and said, "I think I am crowning. Could you please deliver my baby?"

I didn't laugh. I felt impending doom that we were out of the race. No human could endure his pain. Yet he simply said, "Just shoot lidocaine in it, and I will get it done." So, with needle and syringe, Doc Shea delivered a mountain-bike baby, complete with a spank on the ass for good measure. Seeing him cringe settling onto the bike seat made me admire the commitment of SEALs, and his mastery of his own thoughts—his ordeal would have made lesser men quit. If his own Internal Dialogue was anything like what he projected on his "loudspeaker," no mere mortal could have stayed the course.

My focus was terrible, gone. Our brilliant strategy had, like so many other great plans, met reality. The overall plan had been divided in two. The first part: eat and drink methodically. Clearly, we all had learned through SEAL training that the body could go for a long, long time when well hydrated and fed. We had separated food into eight-hour bags filled with GU packs, jerky, Snickers, and such. Water was also an easy plan. We all carried three-liter camelbacks and two water bottles. The plan for eating and drinking was simple: consume 150 calories every thirty minutes, and drink five swallows of fluid every fifteen minutes. We would replenish our water when anyone noticed they were below half. Initially, replenishing water had been easy—streams and wells were shown on the map—yet we didn't see water for three hours. I looked again at the map, in a state of, "I just want the pain to end," but I could find no more water shown for the next fifty miles.

Finally, at the bottom of a long uphill section, I stopped and brought this water problem to everyone's attention. Each man had a chance to look at the map and get needed rest from the punishment of being in the saddle for seventy miles of brutal single-track. The decision was clear: divide all the water and food into quarters, slow down, and hope we could find water. Then the bomb hit. One of my guys noticed he had dropped one of his eight-hour food bags. He thought it had been at our last stop, twenty-five miles back, at the top of a 10,000-foot peak.

"Thom, um, I only have six hours of food left. How many more hours to go?" he whispered.

"You don't have two bags? The rest of us do. We have at least twelve hours left, and the terrain from here to the transition is grim. Gonna get hotter and . . ." I can't repeat what I said and thought.

With that, we threw all the food into a pile and did the old one-for-me, one-for-you trick. After everything was shuffled we realized a sick truth. We had seven hours of food and five hours of water, but twelve-plus hours of mountain biking through the heat of the Utah high desert. We sat silently for several minutes. I lay back on the ground, looking up at the clouds, and let the facts sink in. It was no longer safe to continue, and no longer safe to go back. We were at an impasse.

Oddly, we had not seen another team for six hours. We all knew exactly where we were on the map—it was clear as a bell—we were in hell. "We can't just sit here. Give me the map, let's see if there is a road we can get to and flag down a car, and get the hell out of here," my buddy suggested.

Sitting in utter misery wondering how we had allowed this to happen, I said, "Let's just get on the bikes and find water. The deer must drink somewhere, even without a map."

Instead of mounting up, we just pushed the bikes up the hill and rested when one of us needed it. We did this for the next twenty miles, off and on, going from shade to shade. Finally, we saw two teams sitting on the side of a fire road. We limped up to the group and asked if they were OK or needed anything, though we had nothing to give them, and no intention of giving up our precious water.

An interesting thing happened. The two teams had quit and called the race director on the emergency satellite phones provided. We had not thought to ask or call for rescue. They said if we waited with them, the truck would be there within the next two hours.

Simultaneously, we four looked at each other and smiled. I looked at the two other team captains and said, "I'll pay you $200 for all your food and water. We ran out, and would appreciate help." With that, we extended our stores another four hours. This seemed like a victory as we pulled away from the "foolish quitters." I didn't realize for another hour that we still didn't have enough food and water to complete the leg.

Consider the phenomenon of being closer to the finish line or the end. The finish calls to you. Maybe this is what people summiting Everest go through, and why so many die so close to the summit. All these thoughts went through my mind . . . we were going to die here. But I became angry—not at myself, not at my men—just angry. I told myself not completing that leg was NOT an option. We would simply find a way to make it through this hell.

Cresting a hilltop, we found the last place with trees before the descent into a bowl and a lake, where the transition area was set. I suggested a pause until the temperature cooled down. It was 3:00 p.m., the hottest point of the day. So we pulled off the trail into a shaded section of pines, pulled out our bags, stripped off our shoes, and lay there drifting in and out of consciousness. Around 7:00 p.m. we all came back from la-la land into hell, and the temperature was markedly cooler. Clouds had moved in. We packed up without speaking, mounted up, and headed out. Two hours later we ran out of food and water, and the sun went down.

Somehow—I have no idea how, I cannot recall looking at the map or even riding my bike—we turned a corner and saw the lights of the transition area right in front of us. When we checked in with the event staff, they were wide-eyed and clapping. Somehow we had been one of the four teams to make it. Thirty teams had quit, and twenty-four others were still out there somewhere. I felt for them . . . **not**. I didn't feel anything at all.

The race director walked up to me and said, "Wow! How long have you all had flats?" We looked at him, wondering what he was saying. Then we looked at our bikes and saw not one single tire was inflated. The funny thing was, we had ridden into the TA.

We had nothing left inside us. When our crew saw us, they hugged each of us saying, "You look like hell. What can we do to help you? The showers are over in the bathroom, and we have tons of food, water, and cold Gatorade."

I cried for the first time. Yes, I cried. Not because I wanted a shower or food and water. I cried because of another thought: I was going to see my kids again. I had not let myself consciously say so, but what truly drove me to get to the end was my kids.

My shower hurt every cut; the cold water at dinner hurt the cuts in my mouth; the food gave me diarrhea. No sane doctor would have let us continue. But we slept until we were rested. After eight hours we awoke, stiff and swollen and ready for breakfast. This time the food stayed down, and we hydrated until we were full. As I finally looked at the maps, I laughed out loud and called everyone over.

"Guess what, gents? We have twenty-eight miles to hike today, and the first half is back the same way we stumbled down last night. At least we know where the water isn't."

Several other teams had arrived while we were sleeping. Two had already left, and the other early-arrival team was still sleeping. We packed extra food and water since we had the strength and size to carry more than the smaller endurance athletes who usually make up adventure racing.

Though we were enthused by our new-found position, I knew as a SEAL corpsman that we were in trouble physically. This next leg of the race would bring out all the pain imaginable. I would have to navigate perfectly so as not to waste time or effort retracing our steps. We would all have to help each other, both physically and mentally.

Pulling out of the TA and getting into the rhythm of walking, eating, and drinking, I noticed my point of view about the whole race had shifted. I was no longer looking at it, or even the legs themselves, as total distance. I was looking at the map in four-mile sections only. We could average four miles per hour, easily. Planning out food and water in four-mile sections, which translated to one-hour sections, was simple. With that shift in perspective, our mental and physical reality also shifted; we were absolutely elated when each hour passed without incident.

The physical facts were sickly apparent: swollen hands, throbbing feet, chafing in my armpits and between my legs. Knowing that all I had to do—all we had to do as a team—was walk for an hour made it somewhat bearable. The ease in doing this sick thing together took another form as well. Each time one of us would fall back more than twenty-five meters, we would stop and tie a ten-foot tether to the "man in the barrel" to keep us all working together as one.

We accepted we needed each other. No one felt less for asking for help now, though we had scoffed at help for the first three days. I look back now and realize our earlier independence of each other contributed to the exhaustion and breakdown of our overall effort. This was a critical learning point I would never forget . . . *ever*.

Teamwork is not what each team member brings to the group. Four gifted athletes are nothing compared to the power of controlling, focusing, and altering an individual's Internal Dialogue. Mine had shifted from looking at the various realities of the course—distance and calories and what the other person's physical abilities appeared to be—to simply telling myself and the others what we were doing, shaping our goal with language. This was a subtle shift, but what we were each saying to ourselves and to each other about our goal bridged the gap between our abilities and the level at which we could perform.

For example, while looking at the map, we would literally tell each other aloud, "We *are* here, we *are* going there. It *will* take about an hour. Our legs *are* strong, we have enough food and water, and when we get there we will rest for five minutes." When each step hurt, or someone would stumble or wince in pain, someone else would say out loud, "Bro, in just another thirty minutes, we will feel better."

We went on this way for six hours, without breakdown. The pain was silly stupid. My feet were bleeding in my shoes, but my mind was at ease, filled with words and thoughts of simple creation. I don't know any other way to describe it. Internal words are the most important things you will ever have to master and develop. Take time to learn and use your Internal Dialogue to bridge the gap between where you currently are in the world, mentally and physically, to what is ultimately possible for each of you.

Smiling, with a great sense of accomplishment, we pulled once again into the TA, greeted the crew, then ate, drank, and slept without incident. After the morning wakeup and more food and water, we oriented the maps and loaded our gear for the last paddle section. When we finally pushed off from shore, we were in fifth place, and could see two of the other teams on the lake.

The wind was blowing down the lake, straight into another bay where there was a marker. We met the other two teams at the marker and noticed they were headed back into the wind. My team was eager to push off with them so we could keep pace and not lose sight. I smiled and said, "Hold on," I said, "Let them go. I have a better plan that will put us ahead of all of them. Trust me." I broke out the map and showed how the lake turned north and the wind was blowing south. They saw immediately that if we portaged the kayaks cross-country, we would only have to walk four miles instead of paddling twelve miles into a ten-mile-per-hour headwind.

Though portaging overland and up and down a rocky cliff took every ounce of effort, when we got to the other side, we were six miles ahead of the two teams. We could see another team a quarter mile ahead. We lay second. Before jumping into the boats, we dunked in the lake to cool off. Somehow, portaging two kayaks in 90-degree heat in shorty wetsuits makes you hot. Go figure.

Our legs were done, but our arms and backs were fresh. Within twenty minutes, we passed the team ahead . . . our friends the French. I couldn't see under her wetsuit top, but I don't think the French girl had shaved her pits yet.

We pulled into a modified TA to drop our boats and paddle gear and to pick up our mountain bikes and gear for a short fifteen-mile ride. We took our time, and let the other team stress out about being passed so they'd have to eat and drink fast and leave without a break. As they pulled out, we got on our bikes and easily made our way up the road and the next big TA. We did not try to overtake the Frenchies. The stress we put on them would push them without overt effort on our part.

I cannot recall the fifteen-mile ride in detail, but at the TA, our crew looked oddly excited. After we checked in, our crew hugged us and said we were second. Two of the top teams cut their feet up badly on the lake swim and were out of the race. We sat down at the dinner mat they had prepared and talked about what we needed, and didn't need, to do.

Swim section rules specified each of us had to swim out to an island, mark our cards, and swim back, which seemed easy. The girls said the other teams had elected not to wear shoes, and the rocks on the island had torn their feet up. Nothing like letting others fail so you don't! We put on our full wetsuits and hard-soled boots, and swam the mile to the lake. The water was so cold, and we had no energy reserves, but cold water is nothing new to SEALs. Shivering is a rite of passage for us but somewhat novel at an air temperature of 90 degrees.

When we came from the lake and returned to the TA, the only teams around were us and the Frenchies. Maybe armpit hair helped? They had not completed the swim section, so we were happy to rest and eat. Our plan: rest, eat, and prepare our bikes for what looked like a sick twenty-eight-mile, single-track leg. Our deceptive plan was to let the Frenchies come in and see us sleeping. We had told our crew to watch them, even talk to the French crew and tell them we were sick and injured and were going to sleep for four hours. Once the Frenchies fell asleep, we would leave.

We still needed four hours of sleep to recover. Once out of the TA and on the mountain bikes, we pressed on for an hour and pulled off the trail just as it was getting dark. We pulled up into the trees about fifty yards off trail and got our sleeping systems out. Just as we were slipping into our bags, we heard the French team talking and could hear the urgency in their voices. As they passed, I said to my teammates, "I bet they break and quit, 'cause they can't find us. No way they can push at this point without sleep." I drifted off to a four-hour sleep, smiling.

We awoke to darkness and chill. Exiting a warm sleeping system into a cold shiver is harder than facing the enemy in combat. We all shivered for the first twenty minutes of the ride. The night was a blur, but nothing dramatic happened. We were working well together, and the miles seemed relatively easy, but at the next TA, the reality of the upcoming section hit like a bullet to the skull. We would get one horse, and with four people, make our way to two separate markers and back. Reading this from the comfort of your chair may sound easy, but our feet were done. We all knew riding horses causes your feet to swell, and that was scary. No one wanted to ride.

The decision to simply load our gear up on the horse and walk next to him seemed like the only solution. Again, the best plans made in comfort don't survive the reality of pain. We ran in front of the horse, and when I tried to help him up a rocky section, the beast stepped on my foot. Unbelievable! As I pulled off my shoe, we all looked and saw the damage.

One of my buddies said, "Wow, Thom, um, aren't you supposed to have toenails on those three toes?" I sort of laughed. So the mount-up bugle sounded, and up I went. Let's just say I don't like horses.

Now the end was near: just three more legs to go. The first: an 18-mile hike; the second, a climb up to a rappel; then, finally, a ten-mile ride on hard pack roads to the finish line. We were in first place.

My feet hurt so much, I had to switch from trail shoes to boots to make my foot flex less and allow for the inevitable swelling. The route went from 6,000 to 8,000 feet, then back down, twice.

All I can recall is how my feet hurt with every step. I staved off the pain as long as I could, but heading up the last steep pitch to the final summit, I sat down and cried again. The boys came over to help, but the trail was so steep, they really couldn't do anything. Going uphill at this steep angle meant forcing my toes into the mountain to get purchase, then stepping onto my toes to force my way up. I had tried walking up backward and sideways, but I fell more than I gained elevation.

I drifted in and out of some sort of altered consciousness. At some point, I recalled the start of the race when I was focused and could hear the sounds of the dirt grinding under my feet. Now all I heard was the sound of my bloody toes squishing in my boot and my ankles grinding with the massive pressure of the swelling. Those were not sounds I wanted to hear.

So the three left me to my misery and climbed to the top, only 200 feet, and I worked my way up. I endured forty-five minutes of repeated step with left, bring right up to left, then step again with left. When I got to the top, I walked past my teammates, and headed down without talking. I suppose I can be a real jerk when in pain, and I give it to them; they didn't say a word until we got to the TA for the rappel.

At the rappel, we grabbed our climbing gear and headed up. About an hour before dark, I said, "No waiting. We don't want to do this climb at night." The climb was the most dangerous I can recall. It seemed like a sheer cliff. At one point, I was forty feet up, trailing the team. I looked around and saw we were climbing a 5.8 climb. I was shaking like a dog when I topped out. We found an easier path over to the rappel site, but when we arrived, it was thirty minutes after dark. The race crew stopped us and said rappelling at night was too dangerous, so we had to climb down.

What happens when you are utterly exhausted? Your thoughts somehow make it to your loudspeaker, unfiltered. One of my teammates laughed and said, "The climb down will surely be more dangerous than rappelling off this mountain."

Sitting there, bewildered, we heard the race crew's radios proclaiming the French team was heading to the race crew zip line and bypassing the rappel. So we jumped up, saw their headlights, and literally sprinted to the zip line point.

Earlier, and throughout the race, we had several interesting conversations with the Frenchies. Now we found ourselves waiting in the dark, behind the Frenchies, who had not done the paddle and had obviously lost the battle with their own Internal Dialogue. The tension was that sort of electrical kind when the principal makes you shake hands with the boy you had just fought with at school. But now you are a grown man with no sleep and tons of frustration.

Just then, the funniest thing happened. The French girl said to us, "You all are not adventure racers. You push too hard and are too big and fat." I think the poor girl was hallucinating. One of my teammates replied, "Careful, dumbass."

As a fighter, you have a moment, facing a punk in the street, when you realize it will come to blows. You just sense it. We all sensed it. I don't think the Frenchies did, but don't bring a knife to a gunfight, right? So in the silence of the still night, one of my SEALs said plainly, "When we get down, we are going to kill you." Maybe the great acoustics of the ridge or some other phenomenon intensified this, but "kill you, kill you, kill you" echoed down the mountain.

We had little energy starting that rappel section, but when we all got down off the zip line, there was a new sense of painlessness and energy. We literally sprinted the two miles to where our bikes had been dropped off for the final leg. Maybe the mob brain is real, where something you would never do makes sense in the stupidity of the moment, but had we caught the French team, I don't think it would have been for a spot of tea. Yet when we ran into the transition area, the French team was not in sight; just several race crews and the race director were waiting for us.

He informed us we had broken the race rules by threatening another team with physical harm and were officially disqualified. I calmed down and said, "The rules specify a one-hour penalty—no damage was done, just words exchanged." The director wouldn't listen and threatened to call my captain. I may have even encouraged him to make that call, blithely adding, "He [the captain] will laugh at you." I don't think that is what he wanted to hear.

Nine days through hell just to get kicked out of the race ten miles from the end. I cannot imagine why those poor Frenchies were scared of four Navy SEALs who were alone in a foreign land—who were in pain and sleep deprived—and who had threatened to kill and eat them. I mean *really*? Total victory to a Navy SEAL group. Now I know where our collective reputation comes from.

§

Here ends the physical side of the story I wanted to share regarding my first great attempt at overcoming what was physically impossible for me. I share not to show how great I am, or to cause you to dissuade yourself from attempting something equally impossible for you. This is a story of how Internal Dialogue is the critical key in the first task of overcoming impossible physical barriers you will face at some point in your lives. Every man and woman must get over his or her own physically self-imposed barriers. Perseverance will expand the known world into a bigger unknown world full of possibilities.

I have much more to share about the race—many great conversations and events that would be fun to read—but time is short. After three days of writing and waiting for this C-5 to take off, I am out of time. Before I go and load this already broken plane and head out across the Atlantic to Germany, I want to give you three detailed tasks for gaining access to your physical abilities and a very real relationship with your own Internal Dialogue.

The first thing I ask of you is to actually begin. You may think this sounds silly and easy. Trust me, you will immediately, within a week, see how your Internal Dialogue plays a mighty role in what you do physically. You can start this lesson at any age.

As I thought of an emblem to represent in one single piece what I was trying to tell in this story, I uncovered a short story denoting how things grow in nature. What captured my attention was the point that everything grows from one small whisper, then takes form and yet is, at first, fragile. As it grows the growth ties into the earth and air and multiplies. In the end when that first whisper stops growing, the whisper has become hard and unbreakable. An inverted pyramid represents that for me . . . the bottom is the whisper of Internal Dialogue and moves up toward a solid base and a mastery of your life. The downward facing trident comes from an old American reference to when a warrior pushes his spear or arrow into the ground saying he is at peace. My arrow is the trident. The thirteen blue bars inside the emblem represent the thirteen lessons in the book. And thirteen is a powerful number. And gold and blue remind me of the sun meeting the water off the coast of Coronado.

ADAMANTINE LESSON ONE

Keeping your word

For one week, each morning after you get out of bed, and each night before you go to bed, do five push-ups, five sit-ups, and ten squats. Pay close attention to everything you say in your head. Write down what you say if you find it easier, though most men and women lie and cheat. Do this exercise until you sense your Internal Dialogue. Notice what you say to yourself about the task.

After a week, re-double each effort, and for one week, pay attention to your Internal Dialogue. Observe how the task is going. Are you starting to cooperate with yourself?

On the third week, triple the original number. Note seriously what your Internal Dialogue is saying. I assume one of two things is happening: you are allowing real life to alter your plan, or you are getting stronger and encouraging yourself. Since the first is actually what you are listening to, like a sorrowful trumpet playing taps, don't be distraught. It is normal, and is actually what I hope you are listening to. While listening to your Internal Dialogue gives you valid reasons not to do the task, you need to be telling yourself the exact opposite and completing the task anyway. If your Internal Dialogue is saying, "I don't have time." Then simply switch the words, because they are your words to begin with, and say, "I do have time." And do the task . . .

Having seen so many SEAL students undergo this initial transformation, I want to share with you what is going on and warn you. After training so many SEALs, I know the human body, the human paradigm, resists change at the genetic level. It wants to keep the past alive at all costs. It does this by using Internal Dialogue to subtly make you avoid pain; unfortunately, it also prevents your goals and dreams from happening.

Seventy percent of all students who start SEAL training, who dream of becoming a SEAL, get caught up in their own Internal Dialogue in the form of quitting, getting injured, or failing. As you go through this first test, you may start thinking, *I don't have time. This is stupid. I am tired. I don't want to anymore. Ouch, I am injured.* Those thoughts invariably lead to the most deceptive one of all: *I am hurt.* Other forms of Internal Dialogue will speak at you, but I am sure these are the ones talking to you now.

So, each time your Internal Dialogue steers you away from the test, acknowledge it, say to yourself the exact opposite, and do the task. Continue this until you have made it through the first three weeks without skipping a day. How long it takes you to complete the task is not important. I took three months. Though my numbers were higher than I am asking of you, it is the same task. Don't let your Internal Dialogue stop you, even on the simplest task.

ADAMANTINE LESSON TWO

Facing your fear

The second task is to overcome your fear of heights by rappelling off a 100-foot cliff, then climbing back up using a rope. Here, I am hoping you feel the fear. I pray your body shakes and your palms sweat. Obviously, someone must teach you and provide appropriate safety precautions. I want you to feel your body's response; more importantly, I want you to notice what you are saying to yourself. This voice is loud, and it screams frequently.

Once down, you will also physically feel the effects of overcoming fear. Remember to breathe. At this point, notice what you are saying to yourself about overcoming fear.

Next, climb back up. Make it a somewhat doable climb. I would say a 5.4 to 5.6 climb. If you don't know what that means, find someone who does and enlist that person's help. Here, I want you to feel the physical exertion needed to overcome fear when the feeling you may fall overtakes you. Feel it. Touch the void surrounding you, physically overcoming the fear of falling. Notice the words have shifted once this is complete—as has your life.

ADAMANTINE LESSON THREE

Pushing beyond comfort zones

Finally, the last task is simple in concept, yet seriously demanding. I want you to walk for twenty-four hours without stopping for more than ten minutes at a time. This test is designed for one thing only. Now that you are gaining control over your Internal Dialogue and what it says in times of fear and discomfort, and how it tries to use real life to stop you from attaining your goals, I want you to use it to get to the end, no matter what. When your Internal Dialogue tells you something other than to keep going, replace those subversive words with your own words telling you to continue. This task took me three attempts.

On my first attempt, I got terrible blisters, ran out of water, and quit. I didn't try again for two months. The second time, it rained for twelve hours, and I felt like I was getting sick, so I quit. On the third try snow fell, and I got leg chafing so badly I walked like a man who had pooped in his pants, but I did it. My own Internal Dialogue was screaming at me the whole way: *Thom, you are stupid. No one cares about this but you. You are not proving anything to anyone, especially yourself, and you are hurting yourself so badly you will never walk normally again.* My own, revised Internal Dialogue, which I had learned to tell myself was, *Make it to the next tree, then to the next hill.* Finally, all went quiet, and I thought only of the trail ahead of me.

SECTION TWO

GROWTH

JOSÉ ORTEGA Y GASSET, *Meditations on Hunting,*
Spanish philosopher & politician (1883–1955)
*"One does not hunt in order to kill; on the contrary, one kills in order to
have hunted . . . If one were to present the sportsman with the death of the
animal as a gift he would refuse it. What he is after is having to win it, to
conquer the surly brute through his own effort and skill with all the extras
that this carries with it: the immersion in the countryside, the healthful-
ness of the exercise, the distraction from his job."*

In the process of writing the first chapter and taking the time to fully
convey my points on how important Internal Dialogue is for overcoming YOU physically, Task Unit Trident has had eight days of delays.
Our temporary delay in Dover extended the pain of waiting into another four-day delay in Germany. Nowhere in SEAL training does anyone
overtly teach patience, yet you have to become patient as a matter of fact
due to mechanical breakdowns and organizational failures. Hell, even
sometimes personal "oopses." The universal team guy point of view is
simply this: better be ready when it happens because it will happen. My
own perspective is even baser: I love to hunt, and sitting doing nothing
is part of it.

This is our last "safe" leg of the journey to hell. When we land in hell,
our advance party already has a mission planned for us. Oddly, it is no
big deal, at least mentally. When back in the States, our limited time to
train is a form of practice for real life, or for hell in this case. When I look
at my platoon, I truly cannot tell we are hours away from landing in hell.

We seem like we are going to Las Vegas, with all the smiles and quiet determination, like a group of men going to *Zumanity* . . . you just know you are going to see something, whether you want to or not.

HELL

We have been on the ground for two and a half days; I have only slept nine hours. Much of my time has been spent unloading our gear boxes, making up my "combat bedroom," sighting in my rifles, and planning every single detail of the first handshake with the devil.

As I share what I am doing over here with you, please realize most of the details, names, and places must remain vague. Actually, they matter little within the scope of what I really want you to know. I want you to know *me*. I want to share a part of my life you may never have been able to know, and I want to show you how I personally deal with the issues of life.

Within hours of hitting the deck here in hell, my lieutenant and I were pulled into the combat center and given a briefing on the combat operation planned prior to our arrival. As you go through life and become an expert in whatever field or skills you choose, you will find that anytime someone else plans something for you or your group, they always miss the mark because they lack awareness of the details which make you and your group good. It's not their fault. The task is especially hard for SEAL platoons and Army Special Forces (Operational Detachment Alphas: ODAs). We all breathe air, but aside from that, nothing is the same.

For this mission, we were to fully integrate within the ODA effort, sharing the breaching, shooting, and intelligence collection efforts. I mean to say that even in the order of march, they lined us up one ODA, then one SEAL, and so on. I could just feel the bones breaking and grating. None of it made tactical sense to me. One of my pet peeves is never to separate forces inside the target area at the beginning of the operation. We practiced this method many times in training. Every single time, one enemy running around in the middle of the separated "friendlies" caused us to either shoot each other, or delay shooting the enemy, which in turn allows the enemy to shoot one of us. Well that was in training . . . right? But as professional courtesy, I said nothing and hoped my point of view was just skewed from lack of sleep and tension.

After the briefing, I spent the rest of the afternoon altering my combat bedroom into a place locked away from the stimuli of hell, and instead, reminding me of Stacy, home, and my kids. Albeit, I had six guns mounted on the wall, two grenades, hundreds of rounds in my ready box, and my body armor and helmet set and ready to go. However, I did have white Christmas lights to remind me of God, and that, somewhere, presents were waiting for me. On top of my three-inch Tempur-Pedic mattress topper lay Chance's (our youngest) camouflage rain-parka liner embroidered with his name, birth date, birth weight, and height. I want to marry the woman who made that mattress topper.

Once finished with the room makeover, we all grabbed the various weapons we would need for the mission and drove off base to find someplace to sight them in and get our minds ready for the eventualities of war. Sighting in my weapons is an interesting thing for me . . . always has been. It isn't a time to joke or play. Maybe all my years as a boy hunting deer, elk, and squirrels, or, missing so many animals, caused me to take the time to ensure my guns were ready. Today was no joke. When I walked off that range, everything about my guns worked.

As the newness of the environment and the realness of what we were about to do sunk in, the world began to slow down for me. I spent that night going over the plan with my men. At this point in Bravo platoon's evolutionary development, we had an easy way of briefing and listening to a plan. I would brief the plan, much like other platoons would do across the SEAL community, then I would stop and give the floor to the men who would actually have to carry out the plan.

I don't know if mine is a unique style, but I do know many of the leaders in my immediate team have difficulty allowing open, committed conversation about tactics. Early in my career I discovered, as I hope you will, when you ask another person to risk his life, best to let him find a way that works for *him*. The past eighteen months had taught me my men wanted to win, and when I let them find their own ways, winning was easy.

We spent the next hour discussing the flow of the operation, who would be in key places and in key roles at various points of the movement, and most importantly, what would we do when the shit hit the fan and things got complicated. Two sayings in the SEAL Teams seem to hold true: plan your dive, and dive your plan. Meaning, do your best not to deviate and change the plan, and you can wipe your ass with the original plan once the bullets start flying, but take the time to plan anyway. Someone shooting at you tends to make you react in spite of what you wanted to do! An interesting contradiction to be sure, yet often a highly trained and battle-hardened team deviates from the plan just to address the immediate threat, then quickly gets back to the plan. A young team stays deviated after the bullets start flying, and clearly, the bullets were coming.

As the first night wore down, I walked back to my room and slid the makeshift door closed. Once inside, I put my headphones on and shut out the world. Stacy and I had picked out some songs to transport me back to her, at least in my mind. Family, and connection with family, is the most powerful thing a warrior can have. Since the Spartans ruled the European world, that connection has been time honored and literally written in blood. Some in the Teams see it as a balancing act of sorts; when your family falls apart at home, you become useless in war. However, for Stacy and me, we took it to the level the Spartans did—Stacy was fully committed to me being a SEAL and eager for me to count coup. Nothing was out of bounds for us to discuss about combat, and that dynamic, committed sharing over the past three years made me eager to connect to her about the violence of it all.

We had chosen several songs capturing our commitment to each other and our commitment to war. On this first night, as I thumbed through the songs, I stopped on our favorite song and was immediately transported to the emotion and feeling of lying next to her in bed that last night. As I listened to Peter Gabriel singing, "In Your Eyes," I could feel Stacy's warm skin against mine and could hear her saying, "Thom, I need you to come back to us. Do not fear dying. It makes you weak."

I drifted off to sleep that night lying next to Stacy, with my three children tucked safely in the protection of our home, and my brothers who remained in California.

When I woke the next morning, I had clearly not ensured all the holes in the wall were patched up, because I was covered in dust. If this space was going to work as a safe place to get away from the realities of hell, I would have to spend more time taking care of the holes. The exact moment my feet hit the ground, I heard a missile whistle high over our compound, hit, and explode somewhere on base. Not sure I can do anything about that, but I remember saying to myself, "This is bullshit. Islam has no consideration for a man's sleep. Let's see how *they* feel when we wake them up tonight!"

We all had to inconveniently muster at a pre-determined spot and wait for the all-clear call. I found this funny; all the SEALs were in flip-flops and shorts, and all the Army and Air Force men were in body armor and carrying guns. The men in my platoon were laughing. One of us said, "Relax guys, the thing already detonated, and the Taliban don't stay and fight." After that, breakfast was rushed because we had to meet the army SF unit leading the operation to conduct rehearsals.

I do, however, admire the lengths the army goes to in rehearsals. Take note: successful people in every walk of life train and rehearse in order to continue honing their known skills and to narrow down the unknown ones. We pushed through four separate rehearsals and completed with a tactical-leader debrief. The rest of the day consisted of checking and re-checking with all the air assets and getting my mind ready for everything.

After dinner, I called home. Calling home is often mentally risky. I think many young men struggle with the uncertainty of what they might hear and face emotionally. Maybe because many SEALs marry young, sexy women who resent the fact SEALs spend 200 or more days each year gone. That is not the case with Stacy and my kids. I thoroughly appreciate how they all embrace and encourage me being a warrior.

Hearing the love and connection in their voices always makes me realize why I continually risk my life for them and for my Team . . . staying connected is what matters. After the "hello's," and "How are you doing's?" I said, "Stacy, we are going fishing tonight." Her silence was telling. After what seemed like an hour, Stacy simply said, "Do not fear dying, Thom. It makes you weak. Leave your wedding ring on the picture of your family." Then she said, "I love you," and hung up.

When I placed my ring on the picture, I also left any fear of not returning in that safe place. Don't confuse my action of letting my family go with a lack of love for them. Whatever your job is, you will, at times, have to let go physically and mentally of certain things in order to excel in others. In combat, I have always found it difficult to focus on anything not connected to the specific mission. I knew, and know, my family would be waiting for me to return home.

Thus began my six-month ritual of taking off my ring and donning my combat gear. To this day, I find the disparity between a SEAL's appearance and reality extremely amusing. A SEAL's appearance makes such a misguided impression to anyone who doesn't know what's going on under all that gear. SEALs in combat appear lightweight, aggressive, and armed to the teeth with the latest guns and bombs—from the inside, I can tell you, the experience is totally different. Prior to putting on all my gear, I weighed 225 pounds. After loading up, I weighed 310 pounds. I don't know what equations the planners used to arrive at this solution of lightweight, but MIT must mean *Maybe It Translates or Math Is Tits.* Thank God I was an adventure racer and a SEAL!

With the load-up complete, we all headed out to the helo pad and met up with the SF ODA Team leading the mission. I wish I could clearly communicate the atmosphere of the group just prior to loading the helicopters (helos) taking us to hell. This atmosphere is nothing like the pre-game locker room energy of a football game or wrestling match, or even a track meet. This atmosphere is more a deafening silence, intermittently filled with radio communications in my headset—not necessarily music you listen to at a dance.

Slowly, the helos made their way toward us, and once in place, the ramp lowered, and we all shoved in like sardines. Thank God these helos were armed to the teeth, because we surely weren't able to do shit from inside them. The flight time was only thirty-five minutes; I didn't last ten minutes before falling asleep. I still do not know if it was because I was stressed out too much or just used to it. Next thing I knew, my point man was grabbing my arm saying, "One minute out."

Once on the ground, I exited into a thick dust cloud and followed the man in front of me until he took a knee, then we all waited until the helos took off, and the way to the target area was cleared. Looking around, I immediately found the shape and posture of the men in Bravo platoon. We wore different uniforms and gear and walked differently from the others. The familiarity of my men eased the confusion, and as we came close to the first target, I saw the men assume combat posture with lasers on and weapons off safe.

According to the plan, a group of SEALS and ODAs was supposed to be off to my left about 100 yards; I couldn't see them. Another group separated (yes, I know: separation of forces is not good for Bravo), and was making its way along with the main effort, paralleling our movement. However, the group was having trouble with something and dropped back thirty yards. No one was communicating this over the comms, and as I looked at my men, I could tell they were uneasy about the disorganization.

Somehow, the ODA main breacher did not show up to the main side of the street, so my young Texan looked at me, and I said, "Fuck them. Let's do it ourselves." Over the next 100 yards, he, I, and two ODA, breached and cleared twenty-eight doors and rooms. I recall watching my breacher open up the first lock with his shotgun. After the first round didn't break the lock, he laughed and loaded another one–again, to no avail. After four rounds didn't break it, he changed his approach and shot the latch's attachment to the wall. Bingo, we were in. However, we had never practiced on garage-style doors that push up from the ground. As the ODA lifted the door, my breacher and I squatted down, attempting to see in. The ODA sergeant said with a laugh, "Dude, unless they locked themselves in, I wouldn't worry about clearing it." To him, that made sense, but I didn't allow Texas and myself to drop to a lower tactical standard.

After twenty-four doors, I felt as if I was in a gym squatting 2,000 total pounds, but when the door lifted on that twenty-fifth door and my laser scanned inside, I saw a child's face looking out at me. Texas and I immediately moved on him, and once he and the room were secure, I called the ODA over and said, "No one inside. Right. You are now the prisoner handler until target is secure."

With the first section complete, I took the time to check in with my SEALs who were out to my right, supposedly 100 yards or so. Once I checked in with them on the radio, I said, "Turn on your strobe. I can't see you." After a bit of moving around to the back side of the building, (yes, into uncleared space), I found them in a grove about fifty yards ahead of us and to the right. I slowly attempted to retrace my exact steps, and once back to my men, I told them exactly where they were. Texas replied, "Thank God we aren't in a firefight, because without strobes on, they look like the enemy." I wrote that in my mental notes . . . keep us together; keep it simple.

Here is where the plan began to break down. The canal was too wide and deep, and the bridge looked rather mined to me. So we called up the dogs and EOD and let them handle it. While we waited, the three of us (SEALs) took the delay to share some thoughts and jokes and redistribute some shotgun rounds back to Texas. As we watched the EOD gents kneel down, we passed around a can of Copenhagen and Mister All Around said, "I am swimming across. To hell with those mines." With that, the ODA walked the bridge, and the SEALs jumped into the canal and waded across.

At the top of the village, we found another minefield and decided that was as far as we were going to push this combined assault. We put our own explosives on the minefield in order to deny the Taliban their mines. Cascading back through the target, everyone attempted to go back the exact route they had come. When Mister All Around and I got back to the other side of the canal, we looked back up the alleyway everyone had gone down. I could see two of my men, Ground Launch and Carnie, on rear security. Everything seemed to be going well. In a split second, everything changed. I saw two Afghani troops working with us walking next to each other down the alley, then the bright light of an explosion. The ensuing dust cloud enveloped my men and the commandos. Silence.

After a bit, Ground Launch broke the radio silence with, "Hey, I am going to need a medic over here." My heart sank; could it be Carnie? *Fuck.* I grabbed Mister All Around to keep him from running into that minefield, and I called for some EOD and dog handlers to take point. When we finally got up to Ground Launch, he was kneeling over two of the commandos, trying to stop the bleeding. All four legs had been blown off. I scanned for Carnie and saw him kneeling over with his night vision off. Walking to him, I saw blood on his face in the outline of his night vision goggles. Apparently, the bone fragments had embedded into his face and missed his eyes completely.

I walked over and put my hand on his shoulder. He stood up and said, "No more integrating with the ODA, please." I replied with, "Got it." As several of the medics began to work on saving the lives of the commandos, we all moved toward a security mode while we waited for the medevac helo to arrive. My men filtered toward Carnie in order to see him and ensure he knew they were there. Demonstrating your commitment to your buddies makes all the difference, and when I saw them do this, I had the sense we would be OK. That IED sealed our commitment to each other and ensured we would never make the mistake again of decreasing our capability. We were connected, committed, and angry.

The helo ride back and the debrief were uneventful. We separated, and some of us went to breakfast; Carnie went to bed. We all left him alone because we knew the reality of being that close to an explosion needs some time to wear off. Sleep tends to solve a myriad of life's problems, and I knew he needed time to work through that problem. I did, however, poke my head into his room that night and said I was there for him in case he needed me. I told him to call home; hearing his wife's voice would help.

With the conclusion of our first operation, we had time to meet all the key players on base who would have a role in our successes throughout the next six months. Many of Bravo platoon took their own private tours of the base, finding things no one else would find. Finally, I was invited to a platoon outing at a coffee shop hidden somewhere on base. I will be honest: it reminded me of where I met Stacy in Starbucks. The coffee shop became our after combat mission place to remind us all of better times.

Only after things calmed down with Carnie and LT, and I discussed what we would do differently from here on out, did I finally call home. I recall being rather nervous because I couldn't hide things from Stacy. She knew me well enough to get, from my voice only, what I was going through and facing. I am glad for that. I think hiding from your spouse or keeping anything from them is the worst. So, as I dialed the numbers needed to bypass the foreign codes and country codes, I took a deep breath and waited. After five rings, Stacy picked up and excitedly said, "Hello. This is Stacy." I swallowed and replied, "Hi, baby. We are back. Sorry I didn't call earlier." BIG PAUSE. Finally, Stacy said, "Something went wrong, I assume." I said, "We are all alive, but two partners got their legs blown off." BIGGER PAUSE. "Thom, remember what I said. I need you to come back to us. Do not fear dying. It makes you weak." I replied, "Yes, Honey: I remember." Stacy finally said, "I want you to do something for me, please?" I was shocked at her immediately aggressive tone. So I tried to divert the conversation by asking how the kids were. She snapped, "Don't worry about the kids. I got them. Thom, I want you to kill as many

Taliban as you can. Do you understand what I am asking? I want you to promise me that is the only thing on your mind until you come home. Don't worry about us; we are doing fine. Please say it out loud to me, right now." I obliged. "Stacy, I promise to kill as many Taliban as I can," I said. Oh, how a woman can set an Unbreakable Internal Dialogue in a man!

With that, Stacy said, "Call us back tomorrow, when the kids are awake. I have to go now," and hung up. As I moved away, I knew Stacy was sitting in bed crying, but I got her point. She would not tolerate me calling with fear or misgivings in my voice. I do like the way she negotiates.

ADAMANTINE LESSON FOUR

Creating Love

JOSÉ ORTEGA Y GASSET

"Love . . . is eternally unsatisfied. Desire has a passive character; when I desire something, what I actually desire is that the object come to me. Being the center of gravity, I await things to fall down before me. Love, as we shall see, is the exact reverse of desire, for Love is all activity . . . It does not gravitate toward me, but I toward it."

My daughter Autumn—I have some time and wanted to tell you how important it will be for you to be a great mom, when it is time, and a great wife, as you develop into a woman. This will be the fourth task I ask of you. After that mission the other night, realizing life hangs on a thread here, I feel this is rather urgent.

Again, I will share with you my own successes and failures with relationships and women. Hopefully, your mom will fill in the gaps I may leave out. As you grow up, please lean on her when "woman development" situations arise.

Let me begin by saying, the woman makes the man. Many people you meet throughout your life will lead you away from that fact, suggesting either subservience to a man, or doing your own thing as a woman. The latter is the going trend, which leads to the term, "a catholic marriage," where each person leads separate lives yet are married on paper. Both suggestions are not worth the effort, and both lack in the knowledge and practice of using your own Internal Dialogue to create a connecting dynamic for your family, your husband, and for yourself.

Use everything you have been given to create a connection

fundamentally rooted in one unique conversation: need to be *needed* as a way of life. You literally have to have your own Internal Dialogue to say, "I *need* him, he *needs* me, my family *needs* me, and I *need* them." Any other Internal Dialogue will lead to smallness in your own achievements, your husband's achievements, and your children's development. You will *all* be less. And, Autumn, it is all in you and no other person.

Stacy had a well-established, successful career in the investment business. She was living in Pennsylvania. I was living in San Diego, working as a SEAL instructor. I guess that is not something you see or read about every day, and it certainly doesn't always lead to successful marriages, hence the 70 percent divorce rate in the SEAL community. Even Stacy's development as a woman, a wife, and a future mom up to that point wouldn't, to the outside observer, lead anyone to say, "That is why Thom and Stacy got it going on." We were both recently divorced. You could even say neither of us looked like a good investment to anyone with regard to family and marriage.

I was living in a two-bedroom condo, sharing time with my kids, while my ex lived six miles away. Stacy was living with her mother due to her mom fighting cancer, and they were helping each other recover.

I was trying to fill the void my divorce created by racing professionally on the adventure racing circuit. Most of my time, when I wasn't at work or with my kids, was spent in the back country . . . running, hiking, mountain biking, or paddling. Every month, I would pack my car and unite with my team to compete in forty-eight-hour non-stop multisport races, and sometimes, even ten-day races. I think I found intimacy and connection both with myself and others at the level that had been lost in the divorce. My own Internal Dialogue said I needed to race to be whole, and the team needed me. Most successful people find a way to be *needed*, yet never recognize the importance of the voice saying, *"need."*

On the morning I met Stacy, nothing truly significant was going on with me, or her for that matter. She had flown to San Diego for a business conference and had stopped in at Starbucks. By chance, I was in line directly behind her.

I only vaguely recall noticing her—just another smoking-hot chick dressed to the nines. What caught my attention was the drink she ordered

. . . a black coffee with four shots of espresso. I chuckled and remarked out loud, "You are gonna get hair on your back if you drink that. You know that, right?"

She turned and frowned at me, then said, "Does that line ever work for you?" I replied, "Not a line at all. Just a disgusting drink." Stacy looked at me and said, "Sorry; it didn't work," then paid and moved away. I ordered the usual . . . a perfect seasonal café mocha with peppermint.

As we wandered about waiting for our drinks, I introduced myself. After a bit of chit chat and, if I recall correctly, a little suggestive eye contact, we exchanged phone numbers.

I am sure other men and women have better and even more erotic stories of first encounters than ours, but rarely do they lead to marriage, children, and any profound sense of connection. The unique factor separating us from the hoard of mundane was, and still is, the state of mind we both had regarding marriage and life.

The one unique thing about us at that moment in time—and I say that moment in time because it was not always that way for either of us—was *who we were in relationships.* Maybe the old saying that a life of excesses and failures leads to wisdom may actually hold merit.

For me, I wanted to date and marry God. I knew I needed a woman who needed me. I didn't want something less. To that end, I was faced with a dilemma. My Internal Dialogue didn't give me access to a great woman, and my lifestyle didn't either. What woman—what God—would even date a Navy SEAL, divorced with two kids, who races in 700-mile multisport races? For that matter, what stripper would even date one with that track record? I am sharing this because, although I knew I needed a woman who needed me, my Internal Dialogue said women are evil and bring you down. I had enough evidence around me to validate that. You must first learn that Internal Dialogue can create, or it can go with the trend. Practice creating your own Internal Dialogue, designed by *you,* versus letting the world tell you who you are and then following the sheep off the cliff.

The one thing we discovered after actually reconnecting by phone and Internet weeks later was the similarity in our points of view. I had never met a woman who so openly embraced and expressed a desire to be a mom, while supporting a physical and naturally violent man. The connection was electric. Not hiding part of me in order to have love and connection felt good. She gave me space to be me, and, in turn, she got space to be Stacy. So, we both created a new Internal Dialogue, saying simply, "I need you." Our new Internal Dialogue gave us tons of room to have a relationship.

I think most people, when searching for God, do not realize He has faults. And, let's just say the search for God in relationships isn't viewed as a matter of service. Service is truly the state of mind that works in relationships . . . it is *all* about them.

Service is about treating the other person as if they were God. In point of fact, however, God has faults, and what most people do with those faults is deal with them instead of giving a ton of space to those faults. I noticed Stacy and I gave each other's faults tons of space. In effect, we didn't deal with or try to reason with the faults. Instead, we dealt with each other as if the other were God. We dealt only with what we were creating the other person to be.

That mindset, and consequently, those actions of giving space to the bad things and dealing only with the greatness, allowed even more greatness to come out in the other person. Stacy got access to being a great woman, a great mom, and a stunning wife by me not dealing with her *oh, shits* and bad ways. In effect, the things causing her to fail in other relationships most certainly came up during our courtship and marriage, but I gave them *space* and dealt with the greatness in her.

Stacy, in turn, gave tons of space to my failings, my indiscretions—my smelly feet, as it were—and dealt with what made me powerful. She fully embraced and supported me as a violent warrior. I bring that up because current society and politically minded people never talk about it. The Spartan Wife is a cliché or even a bad word. The current trend is to equate the phrase Spartan Wife with the N-word for black people. I hold Stacy, my Spartan Wife, equal to God, and am not ashamed of it. Don't you ever be ashamed of it, either.

In turn, all the space given to fail, to make mistakes, caused many to go away or even die. I know this is truly counterintuitive. Giving space to the bad and dealing with the good springs from the grace of an Internal Dialogue of *need* to be *needed*. Dealing only with the things in others that make them powerful, while giving space to their weaknesses, literally reshapes the other person. Changing the other person never occurs to you. Dealing with greatness signals to the other person they are great, so why not be great?

How does this work in reality? I know words on paper are fun to read and make sense, but in the back of your mind, you may not see a way to make it work. That's why, in my opinion, self-help books don't resoundingly make a difference to anyone. Love thy neighbor as thyself gets lost because you try it, and the neighbor shits on you, then you deal with the shit and give space to others' greatness. You spend every waking minute dealing with shit from others, and you move away from them. Instead, what works is the opposite. The neighbor shits on you, and you give it space. Acknowledge the shit, then give it space. Deal with what is powerful. For instance, Stacy had to give space to my going to war and being alone with two children who were not hers to begin with. She then dealt with me being aggressive and violent, and embraced and promoted those traits. She dealt with being a mom to our kids and embraced it full throttle.

Need to be *needed* works in combat as a rallying point—even for the hardest of men in the worst conditions. Men who survive when others fail have a *need* to be *needed*. The *need* to be *needed* by a woman is paramount for the development of a man . . . any man, really. Also, the *need* to be *needed* works between men in combat. We need each other, not just for combat, but also for the connection to each other. Embracing this understanding does not make a man soft. This is actually what sets successful men apart from failures. History is rife with accounts of successful men having a strong woman; it's equally rife with failures having no woman to *need*. I can't think of one single man who doesn't have a woman behind his successes. That doesn't mean in any way that woman was his wife, but behind every great man is a woman.

Autumn, I suspect you will be the same. You will make your man. I don't have to be around for that to be true. You will find intimate moments of connection . . . times when your man is alone, yet he can feel you near him. Your nearness will make him powerful and successful far and above what he would be without you. I suggest his endurance in business comes from the *need* to be *needed* you will provide him.

I don't think buildings would be built if men were alone. Hell, why even make a fortune if you have no one to share it with or do it for? I know I wouldn't achieve anything difficult if not for Stacy, who fosters and embodies that need in me.

So my fourth task for you is this: find, discover, and create an Internal Dialogue with a man that says, powerfully, "I *need* him, and he *needs* me." I know this will take a great deal of time, and yes, mistakes will be made. Men will not know what to do with you. I suggest they will ask less of you or push you toward subservient crap. Be patient, strong, and never settle. Hone and reshape your own Internal Dialogue, and do your best to push away those who would lessen you as a woman. Don't fall prey to sex as the only way to connect. And trust me, that will be a hard feat in itself. Oh, don't confuse love and lust with the power of how your own Internal Dialogue will connect all things. Look to Stacy as a guide.

SECTION THREE

Movement

JOSÉ ORTEGA Y GASSET
"We do not live to think, but, on the contrary,
we think in order that we may succeed in surviving."

After four days of sleeping and tending to his face wounds, Carnie re-covered and engaged with life again. I had been keeping my eye on him. LT and I talked often about how we should deal with Carnie. Paying close attention to those around you is vital; yet equally important is not indulging in the drama of emotions. Now, that may seem hardened and cold, but in fact, it is the opposite entirely. Tough physical and emotional times make you even more sensitive to life and living. And, as Carnie slept off the emotions of what could have happened, LT and I continued on and allowed him time to sort through what had happened.

I personally do not put much stock in seeking psychological coun-seling, because when you focus on the drama and a bad situation over and over again, tying how you feel to the bad situation, emotional upset becomes practice. Your focus will become your reality. So as the days progressed, we began to task Carnie with doing his job in the platoon and did not talk about what had happened in any serious conversation. All I would say to Carnie was, "I need your help with getting my sniper rifle set up because I need you to carry it in for me on the next target." I needed him to focus on what he liked to do and what others needed him to do.

Eight days after the IED had exploded and blown bone fragments up in his grill, we were inserting once again into hell. We had pinned down a certain Taliban leader in an area no other forces would go. Letting this man roam around wherever he wanted to just didn't seem right, so as we watched him go to bed that night, we jumped in the helos and began our infiltration into what we later called Afghani-nam.

When Nike again woke me at the one-minute-out call, I rubbed the dust out of my eyes, clicked on my night vision, and gazed out the back of the helo. To my surprise, and to Nike's, this beautiful line of machine gun tracer fire crisscrossed the sky behind us and snaked its way right into the side of the helo. I jumped backward and landed on Lawyer, who had not seen the light show, and who jokingly said, "Jesus, Chief, your radio isn't that heavy." Before I could speak, the helo landed, and unbeknownst to most of the passengers, we had just been shot.

Since my comms never worked anyway, I couldn't warn them, so I decided to just get out with them and let that fact sit in the deadness of my radio. Once off the helo, the dust enveloped us all, and the power and noise of the blades lifting the helo skyward drowned out the screaming voice in my head yelling to take cover. At 100 feet in the air, the helo Gatling guns opened up, and we all ran toward the nearest trench. I recall looking up and watching the red arc of bullets heading off into the distance, opposite our direction of travel, and thinking to myself, "Shit, we have four miles to go, and they already know we are here."

But as I turned to Nike, I saw my platoon and Nike already moving silently in the direction of our target and fanning out into an aggressive pattern that would be our trademark response to encountering the enemy at night. It was simple: keep your eyes open, and don't return fire unless you see someone to shoot at. We owned the night with our night vision, tactics, and our eyes in the sky. Therefore, we pressed on.

I laugh as I write this, because hell is supposed to be a desert, but within 100 yards of the helo insert, Nike had already found a river and was knee deep, walking close to the bank. Damn, I love that man. I liked the feel of the water and seeing my platoon moving in rhythm with each other, feeling their way, and most importantly, making their way when nothing else worked.

After two miles in the river, deep in filthy, rushing water, I stopped liking Nike. I waded up to Nike and said, "Bro, I think it is time to get on the bank. We are not going to hit the target at the designated time." He smiled and said, "But walking in the water is much cooler, don't you think?" We laughed, then helped each other up the steep bank into Afghani-nam.

Once up top, we discovered the fields had just been irrigated and were now two feet deep with mud and water. We had not planned for the swamp, but we did plan for the twenty-two canal crossings we had seen in the route planning. We constructed two ladder/bridges to get across the canals and to scale the walls outside the target. As we pushed the first bridge across the first canal, the stupidity of this idea resonated with the snapping sound of the wood when the second guy, who weighed 300 pounds, fell into the deep canal. As he worked his way up the far bank, he calmly reached down and pulled the broken ladder/bridge over to his side, and spinning like a discus thrower, launched the would-be bridge off into the darkness of the night. We all laughed and jumped into the canal to swim across. Who would have thought SEALs would be swimming in hell?

Our patrol extended out to cover about 800 yards from point element, which I was in, and the rear security element. My point element was me, Nike, our EOD, Carnie, All Around, and Texas. We had separated ourselves about 100 yards ahead in order to allow for more ease in movement of the main effort. We often "bird dog,"—move left and right—and often stop and retrace steps to find the best path. More importantly, if we walk into an ambush, the rest of the force isn't caught up in the killing field and can easily maneuver to take vengeance.

Throughout the years of training and deploying as a SEAL, I've always found that no matter how well you plan something, it is always different when you actually get there. The desert had turned into marshland—fully equipped with 10,000 mosquitoes for good measure. After wading through two feet of muddy, irrigated swamp, I was covered in bites and muddy up to my thighs. My gun was still clean, so at least I could fight from the swamp, because I sure as hell couldn't move fast enough to run away. Approaching the target area, I breathed a sigh of relief—it was on top of a hill, which meant no more swamp.

Now is the hour of calm, when everything makes sense and all the pain and frustration goes away, and you truly live in the moment. That unforgiving moment matters more than anything else in combat. In that moment, the bugs do not matter, the pain seeps away, and the sock that was bunched up near my toes just isn't important any longer. Right now, is just the men and the enemy.

My boys were supposed to lock down the target so the main assault could go after and find the bad guys inside the buildings. We approached the wall around the compound, and Nike and Carnie extended the ladder. "For Christ's sake, the fucking sticks extend three feet out from the roof," Nike laughed. I looked at Nike and said, "Who cares. Get your ass up there. Break them or saw them, but I need eyes in that compound right now."

> I am sure the dad you all know is often short with you when you don't do what you say, or make excuses when you fail. I frequently want to apologize for being blunt and forceful. I suppose this is my form of love. Please know I do love you, and being a daddy is difficult, no matter how much a dad is or isn't home throughout a child's life. As you think about what you have read, and as you continue to read what I am going through, know being in the moment and using your Internal Dialogue to get you through the tough times is what matters—to get to the times when things work.

> Your successes will never be a matter of simple physical ability or brute strength. Find your Internal Dialogue, use it, and learn to shape it, so you can alter the outcome of your life. Trust me, the tide of battle isn't shifted with who brought the best guns; it is altered by force of will through use of Internal Dialogue saying, "I need to come back to my family. I do not fear dying. It makes me weak."

§

Carnie and I pushed Nike over the lip and broke some branches in the process. We ended up on the roof, and no one in the compound was awake. When the main assault came up to the gate, I halted them and suggested two men climb over the gate and open it from the inside, instead of blowing the hell out of the gate. Although blowing things up is always fun and causes chaos, it also wakes up everyone within earshot. Since we had the drop on them, I figured we should keep it and not wake the bad men up as they slept.

As the initial entry changed, I moved around the wall toward my final position to check on the rest of the men. For Christ's sake, I do hate the uneven ground in rural countries. I stumbled my way toward Jake, who was on top of the ladder, looking into the compound. On the last two steps toward the ladder, I fell through a rotted footbridge. When I looked up, Jake, with his ever-disgusted look, said, "Fuck this place. We need to make it a glass factory," then calmly looked back into the compound.

Once I righted myself, I walked by the ladder and shook it, excited to hear his creative Internal Dialogue on loudspeaker. He didn't even look down. But after four more steps, I heard him mumble, "Pussy." That is the Jake I love . . . everything was going to be OK.

We had been on target for three minutes at this point, and I was close to my final position when I heard the voice of the assault lead say he had secured the two primary bad guys. We had three hours left until the helos were to return to pick us up, which meant we had more time to clear more buildings and more time to pick a fight.

Looking through my sniper scope and night vision, I could see movement on the final target building. Or did I? Multiple targets and three elements maneuvering throughout the battle space is always complicated. I wasn't sure where my boys were, and I couldn't tell if the person was carrying a weapon. I waited . . . and waited . . . and waited. Wow, the eyes do play tricks on the mind, but I waited longer.

I had pushed out on comms to the assault element what I had seen, and after an hour, the person was gone and no shots had been fired. Although you may hear SEALs and the military just kill and blow up everything, this simply isn't true. In the confusion of battle, shooting without 100 percent target identification is never a good idea. I sure as hell wasn't willing to kill one of my own men.

Finally, the entire target was secured, and we were beginning to organize for movement off target. Again, we had people spread out over a 700-yard area and eight separate buildings. I called for my team leaders to check in, and within one minute, we had a full head count and were poised for movement. We also called the helos to ensure they were ready and that everything was normal on their end. Nothing is worse than no one being there when you are ready to leave. Even in the airport where people miss a flight, people get a bit aggravated. In combat, things get worse.

Everything was going perfectly; we had the two bad guys and were ready to blow up all the drugs and weapons found on target. We now had to move some distance to where the helos would pick us up. Yeah, right.

When we detonated the leftovers, all the lights in all the houses within a kilometer turned on. Someone said over the radio, "Wakie, wakie. Eggs and bakie. Game on, boys."

My element again took up point and briskly put some distance between the target and us. Again into the fields of mud, again jumping across canals, and again kissing the mosquitoes. At helo pick up point, we fanned out into security positions and waited for the ride home. Nike and I shared a Copenhagen, and he looked at me and smiled, saying, "Chief, it would be a bitch if the helos got shot down, wouldn't it?"

I looked at him, paused, and finally replied, "Why would you waste a good dip of Copenhagen on that?" We sat looking in the direction the helos would come, trying to smile, and waited. There is always waiting. There will always be waiting.

Finally, I heard the sound of the helos and saw the first of two rise over the crest of the hill nearest us. Nike grabbed my arm as a rocket propelled grenade launched from the ground and hit the helo. For a moment, neither Nike nor I moved. The helo opened fire on something unseen to us and started to land.

Let me tell you something: until that point in my life, I didn't think running on top of the water like good ol' Jesus did was possible, but suddenly, Nike and I were up and running across the mud and swamp as if it were the Olympic 400-meter dash. And trust me, we only took forty seconds to cover the distance. As the two helos landed and the ramp lowered, we jumped in and slid across the deck, getting our final head count. Since I was the last man into the helo, I smacked the crew chief on the back and said, "Bro we owe you a beer. But, seriously, let's get the fuck out of here!"

Although the helo had just been hit with a dud RPG, and we had tons of excitement on target, I again fell asleep mid-flight. When Nike kicked me awake, the sun was just coming up as we landed. Sunrise did not make the big dent on the side of the helo any less ugly. Bravo platoon had made it through another close call with only dents and scrapes. LT and I debriefed the boys, talking about what we did right and asking the men what we could have done better. After the men left the room, LT and I sat for a minute, not talking.

"Chief, what are your thoughts?" LT asked.

I replied, "I think we are still being reactive to both the environment and the enemy. Now that the men have seen the terrain and we are acclimated, we need to ensure the enemy does everything we want them to do. We need to find ways to force them to be reactive and predictable. I have no ready solution to that end, but I think if we simply state the intent to the men, we will have solutions. Things could have been much worse. We have some sick luck on our side. Let's let the luck fairy fly around, but let's not depend on it."

With that, we separated, and I cleaned up and went to breakfast. Sometimes the thought of prepared eggs and some good coffee are the best thoughts on the planet—always a great reminder of sitting down with your family around the table, connecting and listening. Meals were my way to reach across the thousands of miles and imagine those I loved were at the table with me.

After breakfast, I headed back to my room and, as I always did, put on my ring, opened my computer, sent Stacy a message, and waited for her to respond. While I waited, I turned on the pre-programmed music to connect me to my family even more. I was exhausted, yet I needed my kids . . . I needed Stacy. After ten minutes, I saw Stacy's response, "We are here, baby. How is everyone?"

We feverishly talked about family, the platoon, and life in hell. After initial talk about the day and life, we began the necessary, intimate, flirty, talk every warrior needs. I share this with you because couples so often tend to neglect sexual connection as a need. Stacy is artful in her ability to keep sexual tension high and constructive. I think the Spartans must have understood this and used it to their advantage. The older I become and the more I get to know other successful men and women, I see sexual connection as one of the primary keys to success. Don't ever forget this point as long as you live. Without sexual connection with your mate, you are less. Women who understand the power of that connection with their men, women who hone sexual expression and control the way they express that power, will find in their men . . . anything. Stacy harnessed sexual expression with me and I actually found everything.

As we parted, Stacy typed our foundational words: "Thom, I need you to come back to us. Do not fear dying. It makes you weak."

Several days have passed since my last entry for you in this book to you called *Unbreakable.* The night after the last operation, we attended a late night "ramp ceremony," where three marines had died, and we all saw them off. Hearing about a father or husband dying is always hard. Often, SEALs are viewed as unemotional and calloused to hard times and death. Not true. I believe the opposite is more accurate. We see so much death and loss, we are super sensitive to it. After the ceremony, I could see the energy drained from the men, and we all wanted to distance ourselves quickly.

The very next night, we had another ceremony, sending off four more army chaps who had given their last breath keeping the fight away from the United States. Personally, as I walked away, I said to myself, "This shit is going to get old fast." Nike and I walked to the coffee shop and sat for a while not talking. Finally, Nike looked up and said, "For every ceremony we attend, let's you and I make a pact to kill two Taliban." I spit in my hand and said, "Deal." Sometimes, facing death is better by taking the offensive, and I was not going to say no to a fight.

Later that week, we joined a major operation that would take over the capital of hell. Apparently, military forces could not go into the capital because of the danger, so no one wanted to. Someone decided inserting 200 Special Operations Forces right into downtown to seize all the drugs and weapons in one fell swoop sounded like a good idea. For some reason, working out the problem on the ground took five days.

Flying back to base, I briefed the men and tasked my lead snipers and assaulters with organizing the initial plan to take over and hold the eastern sector for five days. With the summer fighting season hitting full stride, we had to attend another ramp ceremony to say good-bye to three other marines and army soldiers. Resolve was not going to be our issue. Going from an offensive mindset to a defensive one was going to be a major issue. SEALs don't like being static, and we don't really train for staying in one place for five days.

With this new defensive mission in mind, I wanted to sit down and reflect on what I have written and why.

ADAMANTINE LESSON REVIEWED

The most important thing for you to learn is to get a grip on your Internal Dialogue. Simply put, Internal Dialogue is what you say to yourself about who you are. This defines you and shapes your physical and mental actions, literally bridging the gap between your goals and where you are physically and mentally. I have offered you four ways to tap into your Internal Dialogue on your road to becoming Unbreakable. Be brave, be strong, and do the first three tasks so you can begin mastering your own Internal Dialogue. As you begin and complete *Being Physical* each day, notice what you say to yourself. Notice how incredibly hard completing the task perfectly without interruption is. Then, as your own mental and physical fear of *Height* takes shape, use your Internal Dialogue to overcome the fears. Next, I want you to *Push The Impossible* through enduring discomfort and your limitations by spending twenty-four hours moving without stopping. You will find your Internal Dialogue will be loudest here. Listen to what it is saying, and put in place words to alter and affect you. See what your mind and body will do when you shape your own path with words you consciously create. Finally, although I tasked Autumn with the last task, it is meant for everyone. This task is not *Creating Love*; it is finding the power you have, using your own Internal Dialogue, to create connection for you and your mate. "I *need* him, and he *needs* me." Practice it; live it.

I am and will always be a part of you, my children. My genetics flow through you. Learn what I have given. I will be in your language when you say to yourself, " I *am* . . ."

SECTION FOUR

Spartan Wife Connection

STEVEN PRESSFIELD, The Warrior Ethos

Leonidas picked the men he did, he explains, not for their warrior prowess as individuals or collectively. He could as easily have selected 300 others, or twenty groups of 300 others, and they all would have fought bravely and to the death. That was what Spartans were raised to do. Such an act was the apex, to them, of warrior honor. But the king didn't pick his 300 champions for that quality. He picked them instead, he says, for the courage of their women. He chose these specific warriors for the strength of their wives and mothers to bear up under their loss.

Leonidas knew that to defend Thermopylae was certain death. No force could stand against the overwhelming numbers of the Persian invaders. Leonidas also knew that ultimate victory would be brought about (if indeed it could be brought about) in subsequent battles, fought not by this initial band of defenders, but by the united armies of the Greek city-states in the coming months and years.

What would inspire these latter warriors? What would steel their will to resist—and prevent them from offering the tokens of surrender the Persian king Xerxes demanded of them?

Leonidas knew that the 300 Spartans would die. The bigger question was, How would Sparta herself react to their deaths? If Sparta fell apart, all of Greece would collapse with her. But who would the Spartans themselves look to in the decisive hour? They would look to the women—to the wives and mothers of the fallen.

If these women gave way, if they fell to weeping and despair, then all the women of Sparta would give way too. Sparta herself would buckle and, with her, all of Greece.

But the Spartan women didn't break, and they didn't give way. The year after Thermopylae, the Greek fleet and army threw back the Persian multitudes at Salamis and Plataea. The West survived then, in no small measure because of her women.

The lioness hunts. The alpha female defends the wolf pack. The Warrior Ethos is not, at bottom, a manifestation only of male aggression or of the masculine will to dominance. Its foundation is society-wide. It rests on the will and resolve of mothers and wives and daughters—and, in no few instances, of female warriors as well—to defend their children, their home soil and the values of their culture.

Stacy Shea

I haven't heard from Thom in two days, and we are all feeling the pressure of our daddy and husband being on a combat deployment. I thought it necessary to document for the family what exactly we on the home front do to connect and promote the work our SEALs—our husbands—do overseas. After Thom's sharing of Section 3 for the kids and me, this may be the last chapter.

I have a unique perspective into the community as the SEAL Team Seven ombudsman. Our women are the very definition of strength and grace. The best relationships are those where the wife fully embraces what her husband is doing and powerfully takes that stand alongside him. I have seen my share of relationships where resentment takes over and adversely impacts the performance of our warriors and the overall experience of family. Resentments can, understandably, begin. As the wife of a SEAL, you must find a way to successfully walk the fine line of fierce independence and the ability to surrender that independence the moment your husband is home. He's gone, on average, 220 days a year. All those romantic notions about being married to one of those uber-tough, sexy, warrior types boils down to spending much of your time without him. Thom keeps coming back to Internal Dialogue, and that's truly where all the power lies. It ain't nothing until I say so. What I choose to say about our lives, our marriage, and our deep and abiding connection is this:

"I am with him always, and he is with me."

When he is on a training trip, I am inside him, loving him, encouraging him, reminding him we need him, and that every day he makes us a strong family. When he is deployed and in harm's way, I remind him of the lyrics from a Dave Matthews song, "The space between the bullets in our firefight is where I'll be hiding, waiting for you."

I never, not even for a moment, feel less than an equal measure of his presence and love in my life. His support and contribution to my endeavors is strong, even on those nights when his head doesn't rest on the pillow next to mine. He is with me always.

With that, I wanted to reflect on my life and what our family does to actively connect to my husband, our father, and our warrior.

The night before Thom left for hell was extremely tense for us all. I know leaving their families behind and going to an unknown country, taking the fight to our nation's enemies, is terribly rough on the warriors. I know it is necessary, so our way of life back here does not have to face war on American soil. I thank God for men like SEALs who openly love to fight anyone, anywhere, any time of year. They are men who don't fear death; they just fear dying and leaving their families behind, or having some other man step into his shoes on the home front.

I think this fact is lost on the greater population of the United States. Since I have known Thom, I have not met a SEAL who would run away from a fight, even if he knew he was going to die or the fight was not winnable. They simply *need* to fight. I *need* that in a man, and I think many of the other wives need it, too.

Anyway, the time we shared around the dinner table that night was anything but happy. For an instant, I saw sadness, and possibly fear, in Thom's eyes. The sight shocked me. I didn't allude to the feeling in front of the kids because I did not want them to learn fear.

Thom must have sensed it as well, and like every warrior, he lashed out with aggression by yelling at the kids for small things. As with most families at dinner time, it caused the kids to be quiet and not express what they were feeling. I did not correct him because I knew he was feeling the tension of separation, not the fear of death.

As we all attempted to cuddle around the TV, the emotions came out, and the kids were free to cry and say to Thom they loved him and needed him to come home. While watching this all transpire, I noted how that expressed need from the kids cleared Thom's eyes and mind. He looked focused after that. His resolve was back.

After the kids were in bed, Thom and I locked ourselves in our room—our cocoon. I am not shy in sharing how sex is the easiest way to connect with an aggressive alpha-male, and Thom is truly available to sex as a way to become connected. As we lay together looking at each other, I could sense his sadness. I also knew sex would not resolve his feelings, so I used the next best thing. I spoke our connection into existence.

> As my children read this, I hope you begin to understand how powerful words are for shaping and creating. Your dad and I have come to realize the words we say to each other, and the words we say to ourselves about each other, are the foundation for what we do physically and what our relationship does, too.

As I saw him begin to cry, I reached up, touched his face and said, "Thom, I need you to come back to us. Do not fear dying. It makes you weak."

As spouses and mothers, we know what to say to our husbands and children to provide them a strong foundation of support. I knew Thom *needed* to hear we *needed* him. I knew those words would be his foundation overseas when times got tough—and times were going to be tough.

I knew I had to tell him to never have fear in his heart. I had learned from his Iraq deployment that if he were allowed to talk about fear with me, he would not be afraid.

I also know most SEALs hate weakness in themselves and others. Consequently, I drove the point home by ending it with "fear makes you weak."

As I spoke these words, I watched the sadness fade and his eyes widen, and we spent the next half hour physically connecting.

Five days have passed since I talked with Thom. Although, as ombudsman, I would be the first civilian to get word if something happened overseas, the sense of "Oh my God," still exists. I think writing down what wives and kids go through while our warriors take the fight to the enemy is important.

The kids and I maintain a solid routine to ensure nothing at home could possibly be a distraction to Thom. My expressed commitment to Thom when we got married was to grow our family strong and provide us all with stability no matter what the world gave us. The world was now giving us some serious tension. I am committed to being the anchor for this family. If I am weak and afraid, my children will be, too. My husband will take one of two routes. He'll shut me out so he can do what he must, or he'll be weakened by my neediness. I'm unwilling to live either of those outcomes.

I came into Thom's, Autumn's, and Garrett's lives after they were established; life in the military was entirely new to me. Thom and the kids had already completed several deployments to Kosovo, and he had just completed a tour as a SEAL instructor. Although he was divorced, I saw something in him which inspired me to create a new life for me, and for us.

I had been working as a stockbroker in Pennsylvania and had also come out of a divorce. Yet, after developing a relationship with Thom, we knew we were perfect for each other. It was even clearer to me I was not giving up my life and financial success; I was creating something bigger. Being a mother and a wife is far more important than any amount of money I would earn alone.

After nine months of "wow dating," we married in San Diego. Garrett (then four) and Autumn (then seven) were our ring bearer and flower girl. We got married in a church with only them and my mother in attendance. I can still see them running all over the sanctuary, throwing flowers at each other and having a one-pillow fight during the ceremony.

I still recall Thom suggesting I sell everything and move in with just my toothbrush. We still laugh about it. However, I had four closets full of clothes I could not part with for any reason. At least Thom gave a thumbs-up on the Victoria's Secret closet.

Before we got married, I remember lamenting to Thom, "What am I going to do for friends when I move? This is so different from my life in Pennsylvania." His response, in classic Thom form, was, "You'll have me, Autumn, and Garrett. Who else will you need?" No, this wasn't an attempt at humor. He was completely serious.

As I began fitting in with his friends and the military, I noticed the good and bad effect families and marriages have on the careers and performance of the SEALs. Thom and I talked often about what we needed from each other that would work toward us being strong. A common theme became clear. The vital key was for both of us to expressly *need* each other without being needy.

This truly seemed counter to everything I had read about relationships. To me, this sounded like co-dependency, that tired, over-used word, and it seemed if we needed each other, I'd have no way out if we fell apart. Yet the formula of not depending and needing the other person was the going trend, and we both acknowledged it was the formula we used in our previous marriages, as well as the one all divorces have used.

Thom has shared with me how SEALs have an 70 percent divorce rate, yet at work he noted they are all dependent on each other. SEALs never look for a way out of the overwhelming difficulties they encounter in training, hell week, or combat . . . they look for a way in. We decided to *need* each other and "go all in, every time." We *needed* to be *needed*. We needed one another. The *need* to be *needed* is a genetic trait within all humans, yet it's one only a few come to realize.

As the days of no communication grew, so did our family's resolve to do whatever we could to reach out and make sure Thom knew at his core that we needed and loved him, and that we were strong and safe. Each night, we prepared a plate at the table as if he were there with us. Each day, we shared our individual thoughts with him in a note to him on the Internet. I think it was more to keep the communication and connection alive than anything mystical. But, the hell Thom was surely in may have tapped into the ability to reach across the distance with love, affection, and prayer.

The kids and I talked each night about daddy and about what we thought he was doing over in hell. I said, "Daddy is fighting bad men and he loves it, so we need to pray he fights hard for us." Chance would say, out loud, "My daddy is fighting. I want to be like daddy someday, so I can be strong."

After the kids fell asleep, I would turn on my iPod and listen to the songs Thom and I had selected. One of my favorites was from Dave Matthews, "The Space Between." Often, Autumn and I would lay there listening to the words and imagine Thom dodging bullets, knowing his family was waiting in the space between the bullets. The song and the lyrics became exactly that . . .

"the space between the bullets in the firefight is where I will be hiding waiting for you."

I would literally close my eyes, and say to myself, *I am here, Thom, between the bullets. It is safe here; do not be afraid.*

This was our routine and our foundation. I thought it was solid until one day I turned on the TV. I just happened to be watching the news on FOX when they showed a huge military operation that was supposed to be the biggest drug seizure in history. As the camera showed images, I dropped to my knees, because I saw Thom. What the hell was going on? Why was Thom on TV? The ringing in my ears was terrible. Did I hear he was dead; did I hear the words "Special Operations Forces?"

I had to hit rewind on the TV to ensure I was not going crazy. After thirty minutes of rewinding and watching, then rewinding again, the rush in my ears stopped. He was not dead, but he was clearly in the special operation, as I had seen Thom and someone in his platoon. A wife can tell—trust me.

The amount of drugs seized and enemies reported killed were staggering. Somehow, Thom's Task Unit and the Army Special Forces had killed over 180 enemies in three days and seized over a billion dollars in opium. I have to admit it actually made me feel sexy. I know it will be hard to read and understand, but OMG: I want that man right then!

The kids and I watched the show several times, talking about what daddy was doing. During the rewind, Chance turned to me and said, "Mommy, daddy is fighting, isn't he?"

I needed a second to compose myself, because I realized that there's a turning point in every child's life where they are taught to be afraid or learn fear. I was not going to allow what Thom calls our "Internal Dialogue" to shape our boy into someone who had been taught fear.

I grabbed Chance and said, "Yes, your daddy is fighting. That is what he does. He is good at it, and he keeps us safe. Let's all get on the computer and write him a note telling him we love him and are proud he is fighting for Americans and for freedom." I saw the questioning look of the beginnings of fear fade to, "Oh. That's just what he does . . . OK." As Thom has often said to me, "Stacy, the small things we do and say to each other shape us."

Several more days passed after seeing Thom and his platoon on TV. Chance and I spent a majority of our time on Gator Beach with other Team Seven wives. We needed each other. We laughed and talked about our families and how we were all coping with the deployment. Inevitably, the shit hits the fan as soon as they leave. Each of us has to humble ourselves, swallow our pride, and ask for help. Oddly enough, this condition rarely, if ever, exists in America anymore. We are prosperous. We don't know our neighbors; we don't need *anyone*. What a lie! I needed the connection with other wives, both in the SEALs and also with other women who didn't know anything about the war over there.

However, some of the wives were really stressed out, sharing how their husbands rarely communicated with them about what they do. I began to notice these same wives worried about infidelity and trust.

Since I come from two previous failed marriages where I had complaints about the situation, and infidelity was always a concern, I also became uniquely aware of the difference in my current marriage. Oddly enough, Thom was right. The small words we say to ourselves and each other really make a profound difference in both the physical and emotional aspects of the marriage itself. I knew, from what Thom was sharing with me and the kids, that Internal Dialogue shapes everything. I saw the effect bad Internal Dialogue had on other relationships.

I spent the next two days researching all I could find on Spartans and their wives. Spartan women played a major role in both family and the society. I think they were the first women in history to actually have a vote in society and allowed to own land. In my readings, I found they, too, openly embraced the warrior in their husbands. Apparently, they also found sex to be a great way to harness the power of the warrior and make the connection with their men unbreakable. I am glad Thom picked the name *Unbreakable* to describe his life to our kids. I would call it "Spartan Wife," but that term leaves out the contribution the husband and children make to the success of the entire family. You see, part of what inspired me to flourish in the midst of my husband being in such dangerous conditions during these deployments was the looks on my children's faces. They were so brave and so strong, and I refused to let them down by allowing any fears I had make an impression upon their spirits or lives.

After all, I had chosen this man knowing exactly what I was getting . . . knowing he would be gone, on average, 220 days per year, and knowing the work he chose (and was so good at) could literally cost him his life. Our babies had no such choice. Yet, I would now teach them to choose *this* life. They were born of a warrior and live their lives with such grace and courage. I would never let them down.

I've had people ask me why I married a man who is constantly in so much danger. For me, it's an honor being a part of what he is committed to. In our relationship, I have found what I've wanted ever since I was a little girl: a man who loves me completely, who is not afraid to be strong and bold, and who makes me feel safe and secure because he knows who he is. To us, and to those around us, everything appears easy between us. In many ways that's true. But I want you to think about something. When we met, I had been divorced twice. Thom was recently divorced. He was trying to manage being a single father of two young children, a SEAL, and the lover of a strong-willed woman. When we got married, we faced what anyone would call insurmountable odds. I was leaving a successful career, my friends, my family, and everything I had known for so long. My new husband would be traveling a great deal for work, and I would have to figure out how to balance the life of a newlywed with spending a lot of time alone in a new place.

Within a year and a half of getting married, I moved across the country, changed jobs, had a child, lost a job, and faced my husband's deployment to Iraq.

Early in our relationship, we came to some agreements. One of them was this:

We do it together, or we don't do it at all.

This agreement was so different from anything I had experienced before. All that mattered in this expression of our love and commitment was what we openly SAID to ourselves and each other about . . . us.

Our agreement created a very connecting conversation. I was a part of everything he was doing, and he was a part of everything I was doing. We left each other out of nothing. As a result, I never had an experience of being left—or of being alone. In all the times he was away on training trips or at war, I was with him. In the challenges I faced in my professional life or in the transition to being a stay-at-home mom, I did none of it without him. The tyranny of distance did not limit our connection and our communication.

As many of our wives do during deployment, I traveled to spend time with family. Being home, surrounded by familiarity, was comforting. During this time Thom and I communicated more than any other. Outside of planning and executing missions, he had a lot of free time. We Skyped and chatted online a lot. I still remember the first time Autumn saw him after he had left for Iraq. She was so excited when I said we were going to be able to see him. She laid on the living room floor on her stomach, propped up on her elbows. The laptop was open, and when she saw him, she got really upset and cried. Watching her so upset was hard for me. I knew what she was going through. So many times when I saw him on the computer like that . . . well, he looked so different when he was at war. He always looked so tired. Many times I thought to myself, *What if this is the last time I talk to him? Is this dirty little Internet room the last place of civilization he'll know before he dies?*

I wanted to make all her fears and sorrow go away. I fought the urge to close the computer and hold her in my arms, telling her that everything would be OK. I knew seeing and connecting with her dad would make her stronger to face that fear. After all, I didn't really know if everything was going to be OK. Her daddy was at war. I couldn't possibly promise her his safe return. It would be an outright lie, and we would both know it. Instead, we faced that fear together and, in those moments, I began to find my deepest connection to Autumn.

Chance and I stayed with my family during the first part of Thom's deployment. Getting away from the house for a while is helpful because life is not the same without him. The thought he might not come home to us is sometimes too much to bear. Like many in our community, we escape for a while to the love and support of family. Living in the San Diego area, if you tell someone your husband is a SEAL who is currently deployed, there isn't much of a reaction. With the large military presence here, half the SEALs being stationed in Coronado, and a protracted war, the local civilians are used to hearing this.

Step outside of this little enclave, and the reaction is quite different. Anywhere you travel as the spouse of a deployed service member, if you share that your husband is overseas fighting, people want to do anything they can to help you and your family. How much people truly love our military and their families has been the most touching thing in my travels. People show they care in brief encounters with us, through random small acts of kindness, and through generous financial gifts to the many groups providing support.

"I got this."

So, here it is, roughly one month into the deployment, and one of the unforeseen things I have to face is the overwhelming fear people around me have about Thom's death. It will come up intermittently until his plane lands and he walks across the tarmac and into our arms.

These fears are clearly harder for the women in my life than the men. I think the women see themselves in me; they wonder how I can do it and be so solid. The men think it will make me falter to show any weakness and, somewhere deep inside, they wish they were taking the fight to the enemy and counting scalps along the way.

My mom and my sister seem to struggle the most. Their tears affect me profoundly. Mom pictures me alone in my house with my babies and without their daddy, and she can't hold back her emotional response. Lisa, my sister, sees a firefight on the news resulting in loss of American lives and calls me in a panic. After all, they're mothers and wives, too, and they struggle with the reality I'm facing. In these moments I find my strength. I do my best to reassure them. They need me, too.

"Thom, don't be afraid.
It makes you weak."

PART TWO

Your Muscles

SECTION FIVE

WORDS

WERNER ERHARD, 1975
"Fuck and spaghetti are just words. It is you who provide the meaning."

"I am here, Stacy," I typed in an email, knowing she must surely be stressed out. I had not left them with any knowledge of where I would be, nor how long I would be gone. I suppose this is the way things are when you marry a SEAL. Especially so in my case. I knew our life would consist of me constantly going to war. I tried to make that clear. Looking back, in light of the last ten days, I should have tried harder to talk her out of marrying and creating a life with me. The last ten days makes clear I will not have total control over when I die.

I *had* made an attempt to talk Stacy out of marriage. For God's sake, my proposal was simple and to the point: "Stacy, we are both divorced. I have two kids who live with me. I am a Navy SEAL who actually likes and enjoys my job and wants combat. I travel 220 days a year, and will surely go back into combat two or three more times before I retire. I may not survive. I love and need you, and I don't want you to suffer in a life you don't want. So you wanna get married, or what?"

Poor Stacy said, "Are you serious? Is that your proposal?" I do recall thinking for a second and finally said, "Oh no, that isn't. I don't have any money, so if you want a ring, you have to buy it." I was serious, and knew for sure she would say no. But, the silly woman said, "Yes, let's get married."

I wanted you, Chance, to know that tidbit about your mother and father, so you might know for sure who your daddy is, and what he said to your mom. Writing this is tough because, as I wrote earlier, I truly had no control of whether I lived or died over there. Each day counts; I am glad for that fact. Every thought I wanted to share felt urgent to write so you could have it later in life when you needed it.

Before I get into what I had gone through over the past ten days, I want you to know this about me. I don't use words like hope and belief. Let me tell you why—and I want you to ponder why I do not. This question is the fifth task for you to complete.

ADAMANTINE LESSON FIVE

Hope and Belief

I want you to begin looking at your language and the meaning of words, both yours and those others use. Specifically, **hope and belief**. My definition of hope is:

> *The feeling that what is wanted can be had or that events will turn out for the best.*

As a result, many people use this word. I did for the longest time. Yet something shifted for me when I became a SEAL. I had to actually make it through very hard times and tasks, and then later, I had to watch and train other men attempting to go through SEAL training. The shift occurred when I realized some people use the word "hope" as a mechanism when they are not actively taking committed action in their life or toward their goals. "I hope I make it through SEAL training," said by every single person who quit BUD/S, helped me move away from that word.

Can you imagine saying, "I feel like I am going to make it through football camp," or, "I feel like we are going to win or lose this game." Sounds completely stupid, doesn't it? So does, "I hope I do well," or, "I hope that girl likes me." Hope is what you have or say when you are neither in action, nor committed 100 percent to what you are doing . . . when you have given yourself a way out. Hope is a word used when you don't act or follow up on what you are doing.

My definition of belief is:

> *Confidence in the truth, or existence of something not immediately susceptible to rigorous proof.*

I want you to look at your language again. What are the words you and others use in the course of living? Belief is a word which will not serve you well. Belief works to make others feel good about something, but in the end is truly deceptive. Don't let anyone tell you Jesus or God used the word. They did not. Jesus was a man of action. Belief and action cannot live together.

Therefore, belief is a disease sucking action out of you . . . sucking the possibility of the actions you take toward goals coming to fruition. Belief is what is left after you fail once, and stop pursuing. Belief is what people say when they have no experience, but refuse to take action.

Grasping and coming to terms with this task will take a long time. Look at language, your Internal Dialogue, and don't fall prey to misuse of it by others, especially with regard to "belief" and "hope." Replace those two words with, "I know I will do this thing . . . not hope," and, "I know God . . . not belief."

§

Well, the last ten days were the most real and most chaotic I have ever lived . . . up to this point. The first five, since I talked with my family, we were placed in "lock down." Due to the nature of the mission and rather high-profile issues, the bosses turned off our Internet and phones for security reasons. I am sort of glad for it, too.

With that said, I am proud of the men for how they planned and organized every detail of the upcoming mission into the capital city of hell. And, trust me, we needed all five days to work through the details. Stacy always says the devil is in the details; now I know why. But let me add: the devil actually lived in this city, and I was going to shoot him in the face.

I am writing this while waiting for Stacy to get my email saying I am alive. I'm trying to find the right words to convey something that happened to me. The last five days were completely out of control by every definition. I even think the god of war looked down and said, "Shit, that place is too dangerous for me. Those SEALs don't need my help."

We loaded up all six helos with 200-plus Special Operators and, after a twenty-minute flight, we landed everyone in two minutes. I have never, ever heard of that many Special Operators landing so fast on one mission in the heart of enemy territory. Let me tell you, it was breathtaking and actually manageable from my point of view. We rehearsed each phase, from insert to hitting each phase line to extracting.

My platoon's specific section was immediate takeover and hold of the eastern sector, then maintain hold for five days. Our part was small in scope, assaulting only one building, but let me tell you: we did not sit down for five days. Upon insert, we only had to move 40 yards to our target, but we all packed food, water, bombs, and bullets so heavily, I could not pick up my backpack and had to drag it behind me. My pack weighed 220 pounds. I had packed ten liters of water, two days' worth of food, six mortar rounds, and a case of linked .50 caliber.

Near the building, we dropped our packs and commenced to "get it on." In two minutes, we worked the problems on that target, seizing those who gave up and shooting those who wanted to go to guns. I have to admit it felt more like twenty minutes, because in combat, everything seems to slow down; I don't know why. However, we had a timekeeper calling out time, and as I heard my men say they were done, I called target secure. As I set some of the men on security, the rest of us rushed out and got all the packs. I do recall saying to myself, after getting five separate packs, I wished I worked out more—less endurance, more power lifting.

After an hour of going over the buildings with a fine-tooth comb, I had already consumed one liter of water. At 5:00 a.m., the temperature was already 110 degrees. At this rate, I would be out of water by noon. I should have taken that hint, because it came back to haunt us all by 2:00 p.m. However, at 5:30 a.m. on the first morning, my snipers were already shooting. We were in our first real firefight in this platoon.

Two separate sniper positions had been set up on the roofs, and holes knocked in every wall, so everyone was gainfully employed. As tactical leader, I moved around the compound ensuring we had all avenues covered, and I also assisted the men who needed help. In a firefight, every man needs help, and every man needs to know you are there for him. You will rarely read in a military journal or heavy combat book how vital that connection is.

The machine gun young Texan was running, jammed, so I rushed over to his wall and took his position while he fixed the problem. Rushing in and looking through a hole in the wall, only to immediately see the enemy shooting AK-47s was an interesting feeling. All my training kicked in, and all the years as a sniper took hold. Guessing the distance to be 200 yards or so, I raised my M14 rifle and looked through my scope. Dialing one minute into my scope, I took a deep breath. Slowly, I took up slack in the trigger, then gradually exhaled until my breath stopped naturally. In the pause between breaths, the waving of the cross hairs on the scope lessened, and the gun fired. I saw the bullet hit his neck and his gun drop.

Suddenly, the wall erupted with bullets, and I ducked. When I looked up, wide-eyed Texas was looking down at me, his chief, kneeling. I smiled and said, "There is enough for everyone, but that dude is dead. You need anything for that gun?" He frowned and said, "Yes, get the fuck out of the way so I can shoot." I crawled away, and when I looked back, he was unloading on someone, who, I can only imagine, didn't realize he was dying.

I moved another five yards to the corner of the wall and looked back for a wider perspective. I saw carnage like I had only seen before in war movies. To my left a ground-mounted M2 .50 caliber machine gun was hammering down the road. In front of me two sniper positions were manned with four snipers, who were calmly shooting their .300 Winchester Magnums, ducking occasionally when rounds from the enemy hit next to them. To my right, Texas was yelling for another box of rounds for his machine gun.

Lawyer was tucked in a corner with LT looking at a map and trying to coordinate an A-10 and an AH-64. I turned to crawl back to Texas, and at that moment, a rocket hit the wall outside my just-vacated position, knocking me down. Texas ran over and pulled me out of the rubble, saying, "Hey listen, don't go over there. It is bad. Stay over here and kill some more with me. If you die, I am going to shoot you."

After forty-five minutes, the enemy retreated, so we continued building up our position, and resting, eating, and drinking. One truth about combat you rarely see in movies or read in books is you are never safe until you are back home with your kids and wife. For SEALs in combat, this is an ingrained truth . . . never stop fighting, never stop making the situation better for yourself and worse for the enemy, and, finally, if the enemy doesn't do what you want him to, MAKE HIM.

While we built up sniper positions with sandbags and more sandbags, until the roof began to dip, I checked in with every single man to ensure he was OK, that his "shit was still tight," and that he was not afraid. Looking into a man's eyes moments after he has shot and killed another man is a hard thing, but I have learned this is the time for the leader to stop and connect with him, even if only to make sure your man is present and living in the now. While hard to describe, the key to connecting to everyone in the middle of conflict is to give him or her exactly what is needed in the moment—even if what's needed is a kick in the ass.

Moving around the compound, I made my first stop at the .50 caliber machine gun position we called the hell hole. KM sat behind the open window the barrel stuck out of. The whole scene was surreal to me. He was soaking wet with sweat, the barrel was smoking hot, and I could see the mirage rising up and hear the metal ticking as it tried to cool. The ground around hellhole was covered with shell casings, and it occurred to me there were over 500 casings. I immediately turned and got two cans full of new rounds, dragging them forward to KM.

Without turning, KM said, "What up, Ridge Boss?" I laughed, "Dude, what the fuck is going on here? You shot over 500 rounds by yourself."

He smiled and said, "I thought all of you were dead, 'cause I shot the first 100 without ear protection, and I can't hear a fucking thing. Other than that, you might want to take a look down that road."

I got out my binoculars to look. My brain took several seconds to realize what I was really seeing. I saw bodies lying all down the road. RPG-7s lay everywhere, some shot apart by KM, others apparently having already launched their rockets. One, two, three . . . seventeen, eighteen.

I went to hand the binoculars down to KM, but he handed them back, laughing, "Let the buzzards come, or let the enemy come get them. Either way, I got this shit."

At that point, our EOD walked in, stopped, and said, "Holy shit, Chief. You've got to come see this." I turned to KM, "Look at me, KM." He did. I said, "Everyone is alive, and so are you. We are going to help you bunker this .50, so hang tight. Don't let any motherfucker with a weapon get in on us. Do you understand me?" He smiled, we hit fists, then I left.

Outside I grabbed our EOD and let him lead me around in front of the hellhole. We stood there for a minute, then looked at each other. Bullets and RPGs had left holes in the wall where they had impacted. Even bigger holes were on the ground, where bad aimers had tried to hit KM on the

.50 but missed.

"I count eight RPG impacts and over a hundred bullet strikes in the wall," I said. EOD nodded, "We have to get more sandbags in the hellhole. He won't survive another volley like that."

I replied, "I agree. You and he are manning the hellhole. KM will need you. Keep him alive, OK?" EOD patted me on the back, "*You* keep *us* alive, OK?"

I returned to Texas and said, "How are you doing, Son? How is the pig working for you?" He shrugged and asked for water. "I left my kit over on the wall and I am parched." I handed him my two Gatorade bottles saying, "Drink up." I patiently waited and began moving into his position subtly. When he was done I said, "I think we are good here. I need you to go to the hellhole and help KM and EOD bunker that shit so that it can withstand a 500 pound bomb, OK? KM needs you; go help." Texas and I hit knuckles, then he grabbed his shit to walk to the hellhole. As he passed his kit, I stopped him, "Hey, take your kit with you until I personally come and get you, OK?"

After Texas left, I walked over to LT and Lawyer, who were still engaged in controlling the jets and helos above us. "LT, the hellhole needs some serious bunkering and we are going to run out of .50 caliber rounds today. I am going around to see how everyone else is doing, but I can assure you, we are all going to run out of rounds today. Better get coordinating with everyone else. I am sure every other position will also need a resupply. I'll be back in ten. How are you doing?" LT looked up and said "OK?" then looked back at the maps. I took that as, "Hey, I'm busy; get away."

Lawyer looked frazzled. He was on the ground on all fours, one hand on the map, and the other on his push trying to reach the aircraft.

I walked over to him and put my hand on his shoulder, "Good job, brother."

I took a second to stop at my own kit and pull out another Gatorade bottle and snacks. In the room where my kit was, I noticed Carnie sitting on the ground in the corner.

He looked up and said, "This is just like hunting deer from a stand." I walked over and sat next to him. He proceeded to tell me the story of his "hunt." I let him talk. As long as men can associate what they are doing in combat with something they like, I think it's a good thing. He got animated telling me about guys shooting at him and ducking behind trees, as if the tree would hide them. So, he shot through the trees. He ended the story with a laugh and said, "I am not going out there to get the horns."

We shared a bag of beef jerky, then I got up, reached down, and patted his shoulder. He and I had known each other long enough that I knew a word wouldn't work for him. I stood there for a moment before saying, "KM got hit by seven or eight RPGs, and has bodies all over the road. Keep your wits about you—your wife needs you. Do you know what I am saying?" He replied, "Yes, Chief, I got you."

Across the courtyard Nike and Jake were in the primary sniper position. I climbed up the ladder and lay between them. They were still looking through their scopes. After a moment I reached into my pocket and brought out a can of Copenhagen, offering it first to Nike. He rolled to his left side and I could see the smile on his face.

"Damn, Chief, this is real sniper work. I've shot 20 rounds. Furthest is 700 yards. This is going to be fun." With that, he opened the can and put half into his lip. Handing it back to me, he told me, "Chief, I need an aspirin 'cause I have a screaming headache. Can you be my bitch and go dig it out of my med kit?" I smiled.

"Jake, what do you need?" I asked before leaving. He replied, "More rounds, please."

I crawled back, then stopped to grab each of their legs. "Don't think you are studs and stay up here. Ask for help. I am not going to tell you how long. This shit is real. Don't fight it when you lose concentration, just ask for help. Do you understand me?" They both replied in the affirmative. "So, how much longer do you think, so I can plan for your relief?" I asked. "Maybe twenty minutes," was the reply.

I slid down the ladder, got Nike's aspirin, and threw it up to him with some bottles of water. At the base of the ladder, I took a moment to think and consider all that had happened and what certainly would happen again. The enemy knew we were here, and exactly what we had to shoot at them. We hadn't dropped any bombs yet, and that would surely change things. We had 40 mm grenades, 60 mm mortars, and 84 mm rockets yet to bring out. When we brought them out, they'd cause havoc.

Time to set up the mortar tube now. I was the only one not gainfully employed, so I broke out the tube and set it on the bipod and plate. I gathered a couple of boxes of mortars and opened the cans. When I looked back, it occurred to me to go separate the cans a bit, so if one happened to blow up, the whole compound wouldn't go into the sky.

After two hours of hard work, around 10:30 a.m., our compound was as good as it was going to get. I had just lay down to get some rest when I heard the .50 caliber light off. Unconsciously, I was on my feet running to a hole in the wall next to Carnie. Immediately, we were spotting and shooting the enemy, who were running around trying to shoot us. I turned my radio to LT's channel and said, "I suggest we use air on this one. They are only 100 yards away, and we have five EKIAs (enemy killed in action) over here. If they get in on us at this point, we are going to be hurting. It's only the first day."

LT replied, "Already on it. First one: two minutes out. Danger close in your sector." Turning back to my hole, I shot two more "gentlemen who came to call," then I heard a 500 pounder thirty seconds out that rocked me back on my chair. Ouch! My finger squeezed the trigger, the bullet hitting the side of the hole. I looked at Carnie, who was on the ground, having been knocked off the chair. He laughed and said, "Dude, that was funny. You shot the wall: what an amateur." Dust came pushing through the holes and totally clouded the entire room, so we stood up and walked out coughing and laughing together.

Looking in the direction of the bomb, we saw a huge dust cloud rising above the trees, and rocks and dirt were being thrown everywhere. I walked over to Lawyer, who said, "I think I came in my pants; that shit was close. Next time I think I am going to get the A-10 to do a gun run."

"What are you waiting for? Do it," I replied.

A minute later Lawyer called out, "danger close."

I continued the count and got my crosshairs on another "caller," and as I pulled slack out of my trigger, a huge bright light exploded right in the middle of my scope about 150 yards away.

Lawyer was talking to the A-10 pilot and you could hear the plane coming in closer. Nike and Jake were still shooting at the devils in their sector as some stupid ass who thought 800 yards was a safe distance to stop and talk to his buddy.

I climbed the ladder and said, "Nike, gun run coming on those guys you are shooting. Tell me where you want it."

After passing the info to Lawyer, I turned around and looked right into the mouth of an A-10 flying 100 feet above our compound. I do recall my eyes getting wide as it passed right over us and erupted with two huge bursts out of its mouth cannons.

I didn't get the chance to see where the rounds impacted because the shells from the A-10 were falling right on me, and knocked me off the ladder. Thank God for body armor. I lay laughing, because in that split second, I knew I was where I needed to be and had spent my entire life training and waiting for—the happy chaos. Afterward, it was clear no enemy were moving, and wouldn't be for a while. By then, it was 130 degrees, so I checked through my kit for water and noticed I had none left. I nonchalantly walked around, noticing several empty bottles thrown around. After asking every man how many bottles of water or Gatorade he had left, it became even clearer—we had no water.

At that point, my own Internal Dialogue truly worked against me. I was pissed we were all out of water, and had not planned for more. I was further pissed because, without water, we would die quicker than with what we faced in combat. Everyone was more than upset, because we all knew in this heat, water means life or death.

I got Nike down from the sniper position and said, "Well, we have no more water. I need suggestions. Do you see anything from up there that would help?" He replied, "Yes, Ridge Boss. A canal is about forty yards to the south. Or we can drink from these yellow containers that were left here in the compound."

We walked to the bundle of yellow containers, opened one, and poured it out. *Yum*, I thought, *Dirty water that's 120 degrees.* Then I figured, *What the hell: I will try it.* I knew that even if it had bacteria, it wouldn't affect me as quickly as dehydration would. So, bottoms up. Damn, it tasted like piss with sand, but it quenched my thirst, and made me feel alert.

We filled up most of the men's bottles, though not everyone was brave enough to indulge in the sand piss. Yet, after a couple of hours, all but LT were gorging themselves.

I was exhausted, to be sure. After the sandy piss-flavored debacle, most of us tried to get rest; no one can fight in that heat. We called in some helos and jets to continue keeping pressure on the enemy. If I recall, the bullets started flying again around 4:00 p.m. We were ready this time, yet we took heavy fire in all the sandbags. RPGs were hitting the north- and east-facing walls.

I had walked to one of the wall ports and was firing on several enemy who were making their way along a wall, from the east toward the west. Oddly, the wall had a big gap where they had to expose themselves to get to the other wall. I don't think those three guys will be doing that any- more. Again, after forty-five minutes of fighting, we had enough jets and helos above us getting after it, that we could lick our wounds and resupply with the remaining bullets. Only twenty bullets were left per man and 200 linked rounds for the heavy weapons to share.

We needed to get to the protection of darkness, where we had the superior advantage, about three hours away. Lawyer, LT, and I discussed the importance of maintaining an active and visual presence of helos and aircraft above us to ensure our survival. Once our ammo condition was made clear to the commander of the operation, and our plan to get more agreed upon, he authorized more aircraft be called in.

One hour before dark, we got hit with a half-hearted attempt by the enemy. You could tell their heart wasn't in it after several A-10 Warthog and AH-64 Apache Helos did multiple gun runs and rocket attacks. It was fun to watch. But, for a moment, I let my guard down and kept my head exposed just a bit too long. A round hit the wall about two inches from my face, spraying dirt and sand into my eyes. I immediately ducked, even though it would have been too late had the round actually hit me. Thank God I had my glasses on, because several pebbles embedded in my lenses. Those would have left a mark! I was not going to drop my guard ever again.

I recall saying to myself, "Sorry, Stacy. I about lost my eyes on that one. Not seeing you again would really suck! Although, I have a feeling you would be OK." Sometimes my humor is sick, but it works for me.

With night came parachutes filled with resupply. However, the silly coordinated effort put eight para-bundles on our position. Each bundle weighed 300 pounds, and each bundle broke apart on impact; the shit was spread everywhere. As luck would have it, our water bundle landed in the canal forty yards from our compound. Several of us immediately rushed out to grab the sinking bundle and throw the water bottles up on the bank. After an hour of wading in the cold water and chucking up bottles and stray food boxes, I was more than ready to go to sleep.

After six hours of continuous work to get all the bullets, bombs, food, water, fuel, batteries, and extra barrels, we were open for business as combat Walmart. As funny as that sounds, not one of my men had slept for thirty-six hours. We were all completely exhausted, and we only had thirty minutes before dawn brought the enemy, all happy to die, and the sun, all happy to kill us with the heat. This was day number two.

I just went into where my gear was and lay on my back with my body armor off. For maybe an hour I just said, "Fuck it." I think I know what often happens in combat when you are tired and hot, the brain just stops caring about anything other than closing your eyes and sleeping. I had nothing left to fight; everything was quiet, and my snipers were in position. While drinking some new, cold Gatorade and eating some food, my eyes just stopped functioning.

Oh, your dreams when you are exhausted are truly disjointed. I was clearly dreaming of mad, passionate sex with Stacy, but I kept looking out the window at an old man with a beard trying to throw a grenade at the window, and watching it bounce off. I recall sticking my tongue out at him, laughing. All of the sudden, I woke up covered in dust. My ears were ringing, and for a second, I didn't know where I was. From where I lay, I could see out a small hole in the wall. I had a hard time focusing, since the old man looked as though he was carrying a grenade, running toward the wall I was looking through.

The real world came rushing in. I rolled over and grabbed my M14, and lay on my side so I could get my cross hairs on him. I aimed at his right shoulder because I knew the bullet would fly low and right from my point of aim. Right when he threw his arm back, I fired. Dust kicked up in the room again. I jumped up and found another hole in the wall. As I relocated him, the grenade went off between him and me . . . much closer to him than me, thank God.

I looked down at my watch. For some reason, I felt numb—a sick numbness. I am sure some psychoanalyst has a name for what I felt, and would be willing to base a PhD on it. Perhaps the numbness was due to having a sexual dream, then being ripped away into combat and killing someone. I began to care little about the dirt, surroundings, or what was going on anywhere other than here. I was truly surprised by my lack of feeling, but maybe the urgency and exhaustion got me. I drank some warm Gatorade, ate an MRE (Meal Ready to Eat), and looked out my hole in the wall.

I don't know how long I sat, but Carnie touched me on the shoulder and said, "Chief, LT wants to talk to you."

"LT, what's up?" I asked.

LT replied, "Nothing in particular. Just heard you shooting, and Nike said he saw a guy blow up with a grenade in his hand."

"Well, one minute I was naked with my wife, and the next I was shooting some stupid ass trying to throw a grenade. So I am pissed . . . how are you?" I said.

LT replied, "Well, we have everyone's bullets, bombs, and supplies here. I called out to everyone and told them it was here and we were busy fighting. If they wanted it, they would have to get it themselves."

I replied, "That being said, I am going to make sure we have more water and food."

"Don't worry about it, Chief. The boys already pilfered the stores. I passed out at 3:30 this morning, and when I woke up, you were lying face down. We are all dead tired," LT said.

I said, "Listen, our men don't need to be awake every second. They are fighting for their lives and each other. If we don't get sleep, we will not be effective. Sleep to stay alive. I am going to check in with everyone. At this point, they only need reassurance and a reminder we will cover their backs. With all this killing, they only need to know we support them—trust me on this."

Before I made my rounds, I went back into the room where I had been sleeping to sit and take a minute to get my thoughts straight. I took this moment, "in the space between the bullets," to reflect on what I had learned over the course of my life. This may be the last time I would actually get to connect and speak to all—or just one of—my men. This was real, no bullshit combat—real life or death. Every single condition played against us. We were in a static, defensive position and would be for the next three or four days. We had already shown the enemy most of the weapons we had for delivering death, and they also knew once the first round was fired, we would have bombs dropping on them. They had tested our position to see if we had any kinks in our defenses, and we had plenty. Plus, we were tired.

Yet, I knew this was a crucial point in human performance I was personally putting all my effort toward. I knew this:

> What a man says to himself in the crucial moment between a perfect operation and falling off a cliff, always tips the scale and shifts the battle. Human performance adjusts and moves toward each man's Internal Dialogue. The format of his Internal Dialogue is also important. His sentences must follow the statement, "I am going to 'whatever.'" A man must *need* to be in this exact condition. A warrior must tell himself, "I am meant to be here."

I sat and closed my eyes, saying to myself:

"I *need* to be here. This is who I am, and I enjoy combat. My men *need* me, and I *need* them."

"I *need* to be here. This is who I am, and I enjoy combat. My men *need* me, and I *need* them."

"I *need* to be here. This is who I am, and I enjoy combat. My men *need* me, and I *need* them."

I repeated this thought until it became a part of me. After a bit, I heard my wife's voice in my ears, like she was actually in the room:

> Thom, I need you to come back to us. Do not fear dying. It makes you weak.

Afterward, walking around, the bullet holes in walls and the sandbags no longer shocked me. This was our place. We owned it, and we would not only survive, we would flourish. The ladder leading up to our primary position had several bullet holes in it, yet no bullet found any of my men. Nike and Jake were in position again. Lying next to them was inspirational beyond any of my experiences.

Nike said, "Chief, could you relieve me? I am tired as hell. I need rest." I looked over at Jake; his eyes were bloodshot, and I knew he was spent as well.

I replied, "Sure, but tell me what has been going on and where you think the enemy is working in on us."

After Nike's sniper brief, I said, "Send Carnie up here, too. Come back in ninety minutes, OK? I need you both to get rest, but I need you here as well. Nike, leave your rifle here. I will put it to use."

Within a minute, Carnie was next to me, and I had him briefed up on the killing field. I felt much better having him with me. He was a hunter, and I knew he would be looking into the dark places for the enemy.

Nothing happened during our watch, and the men were again rested and ready.

Next, I went over to the hellhole and checked in with KM and EOD. They had cleaned the area up and were laughing and joking about something not related to combat. We all shared a dip of Copenhagen and some water—true warrior rations. EOD and I stood up and walked toward the door. He was old, like me, and I knew his point of view would be a good one. I stood silently . . . waiting.

He replied, "Ridge Boss, thanks for picking me to come with you guys. I have never been with a platoon who wants to be in combat like you all. Makes it easy. We will survive this, don't you worry."

Before I could answer, KM started firing the .50 caliber.

I grabbed EOD and told him to come with me to get the mortar rolling because we didn't have any helos or aircraft on station. We needed to keep the enemy at bay for twenty minutes.

Running toward the mortar pit, rounds cracked over our heads, and the snipers were putting rounds on target. With EOD getting the mortar ready, I climbed the ladder and yelled at Nike, "Give me bearing and distance to where the enemy is."

After a moment, he yelled down to us with the bearing and distance. I was shocked: "400 yards, 50 degree magnetic." I grabbed my compass, laid in on the ground next to the tube and said, "Warrant, give me 400 yards at 50 degrees." I prepped three rounds and waited.

"Ready."

"Nike, shot out," I yelled as I dropped the mortar down the tube.

EOD and I waited, and waited, and waited. Finally, Nike yelled back down, "Good hit, fire for effect." I dropped four rounds as fast as I could. After the impact of the fourth round, all the enemy fire stopped, and LT came over saying, "Stop firing. We have two F-18s inbound. Good job on first mortar rounds."

With the F-18s on station, we took time to eat, drink, and resupply our rounds.

Nike came down and we shook hands as he said, "War isn't all that bad. I just wish it wasn't so fucking hot. My balls are turning to scrambled eggs."

Over the remainder of the day, the enemy showed up two more times, but they were not coordinated, and I actually felt bad for them. They were using a motorcycle to carry fighters with machine guns and RPGs across a flat section, from the cover of one building to another one 200 yards away. Albeit, it was 700 yards away from our position—a sniper's dream. I climbed up to Nike and Jake's position, and we worked through the ballistics we needed to engage. After watching this bike carry the enemy four times, we knew they clearly felt comfortable.

"Next time across Nike, you lead three minutes, and Jake, you lead two and a half minutes," I calmly said.

The motorcycle appeared with driver and passenger carrying a RPG. I said, "Stand by . . . 3, 2, 1, execute." The guns erupted and the bike reacted as if hitting a wall, exploding up into the air and launching driver and passenger. After the dust settled, we waited. Someone ran out and grabbed the driver and passenger but, wisely, left the RPG laying where it was.

"Nicely done, gents," I said. "I will buy you a coffee back on base." I smiled.

With nightfall came the C-130 gunship and new resupply parabundles. This time, only four chutes landed, so gathering the bundles was much easier. We had called back to our support crews on base and explained how we wanted the bundles packed. The whole resupply only took two hours this time. All the other positions sent their men to our compound to pick up supplies, and at 0200 hours, all was quiet, so we were able to rest.

The sleep I had the second night was without dreams; it was also without thoughts of combat. However, we did get attacked by a swarm of bugs that literally made Ground Launch's mouth and lips swell as if filled with air.

I thought that was funny until he said, "Damn. I am having a hard time breathing."

We were close to having him evacuated, but he gave himself two shots of Benadryl and drifted off to sleep. His face deflated back to normal.

Before he fell asleep, he grabbed my hand and said, "Don't send me back; I have to stay here. If I leave, I think I will never see you all again."

LT and I looked at each other, and I replied, "Don't worry, brother. We need you here, too."

On day three, I awoke at 0300 hours so I could take watch the first two hours before dawn and relieve the men in the sniper positions. But when I attempted to sit up, I realized I was actually forty-one years old. My arm had fallen asleep, and my mouth was filled with bugs. My family laughs, because they know I sleep with my mouth open. My back seemed to have frozen and didn't want to bend. And, finally, my fingers, especially my trigger finger, had become swollen and could hardly bend due to the amount of mosquito bites. Getting old ain't for sissies!

After a miserable attempt at what I call "disturbed yoga," I made my way to the ladder to the primary sniper position. Jake and Texas were sitting up, talking softly and looking out into the past and future killing fields. The night was moonless, and even though we all had night vision, we didn't see much. Above us, in the sky, a C-130 could be heard flying a big circle, with eyes on every single position.

I called out to them, "Hey, gents! I will stay up here. You all can just get some sleep." But instead of going down the ladder, they both just lay back, took off their helmets, and within three seconds were asleep.

Only I remained. I scanned the surroundings, recalling all the bullets and bombs that had hit our position over the past two days. With much effort, I crawled around the position checking the sandbags; all had holes in them. I grabbed several new sandbags to rebuild the position. A cold beer would have been nice, because temps were already 100 degrees with no wind at all, and gangs of mosquitoes were working their magic on my neck, face, and hands. Too bad we don't fight in cooler climates. I mean, *really*.

Two hours passed, and the rest of the men were stirring and getting ready for another day in hell. Lawyer was checking in with the Lead JTAC, who just happened to be Snowman. I heard KM and EOD checking, clearing, and reloading the .50 caliber. That sound immediately made the compound hum. If the past two days were any indication for the future, we had forty-five minutes until the enemy began their newly-designed assault.

With everyone in place, hydrated, fed, loaded, and ready, I climbed down the ladder and moved over to LT. "Boss, why don't we just call contact now and forego the wait to get air on station. Have the birds loiter five miles out, talk them onto our position, and clear them hot. Let's catch the enemy unprepared," I said with a straight face.

To my surprise, LT replied, "Already done. Two AH-64s checked on five minutes ago and are ready. Wanna make a bet as to where and how many enemy show up?"

"Hell, yes. They are coming from behind building four. Approximately eight enemy. They do the same thing every morning. However, wait for me to get two at the break in the wall. I have taken five over the past two days; same time, same bad channel," I replied.

I moved to my happy spot on the wall of shame and dialed my scope to 280 yards. Then I watched. At 0725 hours, two men with RPGs slowly made their way down the wall, stopping frequently to look at another position where several Army SF soldiers were camped out. I guess the word didn't get passed from the other five guys who died before. As they broke cover between walls and stopped at the tree in between, I fired. The turds were standing side by side, and the round went through one head and the others dude's midsection. He then fell out of my sight picture. I turned around—Texas was shaking his head.

I gloated, "My work is done. I am here all week." It is not cold to have banter in combat because the other side of that cold exterior is probably the knowledge that someone else's life simply ended.

Just then, the enemy returned fire from behind building four. I heard the JTACs working the problem with the AH-64s, and heard the pilot respond with his Gatling guns followed by several rockets. As the second pilot passed over, I heard him say, "Six KIAs."

The majority of the day, we experienced only small, half-hearted attacks across the battlefield in other positions. I heard the medevac bird being called. Some SF soldier had taken a round to the neck, and Snowman had personally effected his rescue. I decided all four of us needed to take a walk into the interior of the target area, check in on Snowman, and see why we had all come to this Godforsaken place.

At noon, I gathered several of my men and told LT where we were going, why, and to expect us back in ninety minutes. Moving outside the semi-protected compound is a funny thing. We absolutely did not trust that every building was cleared, so we cleared our way back through the buildings, looking for Snowman.

After clearing through several buildings, we realized this place was the enemy's version of a strip mall. Each building had something unique to offer, and we felt as if we had gone back in time to the 1900s. One shop made us all stop and smile—it was filled with fresh grapes. Let me tell you, cold grapes in a cooler will bring a smile to the face of the most bitter of men. And we were bitter—and smiling and laughing. I was stuffed when we closed that door behind us.

Once in the center of the capital, we checked in with all the EODs and DEA men who were prepping charges and beginning to burn and destroy all the drugs, bombs, bullets, and guns they had found. Apparently, they had captured over three billion dollars' worth of black tar opium, 800 RPG warheads, and 10,000 bullets. I lost count of all the bags of opium sitting in front of every single store.

I turned to Nike, "Wow, can't buy this in America."

When we stopped to talk to our SF brothers, Nike grabbed my arm and said, "Come with me." He led me over to the arm pump of a well and said, "Shower time, Ridge Boss. And you are first, you smelly animal."

I took off my gear and shirt, got down on my knees, and said, "Pump me, big daddy." Holy shit, that water was cold. It took my breath away, and for a moment, I was transported to some other place.

After all of us took a "hell" shower, we found Snowman. The scene didn't register for a bit. Blood was smeared all over the wall and Snowman. He looked like he had aged ten years. We didn't know what to say; we all hugged him. He was in the middle of talking to twelve aircraft, trying to push the ones who were ready to other JTACs and communicate to the newly arriving ones who was doing what and when. We all dropped several Gatorade bottles and three bags of MREs so he at least knew we cared.

Nike said, "Jesus, that is fucked up. He is the only JTAC up here."

As we pushed back toward our platoon, we noticed a door that had not been opened and was still locked from the outside. We all looked at each other, then I said, "Nike, Texas, cut the lock. Let's clear that building."

Texas produced a set of bolt cutters, opened the lock, turned the door handle, and pushed the door open. I waited a second after the two of them went in, then I entered slowly. While Nike and Texas silently cleared the room, I noticed a leg sticking out from under a blanket in the corner. "Hold," I said softly. When I moved toward the blanket, Nike pushed in, grabbed the foot, and pulled—a bit harder than I would have, but it was effective. An old man went flying across the room in front of me, about three feet off the ground, and hit the wall on the other side of the room.

Apparently, he was barely alive. After clearing the rest of the room, we picked him up and carried him to our compound. This way, we could get some fluid in him to revive him enough to be put back on the alive list. When the interpreter arrived, we found out he was ninety-eight years old, and had not eaten or had water in three days. These people are tough, I have to admit. In America, this man would have died in twelve hours. Most Americans don't live to ninety-eight either. This guy ate shit, drank diseased water, and out-lived all the diet zealots who die at fifty-eight from the stress of hating who they are and what they look like. This guy was worth saving because he was hard to the bone and laughed at death. He truly had no fear of dying or of us shooting him. He even said, "Thank you," and hugged several of us.

Once things had settled a bit, LT and I talked about what we needed to do to take the fight to the enemy, rather than sitting here waiting for him to shoot first. We had noticed a building about 300 yards away which obscured our view of the road. If we pushed south a bit toward the canal, we could see the entire length of the road. Therefore, off we went, Carnie, Nike, LT, and I, to shake the boredom off.

The idea seemed straightforward and easy. LT and Carnie moved to the far side of the road. Nike lay on the near side with his sniper rifle, and I got out my binos and looked down the road. Holy shit! What I saw looked like ants moving their nest across the road. Five enemy walked nonchalantly across, arms full of guns and RPGs. Without saying a thing, Nike opened up with the rifle and Carnie engaged with the machine gun. Due to bullets flying eight inches above the ground, within twenty seconds, we could no longer see anything. Once the dust settled, we saw three enemy lay on the road. *Nice*, I thought.

I don't know what to call this, maybe a sixth sense, but all of the sudden the hair on my head and neck stood straight up. Something was wrong. I looked south a bit instead of straight down the road and saw two enemy running through the trees about 200 yards away from us. I unleashed my M14, though my barrel was three inches above Nike's head when I fired. And I fired like I was about to die. The enemy was at full sprint. I had to fire seven rounds to hit the first one; the second only took six because he stopped at a tree. I think he was tired.

We were taking heavy fire, and were terribly exposed on the open road. The scariest thing was hearing the .50 caliber machine gun open up and the rounds whiz past us just to the left . . . maybe thirty feet away. When a round hit next to Nike's elbow, he and I jumped into the canal. OK—time to get back to the compound. We crawled and sprinted until we were next to the wall, and the room housing the .50 caliber. Getting the .50 caliber to stop firing was scarier than the bullets hitting the wall next to us. Finally, we got KM's attention. He tipped the barrel up, and we ran into the safety of the compound. Once we were in, the .50 caliber continued firing. I thought, *Good luck with that, Mr. Taliban.*

Just that little forty-yard sprint took it out of me. I was thoroughly exhausted. I think we all were, except LT. He is a genetically-freakish athlete; I think he'd have worked out if he had a weight set or bike trainer in the compound.

All of us were truly strung out. The heat, sustained combat, fear of dying, and lack of rest and good food was taking its toll. You may not understand this, but someone always needs to say, "Stop!" or "Enough!" SEALs have a hard time stopping, but I knew I had to keep my wits about me. A bad decision might result in someone getting killed. A lesson I learned in adventure racing is that with exhaustion comes cloudy judgment. I just didn't know how to apply the lesson here. We really couldn't stop, and we had no place to go.

With night came a long, fitful sleep. My dreams were of my family and of not ever seeing them again . . . of watching them attend my funeral . . . of Stacy crying, shutting down, and losing heart. I woke up at midnight and walked around the compound, noticing others were talking in their sleep, or they were coughing and restless.

EOD was standing in the corner, so I walked over next to him. He turned and said, "Thom, I don't know how much more of this we can take.

Everyone is completely fried. How are you doing?"

"Well, except for just dreaming of my death and watching my family go to my funeral . . . I am right as rain," I replied.

"Just one more day. We have to keep everyone active tomorrow, fighting and concentrated on this. Whatever the hell this is," he added.

I replied, "I agree, Warrant. We need to rebuild all the sandbags, whether we want to or not. We need to clean the compound just to stay busy. Gonna have the men gather all their gear and check it, then place it all in a row, ready for extract. Need to play some sorta game, too, to get us all laughing. I am going to get some shut-eye. I suggest you do the same."

My bones ached. A part of me—I cannot really explain what part—was coming unhinged. Part of me no longer gave a shit whether I lived or died, and the other part hung on desperately, looking forward to making it out of here and going home to my family. Just as I was beginning to nod off, LT and Lawyer came in and kicked me awake.

"Chief, we are going to call a fire mission on the wall east of here to knock it down, so we can see beyond it and deny the enemy that position for a fourth day," LT suggested.

I sat up, not fully awake, and said, "Sure, why not? When do we expect this to go down?"

Lawyer said, "Oh, how about in three minutes?"

I got up, straining to stand upright as the tendons stretched in my back and neck. My body armor was molded to my skin by then and most surely smelled like rotted flesh.

Outside, we readied for the fireworks. I walked over to Nike and handed him a can of Copenhagen. I said, "This ought to be funny. The C-130 at 10,000 feet, shooting straight down, trying to hit a three-foot-wide wall with a 105 mm round that may be seven inches wide."

Nike took the Copenhagen, opened it slowly, and scooped the remainder into his lip. "Who gives a fuck? This is getting boring, anyway. Same thing day after day, after fucking day. Don't get me wrong: killing is fun, but we are pushing our luck. A stray round could easily hit any one of us tomorrow morning. Earlier today, a round went through the sand bag and right into Jake's mouth, breaking his two front teeth. He spit the damn thing out into his hand and laughed."

"Yeah, he showed me. I am not giving him a Purple Heart for that."

We both laughed an eerie laugh. "Nike, you know what occurs to me now after all this sustained, in your face, combat? If your time is up, you can't do a damn thing about it." He nodded in agreement.

"I would rather go out doing this than dying of cancer or from AIDS," he laughed.

"You trying to tell me something, Nike?" I tipped my head up. He knew I was just trying to bring levity to this hellhole.

Just then Lawyer called out, "Thirty seconds to tally."

Up high we heard the engines of the C-130. Then the first round fired with a distant, hollow boom. It was immediately followed by a light, then a very loud explosion on the wall. The artillery barrage continued for ten rounds. Without wind, we'd need another ten minutes before we could see what damage had been done. We all immediately laughed in unison. The rounds had knocked down the wall, but directly behind it stood another wall.

I simply turned and walked back to my room—my place to check out—and went to sleep.

In my dreams, I was playing tag with my family. Autumn was chasing Chance. Garrett was screaming, trying to get away from me. Stacy was laughing. I yelled for everyone to stop, because for some reason, I was wearing my radio headset, and Carnie was asking for cover fire. I am sure some will think that was nuts, but it all made perfect sense to me at the time. My family needed me to provide for their safety, and Carnie and I were doing just that.

When I awoke, my snipers were in another firefight. Game on again.

The initial morning fun only lasted thirty minutes. No one was frazzled. I think we were all jaded by then.

We had to take the offense now. LT and I decided to take half the platoon and move east into the rubble of the buildings to get a better vantage point beyond the walls and buildings obscuring our view. The plan made tactical sense. However, we were all so entirely exhausted, nothing made any human sense.

After lunch we headed out. After arriving at our position, it became clear to me: not only were we, as the maneuver element, going to be awake the remainder of the day, but the base element we left behind was also going to be awake all day with no relief.

Due to the nature of the buildings, we had to knock a hole along the east-facing wall, low to the ground, to give my snipers the steadiest position. We used some blankets and linen to stretch over the heads of the snipers, affording them some sort of shade. But at 125 degrees, our aggressive choice was like asking them to sit in an oven.

Each sniper could only last forty-five minutes in that position before he felt like he would pass out. I went out and poured water over their heads and bodies every fifteen minutes. I think my doing so kept them alive.

We were about to call it quits when we started taking enemy fire. I immediately called back to KM to fire at the enemy who was working in on our position on the south side of the road.

Once he opened up, all hell broke loose. Enemy machine gun fire hammered our position. Tracers flew over our heads everywhere. The sound of the .50 caliber machine gun rounds soaring by the south side was even scarier. You could feel the round, and the vibration in the walls was truly freaky. At some point, we couldn't tell if the bullets were the enemy shooting at us, or the .50 caliber shooting at the enemy. After five long minutes, everyone ceased firing, and we all took a long deep breath.

I walked over to LT, "Jesus, what was that? Was it the .50 or was it the enemy?"

LT replied, "No idea, Chief. Let's get an ammo, water, and food count, OK?"

I answered, "Sure, we have an hour left before dusk. I suggest we prep to leave. We are all done, and so are the men we left behind."

After dark, we made an immediate movement back to the compound. As soon as we arrived, I could tell I had made a mistake. Thank God it was not a grave one. We all rehydrated and soon got radio traffic from the mission boss that we were all going to extract at 2330 hours. We had two hours to check all of our gear, get it prepped to leave, and finally—Oh my God, finally—we had to blow up and destroy all our excess ordnance, which was too heavy to carry.

Half of the platoon began the task of picking up and carrying outside all the stuff we needed to blow up. EOD grabbed his "blow shit up gear," and put charges on top of everything.

Another SF element met us at our compound and waited with us to load onto the helo. As the rest of the platoon and the army guys moved out to meet the helos, EOD and I stayed back. We were to detonate the explosives, then run to the helo. After igniting the fuse, we'd have thirty minutes until a big boom happened.

I have to admit I am not perfect. I know you all know this already, but I truly have to say nothing comes close to getting on that extract bird and leaving combat. I'm not saying I don't like combat, but leaving is better than sex. Maybe because leaving combat and coming home allows you to have sex!

I was in a new state of awareness, or maybe of life. The men were, too. We had no hope, and we didn't hold belief in anything. We had passed through the human condition of non-action and mental drama that leads to inaction and arrived in a place of an odd, new power. Flying back to base, I reflected on how powerful it is to actually live through what other people deem hell.

Performing well in hell, or in other difficult life situations, is uniquely linked to your Internal Dialogue. I have been wrestling with how to explain what I have learned because it is vitally important . . . especially since I have the distinct impression I will not return from this.

Sitting on the helo, surrounded by my men, I realized that although we were exhausted, we were also powerful beyond measure. We had not only survived five days in hell, but had taken the fight to the devil. None of us had been injured. I had become uniquely aware of my own Internal Dialogue—how what I said about myself or my men or the situation impacted the physical world. I clearly saw the power of words. When others talked openly or under their breath, disconnecting things about themselves, others, or the events of the day, it would immediately slow down everyone's physical and mental abilities.

Everywhere are men and women who do not get it. You will notice them in your life. They will often make you feel uncomfortable, and even more so, they make your Internal Dialogue very loud. And, since they don't have access to performance in their own lives, they will make your Internal Dialogue differ from what you say externally. The reason I am sharing this experience is so you will know, when you have these people in your life, be clear and commit to your own Internal Dialogue first. If and when this doesn't work out for you and your efforts, push those people away; get away from them, isolate them.

They will cause damage to you, to your efforts, and to themselves.

I learned something from this last week in hell I hadn't anticipated. Internal Dialogue not only shapes your own performance, but the ill-willed Internal Dialogue of others can and *will* have horrible effects on everyone's efforts. The past few days, most of my energy was wasted on overcoming the disconnected, non-combat, non-human-related demeanor of one of our troop's senior leaders. I felt sorry for him. My men were embarrassed for him, and he was dangerous to have around in combat. An Internal Dialogue saying, "I hate this man," or, "This man is stupid," or, "I wish this man would buy a bullet," tends to rob us all of energy and of being available to whatever the moment brings. Obviously, in combat, being 100 percent present counts. I am sure you will find these experiences throughout your life.

Be patient with mastering your own words about people and yourself—it will make all the difference later in life.

SECTION SIX

PAIN

CHIEF AUPUMUT (Mohican)

"When it comes time to die, be not like those whose hearts are filled with the fear of death, so when their time comes they weep and pray for a little more time to live their lives over again in a different way. Sing your death song, and die like a hero going home."

Sleep. Finally, sleep with no one shooting at us. Finally, the hum of air-conditioning, with someone else guarding and protecting. Most importantly, sleep on my Tempur-Pedic mattress. Aaahhh . . .

The first of many dreams was truly the most confusing. I expected, maybe even anticipated, fitful sleep. Since I had been an adventure racer, I learned that sleep was always shitty after you pushed the body and mind well beyond capabilities—past what the mind and body really wanted to do. So it was no surprise I felt like I was in hell while sleeping.

In my dream, I was on my first hunt with my father in Llano, Texas. We went to one of those managed deer hunts, where they drive you to the deer stand, and corn feeders kicked on every three hours. I grew bored with sitting in the stand, so dad said it was OK to play in the back of the stand. I vividly recall building a little play fort with broken sticks. A foolish thing for a kid to be doing, but youth is never foolish, just always busy.

In my dream, and in reality, I recall looking down the field when the feeder sounded. Through the trees, I could clearly see a four-point buck walk out of the woods, and I heard the distinct click of dad's safety resetting to fire. I froze and waited. Waiting was always hard for me, even though some people would now say, "Shea could wait for days without moving."

Then, all of the sudden, I jumped at the loud sound of dad's 30.06 firing. At the sound of the gun, I dropped and immediately crawled toward the sound of gunfire. I was in combat, it was hot, and tracers were flying everywhere. Then, as quickly as the dream had shifted before, I was back in Texas, and dad was crawling out of the stand. "Tommy, did you see that buck?"

"Yes, dad," I said. My heart pounded; the smells of the wind, trees, and dirt were so vivid. I began to walk toward where the deer had been standing when dad stopped me.

"Son, when you shoot at something, best not to pursue it. Let the bullet, and the damage it has done, work on the animal. Sometimes, a wounded thing is more dangerous when it is near dying. Sit with me a bit, and let the animal die alone."

After a while, we walked to where the buck had been hit. Wow, there was a lot of blood. We followed it. The thrill of tracking an animal is electrifying for me still. We could see where the animal stopped, and I wondered what it was thinking or going through at that time. I imagined where it was trying to run.

Dad grabbed me and softly said, "There it is. Don't move!" With that, I was back in combat with Carnie. (That's the beauty of a dream: you never know where it'll take you.) We were watching a man walk slowly through the trees. I softly said to Carnie, "Go ahead, it is your first." Carnie pulled the trigger.

Suddenly, I was back with dad in Texas. He had taken the kill shot. As I watched the deer kicking and dying, dad put a hand on my shoulder, "Crying is OK." I looked at him and asked, "Are you going to cry?"

"No, Son," he replied.

We went forward, and I touched the deer. I lifted its hooves and watched them drop. I saw the long tongue protrude from its mouth, and I recall smelling the ferric smell of the iron in the blood. I helped dad turn the buck over, and as dad was preparing to gut the animal, I danced, holding two hooves in my hand. Dad looked up and didn't say anything. I couldn't tell if it was wrong in his mind, but dancing seemed to be the thing to do . . . for me, anyway.

I woke up, covered in sweat in my combat room around lunchtime. I had been asleep for two hours and was exhausted. Maybe a shower was what I needed. The shower felt good; water always feels good. At least it washed away the dream's lingering sweat.

Lunch was tasteless. None of us talked about the week of combat. Combat was over, and we had already moved past it—maybe because of our years and years of training through tough scenarios. Or, maybe it was the simple fact that we had survived, or we had nothing left to discuss. Either way, we seemed to have moved on.

The afternoon briefing was short. SF command was still figuring out the aftermath of the last operation. Nothing big or small was being planned. After eight years, everyone had learned to not demand anything from operators after a large battle.

Once back in my room, I nervously opened my computer to see if Stacy had read my email. What the fuck is up with emails? Seven hours had passed since I arrived back in camp and sent the email. Nothing.

I went down the hall to check in with the men. No one else had Internet connectivity. Nike was lying on his bed reading some novel. He looked up and said, "Chief, too bad the rest of the platoon is in Iraq and missed that operation. It would have been nice to have them here."

I agreed. "They were sorely missed. You did good, Nike. I am glad you didn't get out after last platoon. I know your last leaders left a bad taste in your mouth. They sure did in mine."

Nike replied, "I don't know how we survived those five days in hell. Thank God we all did Hell Week in BUDS. At least the stress was the same. My body wanted to quit after the first day."

I added, "I am glad we spent all those extra hours shooting our sniper weapons. I know nothing in sniper training helped here, but Hell Week and LRTI at least taught us all to engage multiple targets from fucked-up positions."

Nike agreed, and continued, "Carnie and Texas rocked, didn't they? Could you imagine if this was the first deployment? Kinda like fucking a porn star on your first go: makes all other women less."

"Unless you marry a porn star who devotes herself to you and your family. Never settle, Nike . . . ever," I said. Then I shook his hand and left.

I headed back to my room for another bout of twisted dreams. Maybe

I would dream of a great fishing trip somewhere? Since it is my dream, I should get a choice—right?

I put my iPod earbuds in and lay back. For a moment I concentrated on my body, starting with my toes, then my feet: stretch, flex, rotate, and relax. Then my calves and thighs. Flex, extend, and relax. Then my belly and back . . .

My hands held a paddle. I was in Canada, paddling a canoe across a serene lake. Each paddle stroke surged the canoe forward. The sun was low on the horizon; the wind was at my back. I looked up in the sky at a bald eagle flying overhead. His head tilted, and I looked into his eye. As he flew away toward the end of the lake, a fish jumped, undoubtedly chasing or being chased.

As I continued paddling, I recognized the lake. I had spent a year up there working for an outfitter in my youth. The wilderness was truly untamed and remote. Maybe the last one in North America. No guns, no motors, nothing—just pristine everything.

At the end of the lake, I knew the portage was long and would lead into Agnes Lake and the lower falls of Lake Louisa. The fact I was dreaming also occurred to me, and I recalled asking my family to place my ashes in Louisa Falls if I were to die. I sat awhile thinking maybe if I made this portage, it would mean I was going to die. I stood up and slid the boat forward, walked around a bit looking at the portage, and glanced back at the lake in the direction I had come. I sat down on a stump and laughed.

Here I am, dreaming of what carrying me to my final resting place would be like for my family. All of a sudden, a long-dead friend of my family walked toward me from the portage. Captain Pat said, "Thom, don't be afraid. It makes you weak." He turned and walked back down the portage trail.

I walked to the canoe and lifted out my pack onto my back, then put the canoe on my shoulders and started walking. The first section was always a pain in the ass. Tons of head-sized rocks . . . and uphill all the way. As I picked my way up through the portage trail, I heard a gunshot. I knew this was a dream, so I let the sound die without reacting. Once at the top of the hill, I put the canoe down and rested a bit. I looked down the trail toward Agnes, and heard gunfire and saw tracer rounds. I could see Captain Pat ahead of me, smiling.

He finally walked back to me and sat down. "You cannot avoid death by running from life. Death will come when it wants to. Walk forward and live. Sit here, or go back and die the miserable life of fear." He stood up, smiled, and ran toward the sound of the battle. He looked back and added, "Now, this is life. Let's do this thing."

"Thom, Thom. Let's do this thing," LT was shaking me awake.

"Christ, LT, did I miss something?" I snapped. He laughed and said, "No. The men want to go hit golf balls into the lake. Let's join them."

We all put on flashy golf shirts and drove over to a pond we called the lake. After an hour of hitting balls and laughing our asses off, we returned to camp for dinner.

With dinner finished, all the leaders filed into the combat intel center for the nightly brief. Again, no big missions were being planned, and I think none of us were actively pursuing new intel. However, a new concept was put on the table by our boss. "Gents, I think we have earned some needed respect from Army Headquarters. I am interested in pursuing our own targeting line and mission set for the remainder of our time here. What say you? Also, we just received brand new heavy weapons. I expect them to be up and running by tomorrow."

I chimed in. "Our resources and intel shop is more robust than the headquarters' is. Let's look at going after the enemy where they sleep and feel safe. Sorta break up their ease of living and moving. Keep them on their toes."

It wasn't my idea, exactly. We all talked about hitting them hard at home instead of waiting for some big important man or mission to show up. We all agreed, and that was that. Period.

Now was the time to get the men back into the game. Time to get the weapons out and go to the range to ensure all were working. SEALs like to shoot, and it would serve to get us all back into the proper mindset.

Passing Nike in the hall, I said, "Nike, we are going to the range in forty-five minutes. All weapons—including rockets and mortars."

Nike went to it, telling the men of Bravo it was time to get the guns out and sight them all back in. I went to my room and loaded my .300 Winchester Magnum, my M4 with all the trimmings, and my new SCAR heavy. On my way to the vehicles, I stopped in the armory and loaded all my magazines full of goodness.

I hope you kids will all learn to shoot. I truly enjoy shooting, and I am sad I haven't spent any time teaching you this passion of mine. More sorry when I thought I might not be around to teach you all I know about weapons and shooting.

As I waited, I thought of what my kids' lives would be like in adulthood. I knew Autumn would enjoy junior high and high school. She was more mature than I was at her age, and far smarter academically. I was excited for Garrett to go through puberty. I know how frustrating being a boy in this new-age world can be. Chance, I need say nothing. He knows I will be watching him closely, from wherever I am.

After sighting in all weapons, lasers, rockets, and mortars, we had about an hour of daylight left—time for a little competition shooting. The event would start at the 50-meter mark with the pistol, then run back to the 200-meter berm and shoot with the M4, then finally back to the 800-meter mark and engage with the new SCAR heavy. I don't recall who won, but I remember the smiles and laughter of the men, and I felt like a good time meant more than anything at that point. Damn, these men could shoot well, all of them!

Back in the compound, we set to cleaning and preparing all weapons for combat. With my weapons cleaned and ready, I sat down behind my computer, lifted the screen, and waited to see if we had Internet connectivity. When *Yahoo!* opened, so did my emotions. Emotion is not a bad thing to have.

Emotion is not a bad thing to have. The more emotion, the more passion.
With passion, you get action, and with action, you get life.

After typing in my username and password, I saw an unread email from Stacy. All the email said was: call me please.

I typed in her number and listened to the ringing. "Hello, Shea's." I so love Stacy's voice—all female, all woman, and always light and alive.

"Hey, Honey," I smiled into the phone.

"Oh, thank God you are alive. We prayed twice a day you and your men would make it back to us. Thank you for calling. So how was it? Can you share anything?" she asked.

I replied, "Well, it was exactly what we all were training for, and what I have wanted all of my life. I can't say more than that because we are probably being monitored."

She said, "Thom, it is OK. I get it. We've all been busy and happy. We talk about you constantly, and I let the kids say whatever they want to. Garrett is a bit distant at times. He is trying to work out why you are gone and what you are doing. I don't tell him too much except that you are happy and strong. I think he needs to hear that."

"Yes, I agree. He is at that age where he needs to hear only happy and good things. How is Autumn?" I asked.

Stacy replied, "She cries sometimes when she sees a picture of you or watches the video you made for her."

I ventured, "I bet Chance is uniquely aware of me being gone, and can tell when you are sad."

She told me, "Oh, Thom, he is your son. He is so sensitive to my emotions just like you are. We were listening to the Peter Gabriel song "Father, Son;" you know, the one where he sings about his father? He looked at me with tears in his eyes and said, 'Momma, I miss cuddling with daddy.' I lost it, and we both cried a little. Then he put his hand on my shoulder and said, 'Momma, daddy is fighting isn't he?' He is such a smart boy, Thom. I love him so much. Thank you for giving him to us."

"Honey, we killed a lot of enemy. None of us got injured. Not one. I am proud of these men. It was the hardest thing most of them will ever do," I shared.

"Thom, I am proud of you. I want you to get that. You are strong and they love you, and they need you badly. Don't give up, and don't let your guard down until you are here with us again," Stacy replied.

"Sorry I took so long to get back with you. They put us on lockdown and turned off the Internet."

"Don't you dare apologize! We know what is going on with you. Now that you're in combat, our relationship has no place for worry about me or us. We are living our lives and having fun doing it."

I replied gratefully, "Thank you, honey. I need to hear that sometimes. I need to know you are all safe and happy."

Stacy reminded me, "Remember what I said to you? I am firmly holding you to it. We need you to come back to us. Don't you dare be afraid while you are away. Fear makes you weak. Your men need you to fear *nothing.*"

"Damn, my wife is a Spartan. I just wanted to say I miss you."

"I know you do, baby. Just don't put fear in a sentence. We both know how powerful language is and how our thoughts control our physical stuff."

"OK. I so want you, Honey. I miss putting the kids to bed and locking the door," I added.

"That is the Thom I know and love. I took some bikini photos I will send. Keep the energy up," she teased.

Then she continued, "Thom, I met some new friends who want to work with the SEAL Foundation to put on a gala event in South Carolina raising money to support you all . . . you know, just in case. If anything happens to you guys, I want to be prepared to support all the families. Tammy and Jerry are willing, and want to do this for us."

"Why the hell are you thinking about us dying? And who are these people, and why would they wanna help?" I questioned.

She sighed. "Well, this is who I am. I think it's one of the reasons you married me, you dork. I have to prepare everything for you not coming home, and for your men if they do not come home. And, when Tammy and Jerry came over for dinner, I sorta shared our 'Unbreakable' writings with them. They both were so shocked, they called their friends and everyone wants to help. They just don't know how. So, sit back and relax, it is going to happen and it is for you all."

"Spartan Wife should be the name of this stuff I am writing for you and the kids," I said, and we both laughed. I was so proud of Stacy. She rocks.

I can't remember having any dreams that night or the next few nights. The days went by smoothly, because we were all once again thoroughly engaged in finding the enemy as well as future combat engagements.

Our boss called our skipper from SEAL Team Seven, who was leading the Team in Iraq, and finally got permission to get the rest of my platoon moved from Iraq to hell. We would be united once again.

I was reminded to let my kids know the dynamics that happen with us at home are the same as this dynamic with my platoon. Doing things separately is great, but going on hikes with my family is truly enjoyable, and less drama to be sure. When my family is together, I feel better as a father, and know we are moving forward as a family. Now my platoon will all be together . . . but not for a family hike. The drama created by different levels of ability and maturity exists in any group dynamic. When a family of five goes on a crazy hike up some cliffs at Mission Gorge, their drama is the same as a platoon of SEALs which was divided and has undergone vastly different experiences.

I was happy the platoon would all be together again. We definitely needed the guns and abilities they would bring. Yet, I was concerned at the difference in tactical maturity the new guys to hell would have. Some things we learn in life cannot be taught. More to the point, I was concerned because my 'hell-worn' men would be planning missions the new guys would not be able to do.

Every leader considers certain points about the men under his command. These ingrained rules of thumb were what I considered as the men flew into hell. I want to share them with you:

1. Plan to win every single battle—in detail. Win!
2. Do not mentally or physically plan for the attrition of your men. Bring everyone home.
3. Keep it simple, stupid. Make sure a five-year-old can understand it. Because when you are tired and scared, you act like a five-year-old. KISS!
4. If in doubt, refer to rule number two. Bring everyone home.

These rules will guide you well throughout your lives. Sometimes what you need to do, or what you think, will not be clear. The older I get, I absolutely know that nothing is clear. I laugh at people who suggest hard and fast rules exist that cannot be broken. Physics has many guiding principles that usually work about 99 percent of the time. I recall reading the Bohr/Einstein papers where two of the most brilliant minds of their day talked about mathematical equations. After much heated debate, Einstein pointed out the concept of relativity. Relativity suggests that time slows down for the person or object traveling at the speed of light, yet stays the same for the object observing the other object traveling really fucking fast.

ADAMANTINE LESSON SIX

Relativity

I don't know the whole debate on relativity and quantum physics, but what a fun thought affecting us here on earth. Everything, always, is relative to the point of view of the observer. I know that may sound heady to be writing from combat, but as you work with the rules of thumb, know your point of view determines what you see, what you think about, and ultimately what you will do. The dance is fucked up, I know. I am laughing, too. Work on it.

This is the sixth task for you. Test, challenge, alter, and shift your points of view, using your Internal Dialogue. Then watch miracles happen.

I spent some time in my youth reading the correspondences between Einstein and Bohr. I cannot recall if the writings even had a name, but within the rantings and mathematical formulas, one striking communication happened. They were working on solving a complicated formula, and while I'm paraphrasing this, Einstein wrote: "We cannot solve the problems we face at the same level of thinking we have achieved thus far. We must alter our thinking to another level."

The condition of thinking and solving the day-to-day problems will forever confine and restrict the solution. I personally think the solution and the problem arise out of the Internal Dialogue that first gave us access to that particular action.

Yet for you, my children, when you fall upon hard, challenging times, remember this point: your actions or your solutions are relative to your point of view. And your point of view is exactly directed and shaped by your Internal Dialogue. So shift your dialogue to something greater or harder, and you will see the small problems get worked out rather quickly.

SECTION SEVEN

Appetite

the boys i mean are not refined
they go with girls who buck and bite
they do not give a fuck for luck
they hump them thirteen times a night

one hangs a hat upon her tit
one carves a cross on her behind
they do not give a shit for wit
the boys i mean are not refined

they come with girls who bite and buck
who cannot read and cannot write
who laugh like they would fall apart
and masturbate with dynamite

the boys i mean are not refined
they cannot chat of that and this
they do not give a fart for art
they kill like you would take a piss

they speak whatever's on their mind
they do whatever's in their pants
the boys i mean are not refined
they shake the mountains when they dance
e.e. cummings

My boys return. For days prior to the first boys from Iraq arriving in hell, my energy lifted to the same level of excitement I had prior to the birth of Chance. Long months of watching them grow with many nights spent dealing with the pains of their growing, and ultimately, finally coming to a head . . . so to speak. Nothing is better in life than uniting the clans, so we can do battle together.

We had begun planning the first mission SEAL Team Seven had designed; we broke free from the local SF targeting line and were ready to take a new style of fighting to the enemy. We were going to take the fight to the enemy where he slept and trained.

We spontaneously decided to run more during the weeks leading up to our first endurance mission. I personally found running a nice way to relieve stress and whittle away at the hours and days we were mandated to be in hell. As Nike put it, "PT is the only way to legally have a morphine injection." So each day, we would sleep through the heat and wake at dinnertime. After dinner, we would file into the gym and get our morphine on.

All the days leading up to the boys' return and our first mission began bleeding into a blur of waking up, eating, working out, planning, chatting with Stacy, and shooting. I am sure most people would find that fun and exciting. I just wanted to get back into combat. A yearning for combat was growing inside me. I yearned for the intimacy and smell of battle and movement, and, something wickedly deep kept telling me I would not make it home.

§

Reading this, you kids must surely ask yourselves why your dad would want this life of facing death over and over and over. I do not have an answer. At least my words don't seem to do justice to an explanation. I have been working on the answer over the past two weeks. And though the words may not capture the answer, the space between words is really where all the true meaning lies, anyway:

When you dream, dream of nothing more than living in this moment.
Wake each day wanting your life and no other.
Want your body, want your family, want your life.
Run like you are being chased, and chase like you are hungry.

Love as if in the next minute your mate will be gone.
Do not fear death; it only makes you weak.

Daddy 2009

§

While cleaning up extra rooms for the boys and creating more space for their war goods in our war room, we discussed the upcoming mission and what would be needed to bring the boys up to speed. At this point in our platoon's development and maturity, having a round-table discussion was possible. We put the maps on the table and stepped through the overall plan from beginning to end.

The point of the walk through was not to see if the plan was effective, but to see where and when the new boys would be put into the game, and if they would be able to handle that particular situation. I share this point with you for two reasons that will become clearer. The first reason is simply to share with you what I was doing over here. The second is to teach you to open your minds to planning, and knowing what may happen and when, so you can help at critical points. You will be able to predict what will happen in your life if you begin knowing how you see the world; you will be able to inject solutions when you learn how to use your own Internal Dialogue, and also know how others use theirs.

The original plan was to put the new guys in the same positions we had all been in during our year of training together. However, as we talked through the movement of the operation, we discovered that at several points, the new guys would be by themselves making tactical and life-changing decisions without any of us to aid. I was unwilling to let the new guys have the reins without myself, Nike, or LT there to oversee. I admit I am a controlling bear at times—alright most of the time—however, I was not going to risk anyone's life or test their abilities here in hell.

We actually all agreed without much discussion. We had learned the dangers of assuming ability and skill in this environment. The flow of the plan stayed the same, but the positioning of everyone changed, so the new guys were meshed into pockets in the patrol order where they were surrounded by the survivors we had all become. I finally said, "At no point in time will one of the new guys be out of your sight. Do not put any of them into a condition where he has to make a call or make a decision other than shoot or don't shoot. We have learned too much to tell them during the three days they will have prior to a mission. Trust me on this, gents, the boys need to feel you around them. They should never feel alone and unsupported out here."

With that part complete, we all went to lunch, then headed to the airfield to pick up the boys. The atmosphere was hilarious. We knew the new guys would be nervous and anticipating something far from the truth. We had decided to rush them through dinner and push them immediately out to the shooting range. The intent was to make them think it was dangerous in the compound all day long, so we all had to carry guns with us twenty-four hours a day.

When the ramp lowered from the plane, the looks on all of their faces made us laugh. They were frowning like they were about to get in a fight, and their eyes darted left and right like there was already a fight going on. Then the funniest thing happened: an enemy rocket flew overhead and hit a building about 600 yards away. Alarms on base sounded, and aircrews and other people ran for cover. We all lay on the airfield, laughing. Timing in the delivery in a joke is priceless. Especially when the enemy makes a joke out of trying to kill us.

Finally, a security crew drove over and yelled at us for not taking cover in the bomb shelters. I answered, still laughing, "Bro, the rocket already hit. The damage is done. We need to pick up our guys and get them out of here."

I don't think he wanted to hear that. As we walked to the bomb shelter, the security guard took down my name and my command's name. He threatened to kick us all off base. "So, you mean you have the authority to send me home to my wife and kids because we didn't run scared?" I asked sarcastically. I don't think he wanted to hear that, either. He stormed off without getting into the bomb shelter. Hypocrite!

I just had to share this funny story with my kids. They all know their daddy likes to fight authority, and likes getting up in someone's grill at every opportunity. I know this trait of mine drove off Garrett and Autumn's mom. I am glad Stacy actually likes this degenerate quality of mine.

Following dinner and the night shoot, we found ourselves circled around the planning table looking at maps and going over the general flow of the mission, once again. All the old guys were animatedly talking over the visceral things that would most likely happen. Looking over at the new guys, I saw the confusion and hesitancy in their faces and eyes and noticed they were not saying anything out loud. I think no one else noticed this nuance. But with my years of training SEALs and facing different life-threatening missions, I clearly saw the sign of fear, masked by overt quietness, hiding the inner roar of confusion.

As I do when I am home with my kids, I simply said to them, "This isn't a game where keeping your tongue will keep you alive or make things miraculously disappear. Now that we have told you the entire mission flow, you have to talk out the reservations you have; you have to say what you think you will need to carry out the mission. We may have missed something. You have to tell us what is missing."

With that, many of the new guys talked through basics they thought we had missed, such as, "Why are we just taking four magazines of ammo, instead of ten?" I chimed in with, "In this game, here in hell, you have to be mobile. The extra weight will kill you. And, gents, you only shoot if you have something to shoot at. Do not waste your bullets thinking you are keeping their heads down simply by shooting. Seeing their buddy's head explode next to them will keep them from shooting back at you— and ensure you only shoot to kill."

Another new guy asked, "Chief, if a woman is carrying an AK-47, what is the real Rule Of Engagement (ROE) on that?"

I answered, "Bro, don't be confused. They all know the deal here. If they are making an aggressive move on you for any reason, you have to do what you think is right to protect yourself and me, dammit. Don't hesitate to make the right decision. Stacy will kill you if I die here because you failed to act." We all laughed, but the point was made.

The last question caught many of us off guard, to be sure, "Chief, we are hiking over some high-altitude mountains. We are not in shape for this like you all are. I am not proud to say that we will need to rest several times."

I looked at Nike and we smiled. "I will make sure I am fresh before we hit the target," I said, and I am eighteen years older than you. Trust me, we will rest. This isn't a sprint."

ADAMANTINE LESSON SEVEN

Connection

I learned several nuances about how performance dwindles when connection is lost while I was a student in SEAL BUD/S training in 1994. SEAL instructors hammer home the basic lessons such as the swim buddy rule. This rule is paramount while going through training. It simply states, "While conducting hazardous training evolutions, students will be in swimmer pairs, and no pair will be separated by a distance greater than six feet." I am sure safety reasons come into play for this while in training. Yet the rule, and the fallout from not obeying the rule, ingrains in each student the need and desire to be intimately linked to his buddy. That impression lasts a lifetime.

I also observed, as a student, that during timed runs or conditioning runs, when a student was separated from the group, when he felt he could no longer stay up with the group, his performance faltered considerably. Often students would literally quit when they perceived they no longer could hang with their peers, or were no longer connected physically with the group.

Later, as an instructor while in third phase, on long runs or long backpack runs, I would notice the separation and slowing of the students in the back, so I would circle back and literally pick up the stragglers. Re-joining the class served me well, and I noticed the students in the back would revive and put out once again. I learned physical connection helps with Internal Dialogue and, ultimately, physical performance.

Later, I used this knowledge while adventure racing. The rule was simple. If anyone fell behind the pace, we would literally tether the slow person to the faster ones and stay connected in order to go faster. The subversive mental strain and ensuing shitty Internal Dialogue of being physically disconnected from the group is a death sentence. I observed other teams in adventure racing not following this cardinal rule, and they would always quit or get injured, but most certainly, they would complain and feel separate.

I share this so you can put into practice this important point of connection within the framework of Internal Dialogue. During difficult times, times when mental and physical exhaustion sets in, you MUST connect with those around you. This might seem counterintuitive in every sense of the word, but when you feel pain, you will want to withdraw. When you feel like you are no longer connected, you will want to simply stay that way. I don't know why the mind and body do that to our efforts. Maybe millions of years of programming makes us believe when the weak fall back, they are no longer worthy, and no longer *needed*, I suppose.

But, in reality, this is nonsense. Simply use what I have taught you thus far. You will have to summon your own Internal Dialogue and reshape your immediate condition with words. Those around you will also assist, trust me.

"I *need* to stay up with my Team. They *need* me." This simple phrase is more important than a PhD in anything.

"Hey, I need help here. I am exhausted. Help me make it just a little bit further." You will be surprised how even the toughest men in the toughest conditions will reach out to help. You know why? They, too, really want to remain connected.

Today I am flying out to do an over-flight of the area we intend to walk through. Some local helicopter squadrons are doing a routine flight near our route, and honestly, I am bored with being in camp. Oddly, I don't find flying over the area dangerous with just with my rifle and without my platoon. I simply don't have any fear of dying here. Instead, I have an odd sense of calm . . . others may die, but not me. This is not founded in any hard and fast truth underlying my thought. Maybe I'm jaded and no longer care. The things I have thought about sometimes are odd. I will not be able to talk with my family until after this next mission. They must be strong and know I am in my element. Although the temps are hotter than fucking hell here, they must know I love them all.

We met the helos at the airfield and flew for an hour deep into the mountains. I was actually worried because I didn't fall asleep on this flight. We landed safely in a field, but just as the helos left, we immediately saw headlights of a car moving toward us from the valley miles away. *We were moving toward the lights, and the lights were moving toward us. Not a good combination for them,* I thought.

I extended my lead element about 200 yards ahead of the main force. Moving closer, we saw the car had stopped and men were getting out. We could not see them clearly, but our eyes in the sky reported they had AK-47s. The car abruptly moved away from our movement, but someone stayed behind, and the eyes in the sky could not confirm where the men had gone. As the minutes ticked by, we gained ground on the last location of the car and watched the car leaving the valley we were in. All of a sudden, from the direction of the car, we heard machine gun fire.

My LT confirmed he had also heard the fire, and I suggested we push forward. The men were very alert and doing what we had all trained to do. Nothing to do now but press on.

We observed a building near the last location of the car. I analyzed the route we needed to take and saw no easy way around the building without exposing the entire patrol. I knew not everyone in the patrol would realize the danger of the building, so I ordered my lead element to immediately secure the building and ensure we were all not walking into a trap. Thank God we all had night vision, because two men were lying in there, looking the other way, waiting for us to walk down the road. Poor, stupid bastards.

Not a shot was fired when we snuck up on them and decided to bring them along for the ride. We still had three miles to go. I hoped those guys had a good meal, because we weren't stopping for a snack.

I do recall the terrain made walking a complete suck-fest. I felt every step of the steep moutainside. Going up was steep, traversing the sides was dangerous, and finally, the going down was steep. At the bottom, Nike again found a river to cross. Water is always a blessing in the heat.

As we crossed, I knelt down to get my waist and belly completely wet to cool down. I looked around and noticed everyone else doing the same. I recall thinking, "I do love these men. We all think and do the same things."

We approached the final delay point. We were supposed to stop and wait for everyone to close the distance and get ready for the assault, but the view made something painfully clear. The numerous buildings we were sent to clear were all different heights, and they were surrounded by high trees. This meant clearing was going to be far more complicated than our original plan.

Once we consolidated our forces and had something to drink and eat to ensure we were ready, we began initial clearance of our first compound. The first was the biggest of all the buildings and posed the biggest threat. We snuck in silently, and found men, women, and kids sleeping everywhere. Stepping over sleeping people, walking into rooms, then backing out without waking anyone is a strange experience. The first compound took three minutes to clear, and after waking all the sleeping people, we now had twenty people to manage. I had not truly considered managing that many people in the first building, but life always throws you things to make you laugh. I ordered a squad to stay in compound one, and we continued clearing the other buildings to bring all the people back to the main compound.

The map study we had done prior to the mission was completely wrong. The shit on the ground, the reality, was confusing as hell—twisted and complicated. After clearing the first four buildings in a twisted maze, we had found forty-five more people sleeping. We delayed further clearance, because taking all these people back to the main compound was very time consuming, and actually very dangerous—at least from my point of view.

I moved over to Nike and said, "Nike, you and I and Carnie are the only ones up here in the front. The maze behind us is out of control. We are going to wait until the entire squad is back here with us before we move again."

Nike replied, "Chief, as long as we don't shoot, none of these idiots will wake up. I just hope the men can find us again. Hey, let's have some Copenhagen."

I handed him my can, and we sat and watched, saying nothing. The heat was oppressive. Snores of men in the next compound mixed with the sounds of dogs moving around, and maybe the sounds of cows stamping their hooves. In times of combat, the silence is deafeningly loud.

Time must change, too. I looked at my watch and only five minutes had passed, yet it felt like two hours. I was tired. My feet hurt, my back was aching, and my eyes were tired. However, as we heard the men moving toward us, I flashed them with an IR flashlight. All the pain stopped, and we were back to the clearance.

Mazes of compounds, sheds, walls, and irrigation ditches got us thoroughly twisted. The map I carried didn't aid at all to help any of us find where we were exactly. We did know how to get back to the main building, so that eased our pain . . . somewhat.

The men continued clearing compounds and shuffling the people back to the main building. My job was deciding which compound would serve as our "castle" for the next two days. We were unable to find a compound that would lend us a tactical advantage, and that pissed me off. We'd already cleared thirteen, and not one would work. The clearance was complete, and I had nothing.

I called the other platoon chief on the radio and informed him of our predicament. He, in turn, echoed his total displeasure with what he had found on his side of the target area. We had only one hour left until daylight. Problems 'o plenty!

I grabbed Nike to move into a shed where we could lay the overview map on the ground to take a look. After some confusion, we were able to trace our route through the maze and find the shed we were in. We located a set of buildings further away from the original clearance compounds that might be perfect. The problem was we only had twenty minutes to clear them before the sun said hello.

I informed LT we were pressing to a new compound, which would take fifteen minutes to clear. I also said I'd tell him in five if the new site would meet our "castle" needs. He replied with, "Get some."

I took eight guys 200 yards across an open field and put ladders up on the walls. Nike, Jake, and I climbed up and saw the people here, too, were still sleeping. My men entered the far side without incident and without shooting a round. Too bad, really, but at least this compound was perfect.

"LT, we are in building twenty-two. Bring everyone here. Come in the west side. How many unknowns do we have?" I asked.

"Stand by," he said. "We have sixty-eight unknowns. I will need three of your guys if we want to get this done by daylight."

I replied, "Roger, I will send them now. They are coming along the north side of your building in five minutes. Don't move until they arrive."

"Roger, standing by to receive."

We were in a hurry now to reunite with the rest of the platoon, set ourselves up for the ensuing battle, and get the other platoon secured in one of the other compounds further south of us. We had five minutes. Setting up before daylight is actually a self-imposed deadline. Nothing indicated we were in any impending doom scenario, but we all knew our advantage would go away with the night.

"LT, we need some overhead cover. Call the fires guys back at base and tell them we are in contact and need immediate Apache support. We need at least an hour to set up," I said over comms to the boss. *Why wait?* I was thinking.

I heard him acknowledge and then heard Lawyer get to work on calling in the request. While they worked on air cover, I worked on identifying three positions within our compound that would support our defense. Nike, Jake, and Carnie were put in place when the rest of the platoon, along with several enemy fighters we had rudely awoken to capture, filtered into the back door. With the sun came heat, already 105 degrees and rising. Why would anyone live here?

I sat next to Carnie while he got his machine gun into position and remarked, "You know those ruby slippers in that Oz movie? I bet if you clicked the heels together and said, 'I want to go see how people lived when Christ was alive,' you would be transported right here." For some reason the thought made me laugh, and writing it now makes me laugh again.

A cow was tethered in the compound right where the family was sleeping. Chickens were running and shitting everywhere. The kids peed and pooped right where their parents were being questioned about the enemy guys we had captured. The clincher was the family was feeding curdled milk from open buckets to deformed kids sleeping in a little hole in the wall. *All the comforts of home,* I thought.

Carnie and I were looking at this when he said, "Thom, next time can we fight in Germany? At least those people have wine and beer, and the country is pretty." Neither of us laughed. They were existing in literally the most disgusting human condition I have ever seen a family tolerate, let alone live in. Further, nothing we could offer would be what these people would want, or even know how to use.

I had to remind myself that SEALs are not here to make friends or change lives. We are here to capture enemy, and most of the time, kill them. At least you can respect the enemy. They like to fight, no matter the odds against them. They aren't very good at it, but they don't lack in conviction.

After an hour or so, both platoons were set, and some of us were getting some rest. Now was the long, boring pause before all hell breaks loose. I sarcastically thought how the hot air, bugs, dirt, smell, and half sleep with body armor on all made for happy thoughts and joyous reflections of life in general. I woke ready to shoot someone in the face just for making me be here, instead of not with my family. I sat looking at my muddy boots and a strange looking bug crawling around on them and thought of the movie *Gladiator*. Russell Crowe says, "I will seek my revenge in this life or the next," which truly spoke for my mood and desperation at that moment. Stacy need not worry about fear, as it was reshaped to angry disgust.

Not a single enemy showed up before lunch. What a shame. We continued building up the three positions, resting, and eating. At 3:00 p.m., I again climbed up into a position where Carnie had just relieved Snowman. We sat without talking for a long time, while we both scanned the area looking for the signs of movement . . . or maybe a trained enemy sniper crawling around getting ready to shoot us. Nothing. After an hour of exhaustive work looking and watching, and more watching, we heard what sounded like a motorcycle. Very faint, but we agreed we heard a small engine. Then, it suddenly stopped.

I continued using my binos to spot ways some enemy could maneuver in on us and found about 100 different ways. Or, rather, if I were an enemy, I could have gotten close enough to throw a rock. All of a sudden my skin got goosebumps, and I grabbed my rifle, bringing it up to my shoulder to look through the scope. Something was about to happen. I hadn't seen or heard anything, but goosebumps don't lie.

I looked through my scope at a tree close to a wall about 100 yards northeast, and saw a man with an RPG turn toward me . . . and aim . . . I fired immediately, even as I moved my gun toward him. I saw my bullets impacting on the wall, tracking toward him. With each new trigger squeeze, I realized we were each trying to get better aim on the other. After four rounds, I saw a puff of smoke rise out of the back of the RPG, just as I squeezed off the last round—which hit him in the neck. Then I immediately ducked. Carnie ducked, too, and we smiled at each other as the RPG round sailed ten feet over our heads, and detonated 100 yards south of us. He and I jumped back up and continued firing at the tree and wall the shooter had walked behind.

Snowman worked on getting air support, while everyone else ran to the ladders and their fighting positions to get in the fight. No one was firing, though. The wait was on, and so was the weird slowing of time for me. What seemed like an hour of nothing turned suddenly into enemy bullets hitting everywhere around Carnie and me. The boys fired from all three positions. All my men were getting eyes on enemy with weapons, who had **again** moved in on us, without our seeing them.

Snowman and Ground Launch were now up in the position with Carnie and me. Ground Launch was shooting 40 mm grenades at three enemy in the trees, about 300 yards away. Snowman made jokes about a swarm of bees trying to bite us all: "Chief, I am really allergic to bees. If I get bit, I will probably not be able to breathe within three minutes."

"So, go somewhere else then. I don't have time for this. Kill the bees, leave, or kill the bees and stay," I hated to be short with him, but I was in a really foul mood. Such is the life of a SEAL chief in combat. Snowman got a bottle of bug spray and a lighter out, and proceeded to burn the bees despite at least five rounds whizzing over his head within five inches. I honestly think he wasn't as scared of the bullets as he was the bees.

When he finished killing the bees, he knelt down and looked up at Carnie and me. Carnie said, without cracking smile, "I was about to call your mom."

Snowman replied, "I would rather call a stripper to suck the stinger out. I think one stung me on my cock."

Carnie said, "Still think I will call your mom for that, you pussy."

Somehow the whole scene of bullets flying everywhere, bees being burned, talk of strippers and moms, and cock stings made perfect sense to us. Probably not to any of you, but it did to us.

Strangely, the enemy fire and bees died down at the same time. A moment of no noise and no movement made us all nervous. "Holy shit, what just happened?" I asked Carnie. I stood back from my firing position to look around. Everyone was either looking through their scopes or sitting against the wall, looking at me. I shrugged my shoulders, smiled, and said, "Maybe they are all changing their magazines at the same time?"

Snowman moved slowly over to Ground Launch, then they both aimed their weapons and lifted their heads . . . a bit too much, apparently. Two rounds cracked over their heads. I felt the spin of a bullet and the air of its passing. They immediately ducked. Ground Launch yelled, "You missed me, motherfucker!" Snowman looked at Ground Launch and said, "Do you think it is personal? I think it's personal. I don't think that guy likes you too much." Then, Snowman handed Ground Launch a 40 mm grenade, which he loaded without saying anything. He lifted his launcher to his shoulder, aiming right at the place the round had come from. Then he fired. Before the round landed 200 yards away, he had shot two more grenades. When the first one hit, an enemy ran from his position. We had all anticipated this—nothing like one year of training together. Before the second round hit, Carnie and I had put four rounds in the enemy. As he tumbled, the second round hit at his feet, blowing him up into the air. When he landed from that flip, the third round bounced him up again.

I put my hand on Carnie's shoulder and said, "Nice, brother."

Lawyer yelled, "Fast movers, two minutes out. Give me bearing and distance."

I yelled down to him, "Ninety-eight yards, thirty-five degrees. Have him spot the tree then the wall leading away from our compound. He should find some dudes at the first tree line. Drop a 500 pounder ASAP."

"Roger, Chief." He cut himself off, and I watched him talking into his radio, tracing the lines on the map as he spoke. After a bit, he looked up and said, "Two minutes out, Chief."

I turned to Carnie, Snowman, and Ground Launch, "Gents, this is going to be dangerously close. A 500 pounder is dropping right on that tree line. Carnie, shoot a burst of rounds on the left side so the enemy run back to the right." Carnie shot a couple of bursts and ducked, just as the 500 pounder landed. Wow! The walls shook and the blast wave traveled right over our heads. "Damn," I muttered softly.

I realized I should check in with all the men and reconnect their efforts with the fact we were doing well and staying alive through another round of dealing with the devil. My feet and knees again hurt as I walked around the compound. I guess stress causes endorphins to kick in, and they were now wearing off.

I climbed up the ladder leading to Nike, Jake, and All Around's position. When I popped my head up, I noticed twenty or more .300 Winchester Magnum shell casings on the ground. "Nicely done, gents. How many did you get?"

Nike replied, "I have no idea, but I shot three magazines."

Mister All Around added, "I got one at 500 yards. I think he is still praying, because he is lying facing Mecca." I crawled up and used my binos to check it out.

He was, lying with his AK-47 still in his right hand.

"Ok, what do you all need . . . water, food, bullets, what?" I queried.

Nike said, "Yes, yes, and yes."

I told them, "Jesus, I shot a dude right when he was pulling the trigger on an RPG. Did you hear that thing go right over your heads?"

Jake laughed and said, "Yeah, the thing hit right over in the middle of that marijuana field. Too bad it isn't burning; it'd be nice to take the edge off."

"Yeah, that is all we need to get piss tested right when we get off the helo. I am sure someone in particular would love to see me fall," I said, laughing.

I went to get rounds, water, and food for the men. After years of following and leading, I have found when someone asks for something, the best thing is to immediately get it for him. Get him exactly what he is asking for, in a hurry. When I tossed the filled bag up to them, they all grinned down at me. Those smiles were worth every bad thing I had ever gone through in my life—everything.

After supporting the men and checking in with LT, I was sure we had air support and the men were restocked. I was also very aware I was exhausted once again from staying up twenty-four hours prior to the mission and the long, complicated clearance of the target area. Now around 3:00 p.m. on the first day, I found a quiet place, lay my body down, turned off my brain, and allowed myself to totally check out and dream. I know the thought of relaxing after a heavy firefight seems absurd, but in reality, that is the best time to let go—at least it always has been for me.

I put my helmet over my head and was transported somewhere, anywhere other than this hell. The air was cold and snow was falling down. As my brain settled in the dream, I realized I was elk hunting in Colorado. I recall smiling and laughing to myself, saying, "Great choice of dream. At least in this dream I arrived after that sick hike up the steep cliff." I laughed again. But when I looked down, I wasn't carrying my HH375, but instead had my .300 Winchester Magnum. "Nice! Another good choice," I chuckled, again.

I found the herd I had been following for a day and a half uphill from me. I couldn't see the bull, but I used my binoculars to find the lead cow. When hunting elk, make sure you find the lead cow . . . she runs the herd. The bull doesn't do anything but piss her off and annoy all the other cows. This cow was relaxed, unaware I was present. In my dream, I recall that this point in the hunt was a battle of wills between me and the elements, and me and the herd. I knew I couldn't stay there in the ten-below-zero cold as long as the elk could, but I also knew I could make them move in a predictable way. I would only have maybe thirty seconds to get the bull, though, once I made the action.

I think everything boils down to a battle of wills—or maybe a battle of self. The biggest battle is always with yourself, trying to connect with something outside of what we call the self.

The key to this battle was to first get parallel with the wind and the elk, so when I made a sound, they would at least send some of the herd toward the sound. The rest might push downhill just a bit to smell the wind. The move was risky, but most animals need to investigate with more than one sense before they all run uphill. My prediction was they would run uphill toward the closest tree line. This would take the herd out into the open once they broke the crest of the ridge. On the far ridge was a cliff. I predicted they would then all lay out in front of me at about 300 yards, running past until they could find the way down the other side.

I got out my coyote call knowing that would make them listen; I also got a branch to set down where I could break it. The plan was to make the coyote sound, break the stick, then watch them move. If they took the bait, they would move uphill slightly toward the cliff. If they did, I would run as fast as I could, at the same elevation, about 100 yards, then pop out on the clearing.

I made the sound, broke the branch, and got my binos up to watch. In the real hunt, it actually went perfectly. For some reason, the dream didn't go as planned. I immediately saw the bull right in the middle of the herd. I sat and watched instead of getting my gun up. He was too far and moving too fast to worry about at this point. I grabbed all my gear and ran like I was being chased until I was overlooking the opening and far ridge. I set my rifle scope to 320 yards, threw my pack on the ground, and got stable just in time to see the first cow trot slowly through my scope. Thirty were in the herd, and I counted ten; then I saw the bull. He was now walking, looking back toward the rest of the herd, bellowing. I took a breath, relaxed the cross hairs on a patch of hair where his heart would be, and . . .

I jumped up from my sleep because rounds were hitting the wall next to where I had been so comfortably resting. My helmet was spinning on the ground like a top, and my MK17 was in my hands. I immediately press checked my chamber to ensure a bullet was in there, then looked at my magazine. All my senses came rushing to full alert as I crawled toward the door. I thought, *Oh, we're in another firefight in hell, cool.*

Carnie and Snowman were in position. KM and Texas were working their position. Lawyer was working the air piece. Nike, Jake, and All Around were shooting at something. I recall sitting down next to Lawyer, asking, "Well, I may have slept through the first part of this firefight. How is it going?"

Lawyer replied, "Ridge boss, fuck, I don't know. They woke me up."

We both snickered a quiet, shoulders raised chuckle, saying this really isn't funny, but you still laugh.

We had an F-18 and his wingman immediately check on and drop bombs on those silly enemy. Eight of the silly bastards had moved in to grab one of their dead friends, and must have gotten pissed at us for some reason. They decided to rush us from 400 yards away across an open field. As I watched Nike shooting, the strangest thing happened. Two enemy were left, and Nike shot the furthest one. Then he literally stood up and yelled, "Stop!"

I looked up at him and frowned. Then he said, "Oh, you aren't gonna stop, are you?" and lifted his .300 Winchester Magnum and shot so fast I didn't have time to get my binos up to see the impact down-range. When I finally did get a look, the enemy was falling, dropping the grenade he had in his hand, and Nike was lowering his rifle.

He looked down at me and said, "I tried to tell him to stop, but I fear he doesn't speak English, does he? Maybe next time I should say something in his native tongue?" Just as he said tongue, the grenade the enemy had been holding went off, about 100 yards away from us.

I said, "Nike, you and I need to talk about your delivery. If you are going to run for office some day, you really need to learn your manners. Next time, before you kill someone, say something about his sister or mom."

An hour later, we had calmed down, and so had the enemy fighters. The sun was getting really low on the horizon and that night was going to be a no-moon night, meaning really dark. We were coordinating a link-up with some nearby Army Special Forces guys, and a movement on our part to flex forward into the killing zone, checking the dead and clearing the remaining buildings they had been using as a safe haven.

After five hours of night-time movement and clearing an additional eight buildings, we returned to our main compound. We didn't find one dead enemy, nor anyone in the buildings. The C-130 circling above us also hadn't seen any enemy get their dead or leave. My feeling of being safe with the C-130 up there really died for me that night. At dusk fifteen were visibly dead. Within an hour, they all were gone. Makes you wonder, doesn't it? A false sense of security is no security at all.

The next day was hot. The temperature on the rooftop was 120 degrees. In the shade was 120 degrees. Water was 120 degrees. The food was 120 degrees. I think my brain was 120 degrees.

I decided to walk over to the other platoon's compound to check in with their platoon chief. When I arrived, he pulled me aside, "Thom, we have a big problem, and it is getting worse. All my guys are sick, and I am getting sick, too."

"What do you mean sick?" I asked.

He didn't have to explain. He simply puked all over my left leg. I took a step back and noticed two of his men with their pants down around their ankles, spraying, not actually pooping. I immediately called over the radio for LT to come to Echo platoon's position ASAP. Within five minutes, LT arrived, and we were surveying the surreal scene.

"Chief, we are in trouble if we stay. These men aren't even looking for the enemy any longer, and we cannot spare any men to cover their watch," he said. LT wasn't smiling.

He went on, "Boss, time to make the call and request immediate extract of the entire troop. If not, I can guarantee we'll have some dead SEALs to report. Either we stay here and lose one of them due to dehydration and heat stroke, or, lose one because this platoon cannot even post security." He wasn't smiling, either.

The request went out for any helo crew willing to pick up mid-day in a hostile environment, with immediate movement to the closest hospital. Within thirty minutes, an Australian CH-47 crew said they would arrive within the hour.

As great as that sounded, grabbing all the freely puking and shitting brothers, then carrying or pushing them a mile to the extract point was a total nightmare. But, hey, that was the fun part! The not-so-fun part was we would be walking in daylight, straight toward the enemy. Oh, the memories of combat.

We grabbed all our gear and rushed to the other platoon to help the walking poopers. I was in the lead element of seven guys, and we pushed 100 yards ahead of the main body. When I looked back, I had to laugh. Ten guys were walking with pants down, spraying what looked like brown water all over the ground, but carrying their rifles like nothing was the matter.

When the Aussies arrived, the crew was laughing so hard it made us all laugh again, harder. Only in combat. Only between friends, only between brothers, could this be funny.

An 11-mile hike just to pick a fight.

Silver Star.

Kandahar.

Do not get in front of this thing. Trust me.

A relaxing smoke.

A 1,100-yard shot to rescue an SF Army team.

The "Hell Hole."

A day at the desk in my office.

No M4 for me. The 5.56 mm doesn't kill anyone.

120 degrees at 11,000 feet. You have got to be kidding me.

Too exhausted to duck.

PART THREE

Your Organs

SECTION EIGHT

INSATIABLE

"When the student is ready, the Master appears."
—Buddhist Proverb

"Honey, we survived another brutal operation," I told Stacy over the webcam chat. She was sitting in our kitchen, preparing lunch for our kids. She looked gorgeous, inviting, and completely hot.

"I cannot believe how many times you have gone out and all come back unbroken. I keep worrying your deployment will be like that Ramadi deployment with all those dead SEALs," Stacy said. I could tell she had more than just the words, but she couldn't muster up enough courage to say them. I truly think she was a Spartan woman in a past life: committed, deeply in love with her husband and family, and unwilling to waiver and say anything that would show fear.

"No deployment is the same. We all face different circumstances and have different men and leaders. I didn't come here to fuck around, nor did I come here to make rank. I came here because I want to be here, and the men want me here. Maybe that makes all the difference. I don't know . . . maybe," I replied, knowing my reply sounded odd.

"Well, whatever the reason, we love you and need you to do what you need to, to make it back to us. I can't wait to feel you next to me, to feel your skin again. I dream of us every night," Stacy said with that certain brightness in her eyes. "Thom, I have been talking a lot to Jerry about what you are going through with our men and combat. He tells me stories about how what you all are doing is so uniquely tied to both your genes and your need to endure. I am going to send you some of the emails where he talks about how some men have developed over the past 10,000 years to be able to thrive in the hell you are going through. I know you need this in your bones, and I like that about you. Please read it, and maybe that knowledge will make you stronger."

"Wow, sounds like this guy has some experience with crazy times, having grown up running carnivals. I never knew anyone could make millions in that line of work. Wonder why he and Tammy have connected so easily to you?" I said, sort of not understanding why Stacy had brought this up. Part of me was jealous some other man was talking to my wife. Actually, most of me was. The other small part wondered what point anyone could make that would affect our performance here in hell.

"His understanding of what makes men tick comes from fifty years of making things work at a carnival, as well as making other businesses work across the globe. Apparently, he was the sole distributor of shotguns to Russia, but I think having a mentor who was separate from the military who could give you insight to what makes men who they are would be wise, don't you think?" Stacy stood still, looking into the camera, her hands on her hips like a Spartan Wife.

"Damn, OK. How can I refuse that?" I said. "Send whatever correspondence he has had with you, and I'll read it after chow."

I talked a little longer with Stacy about things I will not write here. The Internet is a great way to connect, to be sure. A great woman makes a great man, and vice versa, a great man makes a great woman. Pay close attention to that. Intimacy, connection, encouragement, fun, and ultimately, words from a great woman are priceless.

"A great woman makes a great man.
A great man makes a great woman."

I was late to chow, and no one in my platoon was around. Several Special Forces shooters were sitting around watching TV and talking amongst themselves. After getting my plate, I sat alone and thought about the boys of Bravo platoon. I thought about how they had come through the various training programs back in the States. I thought about how quickly we adapted from thinking we were going to deploy to one place, then a month before deployment, were shifted to this hellhole. I thought about all the patriotic Americans living a life of liberty and wanting so desperately to help in any way they could.

As I ate, I thought about my sons growing up free from this massive Islamic surge. Their anger toward us surely seems almost genetically bred. I truly felt sorry for the poor children who are raised with such a complete lie about how white Americans are so different from them. I will be able to visualize the hatred they have for us in their eyes for the rest of my life. Negotiating is not possible with a hatred so patient and so extreme. I laughed to myself, and the SF guys looked at me like I was crazy. I smiled back and said, "I think I need a beer." They cackled and agreed.

When I lifted the lid to the trashcan, a hundred flies rose up, reinforcing my opinion of how backward this whole land and people are. Nothing like flies in your grill to ensure a passion to survive. "This fucking place," I said with disgust.

I walked across the road back into the SEAL compound and the planning center. In planning another dance with the devil, it was time for me to call on everything I knew about my men—and everything I *didn't want* to know about the enemy.

Our intel shop had matured so fast, they had found ways to get us into the battle. We decided to coordinate our efforts with a Special Forces Team who needed our bullets and training to move into an area clearly used as an enemy training camp; no Americans were allowed to move through the area. A lot of coordination would have to take place, including a flight up to their base to talk through issues, and some mortar training on our part so we could effectively support their offensive.

Discussing our options, I said, "Shit, yes. I would be happy to fly in to 10,000 feet to set up an overwatch and shoot mortars and rifles while they do all the walking. Who would ever have thought SEALs would be mortar men for SF?"

After completing our initial talk-through, I headed back to my combat room eager to read the emails Stacy had, no doubt, sent by now to read what a successful, patriotic man wanted to say to a SEAL chief in combat. I was truly excited to have a committed ear to talk to about performance. SEALs learn quickly to seek out other professionals to help us overcome anything not clear to us. As a sniper, I constantly seek out the top long-range shooters, and even big game hunters, to ask the questions only the best know the answers to.

An old saying I read as a young boy is, "If you want to learn how to go up the mountain, ask the man who goes up there every day. Don't read a book about it."

I pondered what questions I really did have about teamwork, human performance, dealing with overwhelming situations, etc. I also wondered if anyone not involved would have any understanding of what we faced . . . of what I faced. Could anyone truly understand this shit—this hell? I surely didn't, and I wasn't even sure I wanted to delve any deeper.

Yet, since I was a child, I've been driven to seek every advantage to win. I have taken responsibility to make sure we win every tactical task the bosses give us and to also find a way to bring my men home alive and well. Tactically and technically, this platoon could go up against any enemy the world has ever had in the history of war. Nothing any outsider would offer could impact us in this arena.

In my time teaching boys to grow into SEALs, I've learned there's something inside a man far more in need of training, far more valuable for him to learn, than any tactic or new fitness technique. After teaching young men in training to overcome impossible conditions, and watching them endure terrible pain, I noticed the key wasn't how hard the man was, but how malleable his mind was—how he harnessed his thoughts before, during, and after these times of hell.

A hard mind is breakable.

A malleable mind is Unbreakable.

Much effort has been spent by our SEAL community chasing, very successfully, better technology for improving our ability to find and kill enemies. We have spent years using physical performance and toughness to make our SEALs the best in the world. We arrived at a solution of mental mastery by breaking down a man's physical abilities. Throughout history, most nation's warriors achieved this same mastery of mental state by crushing or breaking the body. Hell, some religions even push minimizing the physical body in order to get to heaven—or whatever state of awareness that discipline deems great.

In training these men, I chose to train their minds directly by teaching them to use their Internal Dialogue to bridge the gap between failing, on the one hand, or toward powerful performance when the body fails or when the odds of success aren't in their favor. During hard training days, I saw how the quitters lost control of their own Internal Dialogue, and would quit the task for one or every reason they heard in their thoughts. Yet, what the non-quitters were saying to themselves wasn't clear at first because we didn't interview the winners! So I started interviewing the winners—those who would not quit no matter what.

My task was made more difficult because the winners didn't pay any attention to thoughts that might make them quit. Often, they would not even let themselves say out loud what they were thinking. This simple act of not being comfortable speaking about quitting—or even acknowledging such thoughts of quitting at all—struck me as a far more important discovery.

So, on that day, I sat down to share that very point with Jerry to see if he had any insights.

Reading the introductory email from a man and woman I didn't know, from a place so far away and so far removed from hell, I was immediately shocked by his first paragraph. I have copied and pasted it here, directly quoted:

> *Thom, I will not waste your time with unproven, useless words. The work you have to do needs every ounce of your attention and experience. Your family is safe, I personally assure you if they need anything, we will move heaven and earth to help them.*
>
> *Tammy and I simply offer all of our years of experience in business, with honest conversation about losses and victories, and what we have learned from both. The nation is behind you, and we in particular, will help where we can.*

Stacy has shared some of the emails you have sent your family. We are ready to listen and engage on one particular subject where we know we can assist. We know what it takes to get a group of people to excel.

Very fine, I thought, reading the last word. But in hell, something always pulls you back to reality. A distant explosion triggered the base alarm system, so off I went to the bomb bunker to wait thirty minutes for the base to confirm what the rest of us already knew—the bomb missed, and the enemy was long gone.

I had much to ponder after Jerry's email, but we were off to planning and training. Our next mission matured to the point of having a day and time set. The men always seemed to get electrified when those were set. We had clearance to send a small team up to the SF base to meet and coordinate the entire plan.

Before leaving base, I hastily dashed off an email to Stacy.

Honey, I will be gone for a couple days. My email and phone silence is nothing critical—unless the helo crashes! Just kidding.

My trip away was solid. The men of my platoon are operating beyond the need for my control. I have to admit I am proud of them, and now know I only play a management role, holding the reins. The analogy is fitting, because they are no longer acting like a herd of cats, but as a team of horses, all pulling together in one direction. Sometimes, I ultimately feel I am holding them back. I suppose leading warriors is just that way—holding aggression in check.

We finally met a SF officer who wants to go after the enemy and doesn't care if it is dangerous. The SF battalion we operated with in Helmand was that way, but they are gone now. Now we're smiling openly, knowing we are going to get into some good fights over the next few operations. Time to get a good grip on the reins.

Now that I am back at camp, I have time to get back into working out and talking with Stacy and the kids on the computer or phone. I find myself needing this routine to stay rooted in family and to be fit and available for combat. Mostly, I selfishly need the connection with Stacy.

The men have already completed organization and initial tactics required for loading us up and getting us back home after the operation.

This one has moving parts and logistical delays to this operation, but the tactics, once on the ground, are simple . . . at least at this stage of our combat lifestyle.

Tomorrow night we leave, and I predict we will be back within thirty-six hours. I decided to see what my new, wise mentor may have to add to my experience leading men and to making sure we get back alive.

My short email to Jerry:

> *Jerry, without going into detail, let us talk about what you have learned regarding leading men and making them capable. I just want to know what you think about or talk about with your companies' employees to make them perform.*

Jerry's response:

> *Thom, I will admit I have never led men in combat, nor have I encountered any situation where I have killed or asked a man to kill. I will, however, tell you what I have learned about how we have developed over the millions of years of evolution, and maybe, just maybe, some bit of information will fit in with what you face.*
>
> *Over the millions of years of evolution, some breeds of men have evolved a need to endure hellish things, as you stated. I suggest you don't fight that need; give in to it and give it to your men and embrace it. Don't worry that many people back here don't understand it or want you to be that way. Be that way because you need to be that way.*
>
> *I see that you called your wife Spartan Wife. Keep calling her that—it makes you embrace who you are and who you need to be, and your men will see that. I also think Stacy needs you to be a Spartan.*

Well, that was all he wrote. Don't fight who I am; embrace it. The men will see it and thrive, and the wife needs you to be that way, too. Sometimes I wish wise people would just tell the young "how to," instead of this Yoda shit.

Standing in line for chow, I thought about the mission, about the men, and about my new-found knowledge. I needed to be here, and so did my men. I knew I needed to be here. I had spent twenty years in one war or another and felt at home, even though it sucked, and I would often rather be in bed with Stacy.

I think what I do with the men actually reinforces not only that what we are doing is what we need to do, but also demonstrates the respect I have for each of the men for being here. During the Helmand mission, they showed me, and themselves, they were capable of doing quite well here in hell.

Email to Stacy:

> *Stacy, a week has passed since our last email and video chat. I have so missed my family. Before I tell you what we went through during the last two missions, know we are all here, healthy and unbroken. I so long for your touches.*

The first mission we embarked on was very straightforward. We loaded up our SEAL force and flew to a remote base to link up with our SF brothers. We had an hour on the ground to talk through some of the last details and allow our communications experts to get their final checks with all the assets and other players during the mission.

We have become used to, and relaxed at, the thought of flying into unknown areas, into bad guy backyards, searching through the mazes of buildings we inevitably find. This target area was a maze, too, but the men handled it very well.

The main compound was surrounded by a ten-foot wall, spread out over a 100-yard by 100-yard area. The inside compound was a literal maze of interconnected buildings, with crawl spaces linking some of the buildings to each other.

I found the first crawl hole and could not fit my big ass through, so I backward scooted, then pulled the smallest guy I had over. We call him the Mad Hatter.

He looked at me and said, "Are you fucking serious? Right now?"

"No, I am joking. You are welcome to sit with your back against the wall for the rest of the day, with your thumb in your mouth. The choice is yours," I snickered.

He pulled out his pistol and crawled in. After the light and sound of him scooting disappeared, I looked up and saw LT staring down at me from the roof. I shrugged my shoulders and said, "I bet he is pissing himself about now, don't you?"

"Sometimes being small doesn't pay," said LT as he laughed and walked away.

After two minutes, I could see a flashlight coming back through the space. When he fully birthed himself from the canal, he sat down, and I saw he was soaked head to toe. I didn't say a word, since I knew he'd report when he got his composure back.

Finally, he looked up and said, "Holy fuck, Chief; I about drowned in there. It all of a sudden dropped off. I was head down and couldn't turn around. I dropped my pistol, too. Once I pushed myself up out of the water, I turned and could see my pistol at the bottom of the little elbow. I put my feet in, slid underwater, squeezed my pistol between my feet, and pulled my body back up. I suppose now I know why we do drown proofing in BUD/S."

"Well, get your guns back up, this clearance isn't close to being over. Shake it off," I replied.

I moved back outside to see where all the men were. As we pushed the clearance south along the wall, I grabbed one of my new heavy weapons guys who had missed the first part of deployment and placed him on the right flank security.

I have not mentioned much about these guys. I suppose now is a good time. One guy, Salty, is the toughest and most loyal man I have ever met. When we were forming up the platoon eighteen months ago, we needed one more man. I had a list of potential guys still in SEAL Qualification Training from my master chief. I went to the training building and interviewed some from the list. This guy was at the bottom. He had gotten in a fight with "real" team guys at a local bar and had suffered a detached retina. He had been recovering for three months, becoming disillusioned and pissing off everyone around him. My kinda guy.

As I talked with him, I began to like this dude. The willingness to fight, the lack of fear, and the hatred for administrative leadership reminded me of myself. I offered him an option—only one option.

"Salty, here is the deal. If I take you on, we will have no drinking of any kind from here on out. Unless we are at a platoon family function and I say you can, I better never hear of you being drunk. I expect you to be the hardest, strongest man in the platoon, and I am going to give you the machine gun to carry. If you are ever late, you are out of the platoon. If I ever hear you bad mouth anyone in the platoon, you are out. Can you live by those rules?"

He looked at me and replied, "Chief, I will live by those rules."

"Good. Pack your bags and check into Team Seven Bravo platoon tomorrow morning at 0700 hours," I advised.

Since then, he has done every single thing asked of him. He has become dependable as a teammate, reliable in all weather, and I call him friend. So I set him on flank security and said, "You are the only one out here. Don't let any enemy get in on us. Don't ask for permission to shoot; this isn't a game. Don't drop this position for any reason. I will come get you when the target is secured. OK?"

He nodded, and I walked away.

The clearance went on for another hour of twists and turns, but no shots were fired, and nothing big was found. As we set up for the long day of sitting and waiting, LT and I joked about the tunnels and looked at the really old weapons we had found on target. Flintlock, black powder rifles, and some Russian shotguns from the early 1900s. They may have been old, but they can still do damage.

The sun was coming up as I walked around getting the final head count and ensuring we had 360-degree coverage. Suddenly, I realized I had not gone back to relieve Salty on the flank. "Jesus, Salty, two hours flew by. Next time I won't tell you to stay in position until I get back. Shit, if I had died, would you have stayed here forever?" I asked when I returned.

Laughing, he replied, "No, if you had died, I would have killed the ones who had shot you, or died trying." He stood up and turned to pee. I thought to myself, *Wow, this dude did exactly what he was told to . . . in an age of defiance. Impressive.*

On the short walk back, he grabbed my arm, and we stopped. "Chief, I am here because of you. I will never forget your support. I owe you." I patted him on the back and said, "Go get some rest and sleep. Tomorrow is going to be a long day."

The remainder of the operation was completely hilarious. On the final building, we needed to breach the main gate. My original Leading Petty Officer (LPO), who had been sent to Iraq during the first part of the deployment, had taken the lead to conduct the explosive breach. I think he put in too much charge, poor guy. We blew the entire metal door into the compound. It flew, spinning like a saw, about two feet above the ground, across the inner courtyard, then buried into a wall. The craziest part is the entire family sleeping in the courtyard didn't even wake up.

On the second floor, our snipers needed to breach some small holes in one of the west-facing walls to get eyes on that direction. Again, LPO aided in the explosive breach. I was on the first floor with him, All Around, and Salty. Boom!

"Damn, that seemed a bit loud for a porthole breach," I said with a frown.

All Around turned to LPO and said, "Fuck, how much did you use?"

LPO said, "Just two quarter-blocks."

All Around, who was also a breacher, mused, "Um, that is a half a pound of C4!"

So up we all crawled, back through the 2,000-year-old, hand-molded, mud staircase. I was the last one to climb up. Everyone stood silently. The explosion had lifted the mud roof and twisted it forty-five degrees. The south-facing wall of the room was no longer there. Most interesting—the holes produced were only six inches wide.

I laughed and said, "Good luck," before crawling back down the ancient staircase.

ADAMANTINE LESSON EIGHT

Mentors and masters

Mentorship is a great thing. I am beginning to see, in a small way, my effect on my men, and find myself thinking of Jerry's offer to mentor and affect both me and the platoon. I think great men show up when we are at a place where we're ready to be mentored.

Look for and seek advice and guidance from people who are experts at the things you, too, want to be great doing. Be ready to receive their coaching, their mentorship. I know you kids will all want to go it alone. For a variety of reasons, humans have a natural tendency to do things alone. You have learned to use your own Internal Dialogue to shape your actions. I think this same Internal Dialogue works against us sometimes if we are not careful. Yet, in the case of being open to mentorship, you will have to quiet your Internal Dialogue, as it will most assuredly tell you this person is not going to help, or this person will steal your dreams, or some other self-sabotaging directive.

Don't listen to these sharp words, but also choose wisely who you let into your world. Doing so is not easy. Ultimately, a great mentor will show his or her worth in your actions. Your actions will be far greater with a mentor than they would have been alone.

When we arrived back at camp from this operation, we were immediately brought into the Task Force operations center. The army intel gents were all in a tizzy because some Army soldier named Bo Bergdahl had been captured, and we were to go after him right away, that night. We received the whole intelligence brief and immediately set to finding his location and planning what we needed to do to get there.

This is what we SEALs call a Time Sensitive Target (TST), which, to us, means everything evolves as we go, especially once on the ground. After breakfast, we all went to work planning, cleaning our weapons and gear, and coordinating with the helos retasked with supporting this high-priority mission. After five hours, the information we had compiled led us to a huge village between where he was last sighted and the Pakistani border.

These missions are fun, in that you have to decide if you want to hit the target hard, meaning land right on top, using speed to secure the main objective, or if you want to land really fucking far off and move in slowly, so as not to give the enemy reason to feel scared. We were not 100 percent sure that ol' Bo was there, so we decided to land really fucking far out in the middle of the desert and sneak our way over to the big-ass village. Briefing the men on the mission, I could see their body posture change from "Yeah, this is cool," to "Oh shit, this is going to hurt." The plan called for an eleven-kilometer hike once inserted. Then we had to secure five of the buildings on the east side of the village to block any egress toward Pakistan. They would have to escape six kilometers across open ground to get away, if they were there at all.

After dinner, we calmed down a bit, and I spent my time reviewing the overhead images we had of the village and compounds. Four well-maintained roads led into the area, and one big one led east to a neighboring state. We counted at least 100 villagers moving in and around the main compounds. "God, I hate noncombatants," I muttered to myself. You never know if they are hiding shit, and you also never know how strung out the assault will be in an attempt to manage that many people.

I grabbed Nike and said, "Bro, let's not go fast once we begin the assault. We are not sure where, or even if, Bo is there. They will not be able to run away with him. So. let's just take it one building at a time."

Nike said, "Yeah, he ain't there. This intel is spotty, at best. At least we will get our hike on."

Waiting at the airfield for the MH47s to pick us up, I realized we all truly wanted this life. This life of constantly doing things most people couldn't do on their best day. We all happily wanted to get picked up to fly deeper into hell to rescue some stupid ass. We weren't really into this to rescue him—it was more about rescuing us from the boredom of a mundane life.

The flight was to be seventy minutes long. I knew I was going to get a good hour's worth of combat sleep. I suppose if the helo crashed, I wouldn't recall. I'd just wake up in some spirit world. (Sorry: relaying this thought makes me chuckle.)

All joking stopped when I was jabbed awake at the one-minute-out call from Nike. When my senses popped to life, I was struck by the immediate rush of sound, though I had been on the helo for a long time. Then, I noticed the pervasive green light of the night when my night vision flipped on. And, finally, I acknowledged the numbness of my legs, because they were under me while I slept. These sensations were now the norm of my pre-combat experience.

At the thirty second mark, I drank down my travel Gatorade and tossed the bottle onto the deck of the helo. Once on my knees, the time warp began, and everything slowed down. Mostly, during these time warps, I can hear my heartbeat in my ears, and see the movements and various postures of my men. Still, each experience is weird.

Now on the ground, we all waited for the dust to settle and the world to return to normal after the helos lifted off. All elements checked in on the radios, and I signaled Nike to take the force out on the eleven-kilometer hike. At least this was the flattest land we had seen in months. The first five kilometers were simply in a straight line, keeping the big mountain to our left. The second part was, again: simply turn left and walk the next leg, keeping the mountain on our left. We were in a four-mile wide valley and walking right in the very center between two big mountains. We had several air assets with eyes on us and the target. In reserve, we had two Apaches lying down, with engines turned off, in the middle of the desert just waiting for something to happen. At this stage in the deployment, we were all linked to the tactical mindset of, "Just put us in a hornet's nest and wait to see what happens."

The rhythm of walking, the heat, and the years of working together made the first part of the hike rather surreal. Everything was working perfectly; hell, even my feet and legs felt no pain. However, as all great things don't last longer than the time to spell it, this, too, stopped being great when I got word our C-130 was being called away to another "Troops In Contact" at some other location.

As it flew off, I walked over to Nike and asked, "Did you hear that? Someone else is in combat, and we lost our bird. We have a predator drone (a pred) watching the target. Unless something else fucked up happens, just continue with the plan."

Nike replied, "Well, I would rather just bomb the target area and forego this whole charade."

"And miss all this heat and dirt, and the chance to kill more enemy?" I laughed.

Nike got up and continued walking. I stopped to look back, ensuring everyone else had noticed we were up and moving again. What I saw was a shocker. We were spread out over one kilometer in two separate, long files of men. Forty SEALs, armed to the teeth, moving through the night like ghosts. Without night vision, a person would see nothing.

The village was completely dark. Nothing was reported moving in the target area. No persons of interest with guns were seen by the pred. Still, two kilometers away, we noted a vehicle with lights coming down the mountain pass to our left. Suddenly, on two of the highest peaks, two lights turned on. Well, maybe they could see us after all. Who knows? We continued on.

As my lead element pulled into the final delay point, I knew we had about thirty minutes until all the men trickled in and had time to rest and reset for the final word and eventual assault. Looking around at the place, we had decided to halt and wait, and I realized we were in a cemetery. Several graves were fresh, and after counting over ten new digs, I stopped and leaned over to the EOD, "More dead enemy, it seems."

EOD laughed, "Less of them to shoot at us and plant IEDs."

Again, the plan was to separate the target into left and right. My platoon would take the left buildings, and Echo platoon would take the right buildings. Echo platoon filed in and flopped down to my right. I walked over to their platoon chief, another one of the toughest men I have ever known (mean, too), and said, "Let me know when you are ready. We can move out together."

The men moved out without any radio communications. Bravo and

Echo platoons stood up in unison. The lead element went to the walls to get eyes in the compound. The entry team took direction from Nike, without a word being said. They moved like ghosts from the graveyard.

After the first four lead assaulters entered, I poked my head in to check the progress. All the people were still sleeping, and four doors/rooms needed to be cleared. I turned and grabbed three guys, pushing them inside. I grabbed the last two and put them with a ladder to climb up and get eyes on the adjacent buildings.

After five minutes, the compound was secured, and the marshaling area was set to the first building. As the second squad moved past and began the assault on the second building, I delayed a bit to tell my marshaling leader what would happen as we brought back the numerous people we knew would be in each compound. At this point, they were all women and . . . no men.

I looked up at our guys on the roof and asked, "OK, brother, where is Echo?"

"They are still parallel to us. An alley is between our buildings and theirs. It looks like an easy deal," was the reply.

I paused a minute to take a breath and get myself right. I recall sitting down and breaking out a bottle of Gatorade, already 100 degrees from the warmth of my leg and the air, changing the ice to piss water. I looked around and saw the C2 element sitting in the distance so as not to get drawn into clearance, and kept an eye on all moving parts. Seemed like a good time to call them into what was now the marshaling/main building, but I laughed to myself, "Sometimes making them stress a bit longer is just fun."

Eventually, I stood up, turned on my infrared strobe light, and called out to them over the radio, advising that the main target building was secured and that they should collapse their position on my strobe. While I waited, I looked forward in the direction of my platoon's clearance and saw the guys poised to make entry into the next building. Time to join them.

Passing under the security position I tripped—again—and looked up. Jake was looking down at me all akimbo on the ground. I cringed when he uttered, "Pussy." Love comes in many forms, and this wasn't one of them. He just has hatred for the enemy, burning as bright as ever.

The initial entry team was already in when I neared the entry point. I delayed just a second, listening for harsh language or suppressed shooting, and heard nothing. The walls were sixteen feet high and looked to be rather new—well, newer than 2,000 years old, like the last operation's buildings. The gate was quite new—I think maybe forty years old. How nice to see an upward trend in development, finally.

Inside, though, processing what I was seeing took a few seconds. The inside was forty yards by forty yards. Four vehicles were neatly parked in the corner farthest from the entry point, and at least twenty people were sleeping on the ground. Two men were already moving into and clearing the first room. I moved over to better position myself between the sleeping people and the clearance team.

Suddenly, one of the women sat up fast and moved to stand. I went quickly over to her and told her, in her own language, to be quiet. She either didn't understand my accent, or didn't care to obey. Instead, she moved quicker toward Ground Launch, whose back was turned, so I did what any well-intentioned SEAL chief would do—I grabbed her neck from behind and kicked her knees forward. She fell backward and started screaming. I did what seemed like the thing to do at the time—I turned her over, got on her back, and put her face in the sleeping mat.

Ground Launch turned and ran at a dead sprint, hitting us both so hard I skidded on my butt for three yards. When I got to my feet, he had her in a neck hold, cuffing her hands with his other arm.

"How dare you get in the way of me and a good fight. Ah ha! What the hell were you doing on her back? We can't have you getting involved in this sort of shit. Get up and manage this shit so we all can fight," he stated so matter-of-factly I thought I had offended him.

I just turned and moved to get two more men to join the clearance effort. By that time, the rest of the sleepers were stirring, and additional men would come in handy. The final room was cleared rather quickly, and the rest of the clearance was just shuttling the people all back to the marshaling building. I called for my assistant officer in charge of the movement of the unknown people, then joined the search of the vehicles.

Since we didn't have keys, I simply used the end of my rifle to open the window—very delicately. Wow, more than a handful of AK-47s and PKMs, along with enough rounds to make for a good fight, lay inside.

"LT, be advised twenty AKs and fifteen PKMs, with 700 or more rounds, found in building two. And, there are also some rugged vehicles for getting around," I reported.

I turned to look at Ground Launch, "If I were moving old Bo around, this is what I would use."

He stepped forward, looked in, and smiled. We looked into the other vehicles and found water, food, and bedrolls. He smiled, saying, "No, probably not. They are going on a family vacation to the mountains to sing 'The Hills Are Alive' to the sound of gun fire." He actually sang the title, even carrying the tune.

However, after clearing all the buildings and joining the C2 element, we had not found Bo. In fact, we had found only one male, who had mistakenly attempted to pull the pin on a grenade while Echo platoon moved through the target. We all knew Bo wasn't here.

We had 120 people to interrogate, and I knew none of them would tell the truth. These people only respond to violence, and we did not use enhanced techniques. We had a long day of managing people and setting up over-watch positions. The temperature was already rising, over 110, and the morning had just begun. What a shit hole.

Within an hour, everything was set up, and we began eating, drinking, and getting our rest. Pain always comes when things slow down. This pain comes in my feet, knees, and back. Maybe a sign of age?

To break up the monotony, we brewed some chai tea and toasted another successful night of clearance. The hell minions do have some great tea. I moved around among the men, reinforcing how well they did and asking if they needed anything. I truly don't know if connecting like this made any difference to the men. For me, connection was everything. This connecting nourished me and made me proud to be their chief. I was proud to be a part of them.

At noon, I moved up to relieve one of the snipers who looked exhausted. The field of view he covered was rather enormous. Land stretched out for two miles. Only one road led from the mountains to this village, with nothing in between. As I scanned the area looking for hiding places, I smiled and thought how all those years of sniper training and hunting boiled down to this. I saw many hiding spots for a trained sniper—many ways to move in on us.

After ten minutes of scanning, I ruled out most of the threats within 500 yards. One huge hole was about ten feet wide right outside the compound, and another about 400 yards toward the mountains. I suppose they could have moved old Bo into these underground passages, but it was against the rules to blow them up.

Having settled into watching and waiting, I looked up along the road and saw a truck coming down from the mountains. Since it was still about two kilometers away, I had time to look at it through my scope and see if they had anything resembling a mounted weapon. Tracking a moving vehicle continually disappearing behind hills or dipping down into gulleys is a bitch. The car kept coming.

I yelled down to Lawyer, "Hey, do we have any air on station to look at this approaching vehicle?"

"Um, no. Do you want me to get one?" he replied

I made my decision: "No, that will take too long. I am just going to turn him around before he gets to us. They all know we are here now."

I knew my 7.62 round would not reach 1,500 meters, so I waited. The damned laser range finder I was using could not get a reading on anything due to the flat, sandy terrain. I dialed 1,000 meters into my scope and shot one round at the vehicle to see where it dropped. Dirt kicked up far in front of the vehicle, so I held the impact point in my reticle, adjusted, and shot another one.

I saw the round impact in the dirt 100 meters in front, and I waited until the vehicle was about to pass through that impact point. When I fired again, I saw the round impact near the right quarter panel of the truck. The truck stopped. Two "gentlemen" got out with AK-47s and walked around the truck to see what had hit them. I shot again, dropping the guy who had his hand on the hole. The other ran back to the open door, and I shot the windshield. Then the funniest thing happened: watch the movie *Austin Powers* to see the scene where he was trying to turn the golf cart around inside a tunnel, and you'll know then what I was watching. I stopped shooting and laughed, as eight small turns were required to get the truck turned around.

All Around climbed up asking, "Chief, what you doing up here all by yourself?"

"Oh nothing. Just watching a movie," I replied.

SECTION NINE

EXHAUSTION

PENNY TWEEDY, owner of Secretariat,
from the 2010 movie, *Secretariat*
"He laughs at fear afraid of nothing
He doesn't shy away from the sword
He cannot stand still when the trumpet sounds."

Finally, I had some time to call home and talk with the kids. Until then, I had not taken any time to call just to talk with Autumn or Garrett. I suppose this is a weak point of mine. They affect me so much because I know I truly have not been around for them physically in any meaningful way during their young lives.

During my deployment to Iraq in 2007, simply seeing them on the webcam eating breakfast or saying goodnight would depress me for days. The thought of not being a good dad would literally make me sick to my stomach. Especially when they would say, "Daddy, when are you coming home? We miss you." The worst was the simple statement, "Daddy, why don't you come home? Don't you love me?" I know they said it because they didn't understand what I do and why I do this type of work. I actually avoid talking to either of them while on deployments.

Yet, when Stacy commented in an email that they were having trouble with my absence, I realized I had to man up and be the dad I so wanted to be. As I sat down to dial the number that would connect us, a sense of doom again overwhelmed me, particularly when Stacy answered the phone:

"Hey, Stacy, I got your email. I suppose it is time to talk to Autumn, isn't it?"

"Oh, honey, how great to hear your voice! I read your email about what you all have been doing. Be strong. You are halfway through this incredible deployment. We are all so proud of you and the men," Stacy said, with her always-inspiring voice and tone. "Autumn, has been really having a tough time. I think her mother has been putting you down for always deploying and never being around for her. It is making Autumn very sad, and making her say things like, 'Daddy is always gone;' or, 'Dad forgot Garrett's birthday again.' She cried yesterday when I mentioned how many more months you would be gone."

"Jesus, what should I say; what would make any difference? You are there: what do I need to say or do?" I asked, knowing the answer would not be so easy.

Stacy replied simply, "I don't know. You are her father. Just talk to her."

"OK, put her on," I replied, knowing this was gonna be tough.

"Hi, Daddy—I miss you. Ms. Stacy said you aren't going to come home until November. You are going to miss my birthday party again. You are never here for my birthday." Autumn's first words were already tough.

"Oh, Sissy, I think about you every day. I can never make up for all the time I have been away from you. I am so sorry. How is summer going for you?" I asked, knowing my question was stupid. Autumn wanted me to come home, not ask about what she was doing.

I added, "Do you have anything you would like to say to me? I know you are sad; I am, too."

During the long pause that followed, I felt like I was going into battle. Time was slowing down, and I had an ever-present buzz. I looked around the room and saw other men, like me, talking uncomfortably to someone on the other end of the line. My someone desperately wanted her daddy home, and I couldn't give my daughter what she needed.

"Daddy, Mom says you don't love her anymore," Autumn said.

Damn, I never saw that one coming. I had been divorced from her mother for five years, and we had never talked about the divorce in any direct conversation.

I replied, "No, Sissy, I don't love your mother. I do love Stacy, and she loves me, and she loves you, too. That is the way of things now." God, that sounded so fucking dim to say, but I couldn't find words other than points of fact. I leaned back in my chair saying to myself, *Boy, don't ever be a politician. You can't twist the truth to save your life.*

I continued, "Honey, daddy loves you every minute of every day. That is the truth. I am sorry I have been gone. This is my last deployment. When I get home, I am home for good." I didn't know that for sure. Part of me even felt like I was not going to survive this deployment, but saying so definitely wouldn't help: "Sissy, daddy may not survive this, so stop crying and put Stacy on." Yeah—*that* wouldn't work so well.

As I pondered what to say and what not to say, I could hear Autumn crying. I heard her call for Stacy, and without saying bye, she was gone.

Stacy said, "Oh, Thom, I know that must suck!"

I blew out a breath. "Wow! Oh, how a small girl can suck all the life out of you!"

"Just leave it. You can't make her feel better other than you surviving and coming back to us. You have to let this go, and get back to killing as many enemy as you have to, OK?" Stacy reminded me.

"I know honey. I know," I replied.

Stacy continued, "Remember what I said? **'Thom, I need you to come back to us. Do not fear dying. It makes you weak.'** The men need you. I can handle this until you get back. So get back to killing. It is what you do. I love you always." Then she simply hung up. At least she didn't mince words.

When I hung up the telephone, the time warp stopped, and I noticed my shirt had sweat on it. Calling home and talking to your kids is like a work out! Some day, I am guessing when the kids are adults, they will re-read this, and get it. I don't get it now, but with time, maybe we can both work through the emotions.

Lunch was truly tasteless after the phone call. Even the Dr. Pepper tasted flat. Walking from the air-conditioned space into the oppressive heat seemed the most normal sensation of the day thus far. Maybe going to the range to shoot my rifles would ease the weirdness.

I grabbed a couple of my men, and we loaded our weapons and headed to the range. I think maybe everyone was feeling the tension of the mid-deployment mark or the fact that every single time we headed out, we were in serious gun battles fighting for our lives. Maybe we just liked doing this more than dealing with family. In the end, I think it is a measure of both, mixed with a desire to fight.

§

Stacy Shea

Children, I am writing these thoughts down for you because the last time we talked to your dad, I noticed the sadness from not connecting with you, Autumn, and noted the tension he was feeling from three months of serious combat. His extensive sharing with us of what he is doing and what he is going through, personally and with his men, makes me further worry something big and dangerous is on Bravo platoon's horizon. I am worried we may have caused him to be more concerned with us back home than with his men and his mission.

He so loves you, Autumn. I know your dad has missed many birthdays and special events in your life and how you can think he doesn't care and doesn't want to be here. Even when you ask him why, he seems to lash out and make the condition worse. He is physically and mentally a tough man, so he often attacks your tender requests with anger and hardness. Forgive him so he can find his own peace over there.

I am at my wit's end. We may have said the wrong thing to daddy. My team-guy wives' group seems to be worried about other things, so I think I am going to follow Thom's lead and reach out to Jerry and Tammy. We need help, and I am praying they may have experienced something like this in their lives so they may help us.

I phoned Tammy. "Tammy, this is Stacy. Thom called yesterday and talked with Autumn, and she and he had a bit of a fight. He is so sensitive to Autumn's feelings and wants so much to love her and be loved, and the conversation did not end up with a ton of love. I feel his whole platoon is on edge, and something big is coming up."

Tammy offered, "Stacy, you are a great wife to think about him in this way and not make him wrong for being a SEAL or wrong for wanting to be a loving dad to your kids, though he often says hurtful things. Men are a strange breed. Men who are aggressive and used to being around other SEALs have a hard time being soft, I gather.

"Jerry and I talk every night about what you may be going through and if we can actually say or do anything to help you. I will offer a story that may help. Jerry has four adult children from different wives. I have a daughter, who is not Jerry's. I can tell you each child affects Jerry in different ways. He comes to me often to cry and let out his anger and sadness that he wasn't a good enough father to them.

"So, what I am offering is my solution. Men like Jerry, who are high achievers, who are always looking to make something new and to build a new business, need one thing more than all others. So few women get this point. Men who risk everything all the time need a good woman. It is rooted in their DNA. These men have 10,000 years of evolution leading them to having to have a woman to fall back on. Intimacy, sexual connection, and a woman's openness to him will always lead him to be stronger and more available.

"This open and willing sexual intimacy Jerry and I share makes him healthy, strong, happy, and, ultimately, allows him to actually let go of all his mistakes so he can live in the moment he is facing. I know I didn't make this available to my first husband, and he dwindled from the lack, so we all suffered from my not knowing who I needed to be and how I needed to connect with him.

"With Jerry, I immediately know I need to offer and be available for sexual intimacy when he is going off the reservation, so to speak. It is not a submissive offering; it is a power offering."

I brightened some. "I totally agree. Thom is exactly the same. I learned that even before we got married. I felt like all he wanted was sex, until I realized he needed that intimate contact because of the tons of stress he was feeling. When I would listen to those stresses and issues, I realized he really struggles with not being a good dad and not being around for his family enough. Once we had intimacy, he would actually be a better dad at home, and perform better at work."

Tammy replied, "Stacy, what he needs now is that same thing. I am sure the distance makes that rather difficult, doesn't it? Even for you.

"Think about how men have had to evolve over millions of years. Hunting and fighting off rivals who want his woman. Consider how he had to endure the constant fear of not protecting his family from all the conditions. His body evolved to be stronger, bigger; his mind evolved to be aggressive and hardened to the terrible conditions he faced. I suggest evolution is still present and still going on.

"Women evolved parallel to men, I think. They were always partners in the family, food, and stress, but women did not need the physical and mental evolution men did. She evolved to balance the man, not submit to him, like most women think.

"Neither a woman nor a man can be very effective without the partner of the opposite sex. Each needs the other to perform. They *need* to be *needed*, and have to be 100 percent involved with every aspect of each other's lives. Even the slightest separation causes catastrophic performance degradation for both."

I replied, "That is so true. Maybe I needed to hear that from someone else. Thank you so much. We are going to make a family video and send it to Thom so he can see and hear us and know we are loving and needing him. We'll have to think on how to create sexual intimacy to span 3,000 miles, though. That is risky!"

"Well, I am telling you one thing: his performance is limited only to the level of intimacy he gets from you," Tammy replied in conclusion.

§

"Stacy, I am sorry for the crap the other day with Autumn. All is back to normal now. We are planning another mission into an area with some angry men who need some love from us." I am laughing as I write this. We just watched a predator feed, and saw fifty enemy fighters doing military training and such. They are deep in the mountains, so they surely feel safe.

We are getting our tactics on and waiting for helos to be retasked to support our mission, which could take a week because of some previously planned stuff not involving us. I felt bad because last night, we had another funeral for three marines who died. I wish we had been there to help. We all regret not even being asked to support this Marine mission.

I am back in my routine of working out, sleeping, eating, shooting, and planning. I like this rhythm—it's nice. Often the mere fact of having something to focus on, something to endure other than the impending doom of hell, makes time go by faster. Anyone who has not chosen a life of constant endurance may think that makes no sense.

Over the next several days, all of our effort is going toward practicing and rehearsing, and finally, readying our minds for this operation. Every bit of information about this operation is showing me the entire area is swarming with enemy. Yesterday, we spent three hours searching for a place without enemy to land the helos. Gonna be a really long night and a really long hike through the mountains. Those, too, look to be more rugged than anything we have seen up until now. Our route through the mountain passes and steep cliffs is going to be like threading a needle.

As a result, we have all been working out a bit harder and longer. I even put on all my gear with the intent of lightening the load on my feet and legs, and discovered I needed every single item. After weighing my body fully loaded, I snorted out loud . . . 305 pounds! An additional ninety pounds of shit. So much for being light and maneuverable.

It is 0400 hour, and Stacy should be on the Internet soon. I cannot wait to see and talk with her, and see the new Victoria's Secret stuff she bought. Last night, we went to the coffee shop and there was a pretty British woman who was shaped just like Stacy. Made me really long for just five minutes with my wife.

I sent Stacy the *Yahoo!* chat dialogue between Jerry and me earlier that night:

Thom: "Jerry, thank you for being available for a real-time discussion with me."

Jerry: "Well, young man, I cannot think of anything more important for an old man, who holds the liberty and grace of the United States to be the single greatest thing mankind can preserve, to do right now than support a Navy SEAL in combat. You are doing something over there. Every citizen should do everything they can to support you."

Thom: "That being said, I will get to the point, because we are often cut off of the Internet without notice. We are at the halfway point of this deployment. I have very little left I can teach these men; they are running on their own accord in order to survive and to take the fight to the enemy. So my first question is simple: what have you learned in business that may aid us here during the halfway point? Have you encountered any pitfalls, or anything great leaders or great business ventures do when faced with this mental and physical stage?"

Jerry: "Very few people would ask that question. In the business world, several points are critical and few businesses see the middle being anything more than a place to count their profit or losses. I can tell you of a story I read as a young man, clearly showing how the middle of a big adventure is the most critical time.

"When Shakleton led his valiant journey, he and his men found themselves in the middle of their journey with no food and half a continent still to traverse. He did something which stuck with me like no other sign of great leadership. He told the men a simple thing. He told them they were going to make it, and they were going to all stick together.

"I did not think much of this when I read it other than thinking, 'Well, yeah, who wouldn't say that to encourage his men during desperate times.' But, later, as an adult businessman, I faced an interesting challenge mid-cycle in a particular business venture. We were losing money, and the employees were not happy. I was not happy, and I could not find any reason to say the simple statement: <u>they were going to make it, and they were going to all stick together.</u>

"In my mind, I thought a bloodletting would be required to fire the lazy, disgruntled employees, and I would have to take a big loss of investments. I could not say that simple statement out loud.

"Thom, say that simple statement right now to your men. Don't look for evidence to prove you will all make it. Just say it to your men, knowing you all are bred to react to the words of your leaders and make those words come true. Say it to yourself 1,000 times before you say it to your men. Make it ingrained in your brain."

Thom: "Jerry, I did read Shackleton's voyage and don't recall that. However, what they did was, and still is, impossible. No human can endure those conditions."

Jerry: "Thom, if you recall, he actually went back to get his men, without licking his wounds. He went back because he WAS a man of his word. You have to BE a man of your word. You have said to me that Internal Dialogue runs the show of human performance. So let me ask you, what Internal Dialogue are you using?"

Thom: "Damn, that is a good point. Shit or get off the pot is what you are offering."

Jerry: "No, to the contrary. Don't get off the pot at all. Get on the pot, and get everyone else on the pot. Tell them they are on the pot. Remind them of who they are and what they are doing. Make sure you are also fully in and not looking for a way out. Son, I want to tell you something. Never look for a way out. Always look for every way possible to get back in the game, whatever the game is.

"You asked me the question, and that is my answer. Do it and don't wait."

Thom: "Well, I agree with you. I am in. Thank you for the honest dialogue. And by the way, I want to meet you and shake your hand. Would you honor me someday by fulfilling that request?"

Jerry: "Thom, Tammy and I love you for what you are doing. Stacy and your kids love you—never forget it."

Thom: "Thanks for that. Let's keep this conversation going in two days. Will you be available same time in two days?"

Jerry: "Thom, I am in all the way, so yes. Same time; same place."

§

A note from Stacy, Tammy, and Jerry:

Children, your father missed his scheduled appointment with Jerry for yesterday. He has also not communicated with us for three days. He and I were going to talk the same day he had reached out to Jerry, but we never connected at all. I have been worried. I try not to show it with you three, but when Tammy contacted me that they, too, were worried, I completely broke down.

I want to share here what we were writing with your dad. Jerry even suggested I should convey this message as it may be the last time we will hear from your daddy. I am crying terribly even as I write this.

We three want to write down our special notes to you three, because this is so real and so vivid for us now regarding your daddy. Thom wanted to be able to tell you about his life and his love for you three, and we want to tell you about how he impacted us all.

Stacy's note:

Autumn, your daddy loves you dearly. He and I talk often about how great a young girl you are and how powerful a woman is to the world. I know that may not capture your understanding as a young girl, but later, as a woman, re-read this book and try to see the wisdom in his words.

He has spent every day I have been with him grappling with understanding how and why humans perform. This book has been an attempt to write down for you and your brothers exactly what he has learned, and why it is important. He has challenged you three with discovering those things for yourself through the challenges. He is a teacher, a doer, and leader in his core, and I am sad you may not have gotten to know this and be with him like I have and his men have.

The one profound thing I want you to get from this book is a sense of how to listen to your own Internal Dialogue and how to shape it to make your life generous and moving, like your father has. I have listened to some great men fail miserably while trying to teach salespeople to perform, but I had never seen salespeople immediately perform better than when your dad taught my sales force how to listen and use Internal Dialogue to increase their sales.

Garrett, you are your father's most painful experience. He always feels like he let you down when you needed him most after he divorced your mother. You may not know this, but two weeks after you were born, he left on a deployment to Kosovo, and your mother had more than a difficult time being alone with two kids. He hasn't forgiven himself, nor has he found his own Internal Dialogue to shape a new conversation that doesn't make him feel terrible about not being around for you.

I pray that someday, you read this book and go through the trials so you can see and experience the important things that will make you a strong person and a strong man like your father. I see greatness in you. I love you, and I will always love you, because Thom is in you.

Chance, Thom and I talked every day while you were in my belly about wanting and creating a family and a baby who were strong and loving. I actually used what Thom had discussed about listening to and reshaping my own Internal Dialogue every night as you were growing in me. I wanted you to look and be shaped like your daddy. I must have tried too hard, because you are as strong-willed as he is . . . darn it. But, I love you for that!

You won't be able to read this book and go through the trials for a long time yet. When you do, those trials will lead you to mastering your Internal Dialogue and being a strong and profoundly *moving man. If your father doesn't return to us, know he is in you, and you just need to call upon that part of you deep inside.*

Tammy's note:

Stacy, and my beautiful new friends, Autumn, Garrett, and Chance—

We are all worried about your father and the situation he and his men are in over in hell. I have never met your father, but I have been rather moved by the words he has been writing to you.

Jerry and I have been very successful in our lives and have a deep understanding of what is truly effective when designing and managing people within the framework of companies that must produce a profit. We both are reading and doing (attempting to do) the trials your dad has set forth. I can tell you, when you complete the trials, you will be great at whatever you do in life.

We will be here to help and aid you if your father doesn't return.

Jerry's note:

Tammy says it better than I possibly could. She is spot on about your father's point of mastering your own Internal Dialogue as an access point to your own performance. We three will help you all when the time comes to go through the challenges your dad has set to paper for each of you.

Your father is in a tough spot now. He is in the middle of a very dangerous deployment and is feeling the strain. When he and I last talked over email, I was particularly moved by how he loves his men—and how they love him. Having run several businesses during my life, I can tell you that is not only hard to accomplish, but is also as downright rare as a "red fern." When we finally meet, I will tell you the story of the "red fern."

§

A SILVER STAR

I suppose in hindsight, I would have planned better. Maybe even looked closer at the elevation maps and done a better terrain study. We had been conducting combat operations in the lowland, where you could see for miles without any big mountains. Stupidly, I had used that way of looking at the route in the target area and planned on believing my own bullshit. It looked so simple: fly in with three MH-47s, three separate elements, patrol to the target area, hit the target, and find a building or two to set up shop. Simple, right?

Connecting with Stacy the days leading up to the actual assault was great. A necessary critical habit of ours is to connect with each other as a way to feel needed and to be intimate. Maybe some would say reaching out for such a connection is not good. I personally think it is the most important thing for a warrior to do. Without some sense of *need*, I truly doubt any warrior would last long enough in combat to be of any use to anyone. Thousands of ways are available to be and feel *needed*. That's why I told the platoon to try and capture that essential "thing" that made them connect to their wives and spouses: the connection would charge them up.

§

Stacy, you rock. That intimate hour we spent getting energy from each other kept me alive during this mission. I can honestly tell you that. Knowing you and the kids were safe was as important to me as any other part of the military plan. Kids, when you read this, if you don't think sexually connecting can happen over the Internet, you truly have no access to greatness.

§

As we completed our planning and wrapped up the operations brief, I really felt a shift in the men. I doubt if outsiders would understand or appreciate the way SEALs are before a combat mission. The whole atmosphere is chaos. Fifty different men, with thousands of bombs, bullets, and anger you could cut with a knife, overshadowed by laughter and jokes I wouldn't dare to even write on paper. Suffice it to say that hell is no place for the faint of heart, and a place where SEALs are planning a mission is no place for hell.

We all knew this mission was going to be different. Since I had planned the damned thing, I had a feeling of doom I had not felt before. Impending doom. Enemy outposts were spread throughout the entire route, from insert to the target area. Fighting was inevitable.

I sat in my room preparing my gear, checking my weapons, ammo, and radios. I even took out my grenades. At the time, this seemed odd to me. My grenades sat on the table, and I picked each one up and turned it over in my hands. I felt the weight and imagined the damage they would do on this mission. I had never used a grenade in combat, yet somehow knew this would be an interesting mission, where I might.

Replacing the grenades in my gear, the photo I had on the wall behind my desk caught my eye. Stacy took this picture of the kids and me on our couch the night before I left for hell. What I saw now was the sadness in the kids' eyes, the distance in my eyes, and the physical clinging to each other.

My own Internal Dialogue began screaming, "Don't go on the mission. It isn't worth dying for. All this exhaustion, all this time away from family, all this for a nation that doesn't even care you are here."

I sat for an hour, getting completely drawn into what I was saying to myself. I even cried uncontrollably. While hard to admit, it is true: the sadness overwhelmed me.

Somehow I crawled into my bed, totally depressed, and succumbed. My arms felt heavy; my legs were rubber. Damn the sadness. Fuck it: I am going to sleep. So I closed my eyes and left hell once again.

In my dream, I was immediately at the falls up in Lake Louisa. My canoe was adrift in the middle of the lake. The roar of the falls and the spray were ominous. Somehow, I had decided in my dream to be wearing a pair of UDT shorts, and had a BUD/S issue knife on my belt. I was also wearing the mountain biking helmet I had used in adventure racing. In my left hand, I carried the pipe carved with an Indian head over a perfect carving of *my* head forming the bowl. The pipe stem, leading out of the bowl, was the hollowed-out antler of the biggest buck I had ever killed as a young boy. In my right hand, I had the SCAR rifle I had used to kill so many of the enemy. By the way, I was barefoot.

I could feel the draw of the carved-out bathtub in the center of the falls. I walked over and sat down to look at it. I looked at it for two days. Even in my dream, I recall thinking I had been sitting, looking, and not moving for a long time. In the evening, just before darkness fell, Captain Pat walked out of the mist behind me, and stood looking down.

I looked up and he said, "Why the fuck are you so sad? This is the life you chose, yet you are not choosing it now. Not choosing it now makes you weak. Choose it again, and jump in and live. Staying on the sidelines, fearing to jump in, will cause your death." With that, he walked away.

I stood up immediately, moving forward to jump in, but Carnie was shaking me awake saying, "Jesus, Chief. We are ten minutes out to leaving on the bus for the airfield. You look like shit. Get your clothes on, and I won't mention this to anyone. Oh, and by the way, I cried for three days after that first mission. I get it. Now get up; we need your ass on this op."

I sat up, not saying a word, and Carnie never mentioned it again. We just loaded the bus and headed to meet the devil.

I vividly recall the wait for the three MH-47s. The temperature was hot, and the smell from nightly burning of trash and shit lingered from the lack of wind. The smell of hot jet fuel from the turbines will always be a war smell to me. The feel of the extra eighty pounds of body armor, bullets, and bombs I always carried will also provoke a Pavlovian reaction in me. To this day, when I touch my gun, my mind and body go into a programmed response mode.

After loading the bird and getting the thumbs up from my point man that all of us were, in fact, sitting on the bird, I recall looking out across the lights of Kandahar Airfield and saying to myself, *Let everything go: the only thing that matters is right here, right now. There is no tomorrow. There is no meaning to anything. There is simply facing whatever comes and making due.* I was not making a statement of defeat. To the contrary, I was making a statement of true strength and power. And, I would venture to say all of you would agree that being in the moment is the hardest thing to do in this world. You never truly master it. The moment you think you have mastered the unforgiving moment is the exact moment when you are holding on, and something bad always happens. I was jumping back into the pool in the falls of Lake Louisa.

I laugh as I recall the flight. For God's sake, I can't stay awake during flights. While falling asleep on a flight to hell or into combat doesn't make any sense, I didn't make it five minutes before I closed my eyes. After about an hour or so, I was rudely snapped awake by my point man yelling at me that we had one minute left before landing. So I opened my eyes and said, "Wow, I needed that sleep. I was tired." He didn't smile back; I think he was angry. I could never tell if he was angry with me or just angry in general. He was always angry.

Everything seemed normal. The MH-47 slowed, flared, and landed. I got off, and recall my legs were asleep from being tucked up underneath me for an hour. When I knelt down I could feel the pins and needles sensation of the nerves in my legs trying desperately to fire. The helo took off, and for the unforgiving second, I was covered in dust. I couldn't see anything, losing track of where everyone was. At that moment, all hell broke loose.

For a minute after the helos leave, all is quiet. No one moves while you wait for the dust to settle and allow your senses to come screaming back. But right in that second before the senses rushed back, two RPGs were fired right at the position where the last MH-47 had dropped off the other group of SEALs who were with us. You could hear the whining and rush of air as the rockets cut through the dust, see the bright light, and then hear the delayed explosion of the grenade. My point man was lying right next to me, and we looked at each other and said, "Damn, this is going to be a long night."

Often in movies, and with inexperienced fighters, the immediate response is either shooting back, panicking, or getting up and running. The problem with reality is, unless you have something to actually shoot and kill or know where the enemy is, all that panic and shooting back causes more problems. I was proud of this group; no one said a fucking thing. No one shot back. We all merely slithered away from those nasty grenade explosions, located all the friendly SEALs, and patrolled the hell out of there. Snowman calmly talked to two Apache helos we had ordered to linger miles away. After calmly telling the pilots (and I might add, whoever the female pilot was, she sure sounded sexy) where we were and where the shots came from, the sky lit up with missile trails from the love she was sending us by way of the booms on the hillside where the enemy were trying to hide.

The problem now was how the hell were we going to patrol through these mountains—bypassing enemy fighters, into a target area where they now know we are coming, without getting killed? Patrolling is hard enough with eighty pounds of combat gear through the mountains of hell at 8,000 feet, but now we had to set up a small force to look into and cover the movement of the next force, by climbing up and down the mountains in succession. After about two hours of setting up and tearing down fighting positions, while the Apache helos were shooting and launching rockets along the hilltops paralleling our direction, I was exhausted.

Still, it's remarkable how funny things occur, even in hell. My platoon had a new SEAL dog and handler assigned, and this was their first mission. That poor dog's paws were not ready for the rocks and climbing up and down the mountains. The dog was exhausted, and every time I tried to take a step, I stepped right on his paw, making him yelp. I finally stopped, knelt down, and touched him, putting my hands on his bleeding, cracked paws. Don't know if that helped, but he stayed away from my feet for the rest of the patrol in.

At this point, I have to take a pause. Many things had to happen in the development of my platoon and me, as a man, leading to our ability to function in this environment known as hell, or combat. No brief synopsis of our training would give you access to our level of performance. And no mere lecture series could possibly give you clarity about who we were as men and fighters.

Yet, to SEALs, all is clear, ingrained over years and years of working through problems together in harsh environments. Every single aspect of our days together fosters this identity and is finally embraced by our families in a way unparalleled in our society today. The single most critical aspect of what makes a man able and capable of withstanding the constant pressure from outside forces is the mastering of his own Internal Dialogue. I want my kids to understand this in their bones. To actually perform in this constant hell, we all have learned to say simple things to ourselves that most people don't say at all, and don't think are important. My personal saying is **"This is who I am. Times may suck, but I am a SEAL."** These simple, factual Internal Dialogues are actually the biggest miracle in human performance. Because the opposite is what quitters and non-performers say, such as, *"This sucks. I wish this was over. I hate this place."* Or even *"I can't wait to go home."* A solid Internal Dialogue makes you *need* to be doing what you are doing. A bullshit Internal Dialogue actually makes you need to do something else, or worse, nothing.

Few military leaders, and fewer business leaders, would use these terms. Honestly, even fewer SEALS would break their performance down to this plain level of speaking. The Internal Dialogue making you *need* to be there isn't referenced in any leadership or performance-oriented doctrine. Often this simple fact is shrouded in other buzz words, such as "teamwork," and "practice," or even, "well–designed plans and assets lead to peak performance." But these statements are sales pitches. Human performance is based on the mastery of Internal Dialogue.

The Internal Dialogue leading to the *need* to be *needed*, or the being connected idea, is the fundamental performance truth of mankind. The *need* to be *needed* answers and addresses **why** men achieve anything and everything. Group achievement is founded on this fundamental truth. Each man simply has to tell himself he is *needed* and has to be connected to what is going on around him. He has to identify himself with the thing he does. They must be one and the same . . . no separation, no way out, and absolutely not something he is *trying*. I hate the word "try." Try, by its very meaning, shows the truth of Internal Dialogue, the *need* to be *needed*, and connection. Trying literally means I am not the thing I am doing; I am separate from it. The world is filled with people who tried. We were not that type of men; SEALs are not that breed of man.

For me, in particular, I had sixteen years of passing through the trials of performance. To be exact, I had 220 days per year, for sixteen years, of being away from my family to make crystal clear the importance of using Internal Dialogue for being connected as a measure of my own performance. I *needed* to be *needed* by my family in order to perform in hell. After a difficult marriage, where that was not the case, a woman who understood the value of connection liberated me from the mundane—a true Spartan Wife. The form of connection on her part was all in, no way out; she put every ounce of effort toward connecting with both family and me. Spartans knew the value of fully embracing a woman was equally important to the overall performance of the man and the nation. I wonder what caused the world to cringe and run 180 degrees away from that solution to performance? Poor Islamic women are put in check, so the men never truly flourish.

We were *connected*, we *needed* each other, and we were performing in hell. What more could you ask from life?

At that point, our troop faced some silly odds; we were being shot at by thirty enemy fighters. Our interpreter, who was listening to their attempt to coordinate attacks, learned they were from Chechnya. I liked the fact that they had come all the way here to do what they thought was right for their religion. You have to admire that conviction.

We were exhausted from two hours of movement through the mountains, and we hadn't even hit the target. The Apache pilot, with her sexy voice, told us she saw the enemy carrying blankets over their heads in order to evade her thermal optics, and they were also wearing night vision devices.

This tidbit of info made us all stop in our tracks, literally. We made the call for the Apaches to interdict all targets due to ground troops in critical danger. I thought this was a good call; save our lives in light of the fact the enemy had struck our Pentagon and the twin towers, but, more to the point, we were in no position to do anything except kill the enemy. Enough said on that topic.

The mountains were now the enemy. They were a bit taller than the map had indicated, and punished us by funneling our movement toward the backside of the target area, not the front where we had hoped to start the assault. All this made for a little confusion as we scampered down a series of twelve-foot cliffs to get to the bottom of the mountain, where twelve buildings rested, all snug and warm.

We had arrived and now needed to do what we do best—go after the enemy in their safe havens. The platoons were separated per the plan: Echo platoon was on the right side, and Bravo platoon on the left. After final head counts and weapons checks, we called our silent air asset to scan the target area. Yes, you guessed it, three enemy with machine guns were waiting for us to show up. So, as Bravo platoon pressed our primary target buildings, Echo moved quickly to kill the enemy lying in wait. I breathed a sigh of relief when I heard the suppressed weapons fire with no loud enemy automatic weapons fire in return. Interestingly enough, no communication over the radios was needed. We all knew what had transpired. The general assault went rather well after that. This party was made in hell, to be sure.

WHAT IT FELT LIKE TO BE THERE!!!!

At 0200 hours, I was tired . . . dead tired. We had crossed two streams, my feet were wet, my damn sock had sunk down into my freakin' left boot, and I could feel wet sand and dirt digging a hole in my left heel. *Typical*, I thought to myself as I looked through the green hue of my night vision goggles at my men scattered around the Target Set Point. This was our last opportunity to gather our thoughts and get one last update from the silent bird at 20,000 feet.

What the fuck is a forty-two-year-old man doing out here in the mountains of hell, surrounded by rubbery young killers who never felt pain? I thought.

"Hey, Ridge Boss," my point man nudged my left arm, which for some reason hurt, too. "I smell a cooking fire or something from compound one, and I can see two guys walking around inside. Can I shoot them?"

"Jesus, Nike, we haven't even got the thing surrounded yet," I whispered.

"Well, damn it, I won't be in position to shoot them cause I will be first one to enter; I don't want All Around to get them," he pouted.

Youth, I thought to myself.

Over the radio, the boss said, "OK, Chief. Take it." Again, I must have some sort of Pavlovian response from years of training and saying words that call up an alert response, because for the next hour, I didn't feel that heel being skinned, nor my arm, nor any other pain. We must have some silly hormone or something released to make our senses keen, too. When we started moving, the world slowed down and every detail and danger popped out, clear and distinct.

Off to my left, three of my men took positions to cover their side of the target, and four others moved right to cover, as well. I am always amazed how the men find the right angles and places to go to get after the enemy. As I watched All Around get into position as the assault force, with Nike moved to lead the primary entry, I moved up under him knowing full well Nike had pegged it, and All Around was going to either take them, if they were carrying weapons, or tell me there were two guys in there.

Time always slows way down for me; I could see how this was going to play out, and kept wondering WTF was taking everyone so long.

After what seemed an hour, but was only a minute and a half, I heard the lock snap, and simultaneously saw All Around's feet slide to brace himself. I heard the safety click to fire and saw three flashes of his suppressed rounds leave the barrel.

Over comms, All Around said, "OK guys. You're good to the first door on your right; after that, I have no idea." In reply, Nike muttered, "Prick!"

I could hear the brushing of pants and the opening of several doors inside the compound. After about three minutes, the men left and right of the compound sorta faded toward building two, as Nike said, "Ridge Boss, we're good. Coming out."

I moved, with several others, quickly to building two, to find a twelve-foot wall surrounding the compound. Ladders were pushed up, and the men got eyes on the inside. The entry point was passed to the assault team. Two men stayed behind inside building one to set up a possible marshaling area for women and children, who were the usual suspects during the last ten missions we had conducted. So I moved from my position outside and picked up rear of the assault force, just in case I was needed inside. The compound turned out to be a twisted maze, so "Ridge Boss in," was called. I have to admit: going into a compound when you know problems need to be solved, and solving will include, but isn't limited to, shooting and fighting for life or death, is an awesome sensation.

The damned door to the huge compound was only three feet high, and eighteen inches wide. "Are you kidding me? Who builds shit like this," I grumbled, bending over to squeeze through. And, for some reason, the inside was built like a labyrinth. I couldn't see over the walls, each alleyway was three feet wide, and, after making what seemed eight right turns, I still had not found the assault team. Finally, after a bit of searching for the centaur, I turned the final corner and found four of my men looking down into a hole.

As I walked up to them, Nike laughed and said, "Well, Ridge Boss, at least two women climbed down there. What do you suggest?"

I said, "You four leave it, and move to building three." I pressed my radio button and called, "LT, I need two to hold on a problem as we move to next target. And tell the two coming in to just follow the maze, it leads to me."

When I looked up, the four assaulters had moved away from the laby-rinth and wisely chose to climb over the wall. Waiting always takes longer in my mind than in actual real time, so I stared, wondering what was down the hole. I even cracked a chem-light and threw it down, down, and down. "Oh for Christ's sake, does that hole have a bottom?" When the two men arrived, we laughed about the maze, then I explained maybe two women had climbed down that rope into a bottomless pit. And, by the way, I assume a room is down there.

I made clear, "You will not, for any reason, climb down, throw a gre-nade, or cut the rope . . . period. Now, repeat that back to me, damn it." They both looked at me like I had said something confusing, nothing was registering. "Hey, just stay here, OK?" I finally said.

By the time I climbed the wall and shimmied down the other side, our side of the target was secure. I told everyone to hold in position as we sorted out our next move. Even though I had worked with these men for two years or more, it is always a problem to really know exactly who you're looking at through night vision. All the SEALs look the same, for God's sake. After searching with my eyes, I found LT on a rock overlook-ing the target area. Now a reverse Pavlovian phenomenon kicked in, and I stumbled nimbly up the ridge to LT. The rush of pain in my heel, the sore lower back from carrying extra weight in body armor, and the op-pressive tired feeling all surged through my body like a wave.

Finally reaching LT, I said, "LT, we have a problem. Although the buildings would be a great place to set up for the battle sure to come to-morrow, the damn hills look right into them. We will be sitting ducks for sure. We have a well Nike says two women climbed down. I left two of the boys there. We are going to wait for Echo to get done. But I can tell you these compounds are not our final overwatch positions."

"Yeah, I was thinking the same thing," he said, frowning because he knew I had made a mistake in planning.

After another five minutes we heard over comms Echo's boys were target secure and "No joy for tactical advantage in any compound."

LT pushed out, "Leaders, Consolidate on C2."

We located the C2 element about 100 yards to the rear, and when I stood up, I silently yelled, "Ouch. Ouch. Ouch," with every step.

We all sat looking up at the mountains and out at the valley, and a sinking feeling really swept through me for some reason. SEALs hate to ask for "extract early." Doing so is an unexpressed form of saying, "Pussy." Many suggestions were made, such as, "Well, let's continue clearing compounds until we find one further away from the mountains." Another suggestion was to separate forces, and move some of us to high ground for some sort of tactical advantage. Finally, the only solution was doing both, once we secured a good compound in the valley floor.

Oh, my sinking feeling was ominous. My hands shook because I knew we had no way to get to all the high ground positions necessary to give us a tactical advantage—damn. The boys cleared the rest of the valley floor, only three more compounds. Again, the compounds themselves were perfect, but the high ground was now 700 yards away instead of 100 to 300 yards. I met up with the troop so the overall plan would be set. Bravo platoon would remain in the valley with one squad from Echo, and the other squad from Echo and C2 would press up the closest hill to get some sort of tactical advantage for the day of fighting to come.

As Nike and I walked away, he stopped me. Because our night vision was turned up, I could see his eyes. We looked at each other for a moment; no words were ever uttered. I had never before, and probably never will again, have a louder conversation.

Time was short at this point; we had tons of work to set up our sniper overwatch positions on top of the hill and in the compounds. This work seems to be the most arduous, and definitely makes everyone pissed. Filling sandbags, building the hides, filling more sandbags, and on and on and on. Once everyone was set, and the area somewhat secured, I noticed I was totally spent. I would normally be completely exhausted by this point in every operation due to spending the prior thirty hours planning and talking with the pilots and coordinating something or other. Now, I was even more exhausted due to the release of depression and stress before the mission. Getting shot at during landing didn't help.

Yes, I know you are asking yourself how I could sleep in those conditions: impending combat, hot as hell, and many other reasons that seem important to people who have never seen sustained combat. Problem was, I was and am still to this day, someone who can fall asleep anywhere when I stop moving. So this was MY time—ol' Ridge Boss gonna catch a catnap, boys. Wake me at your own peril.

I actually looked forward to combat for that reason . . . good God, I can finally get some rest. Moreover, I needed to let my brain go, let thoughts wander to other things, other places, other people. Oddly enough, I noticed after the eighty-fifth combat operation, my thoughts would always go to connecting things: things that encouraged me.

My own Internal Dialogue was reshaped during my post-assault, thirty-minute reset time. Never, not once, did my mind go to thoughts of doom, fear, bad times, or bad events from the past. Most often my thoughts went to Stacy, lying in bed next to her, touching her skin, touching, well, other parts. I suppose such thoughts must have been a common thing for warriors over the millennia. Again, I got a sense the Spartans knew the power of a great woman, as well as the relationship between intimacy, sex, and the performance of a man in hell. They surely lived it, and I agree—Stacy, and her power over and in me, created space for the outlet of my other intimacies, like violence and the desire to live in the hell of combat year after year. She actually encouraged and reinforced this side of me.

I lay, tucked soundly into a corner, while the world, while hell, raged outside. I vaguely recall waking to the sounds of Nike snapping suppressed sniper shots at some sad enemy who surely thought he was being sneaky. Nike had an eye for where to look and when to shoot. As I was listening to the comms static in my headset and the sounds of Nike etching his symbol into the next enemy, I rolled over, stretched, and came back from the image of Stacy, naked, into the sights and sounds of hell.

If you have ever slept on a hard floor then you know that, although you may have slept, the marriage of the pressure of your body pushing against your arm, and the ground not yielding, results in the blood to your fingers and hands being cut off. On that morning, this was the case for me, so I rubbed the night's weakness out, stretched my legs, feet, and back, and rose silently. I donned my helmet, grabbed my SCAR-H, and began my crawl over to look out the window and get some sort of visual understanding of what was going on. I hated to use the radio, because only important info should be passed, and stupid questions like, "Hey guys, what's going on?" sorta throws off the whole situation.

After a time, I determined all was safe, so I moved out into the courtyard and crossed to the ladder leading to the sniper position.

"Nike, what you have for me? Do you need anything?" I asked.

"No, we are good," Nike replied.

"So tell me—what is going on out there in your field of view? Do we need to set a demo field or some claymores to protect any of your blind spots?" I encouraged him to answer.

"Actually, yes, come up and I will show you. Oh, and two dead guys are outside, so when you and EOD go out, see what they got on them," he pronounced.

I scampered up the ladder, tucked myself up next to Nike, and surveyed the area, letting him speak until he was finished. Yep, we did have a blind spot to our front about 100 yards out. A nice place for some command-wired claymores and Bangalores we had made to look like tree branches. With that, EOD and a couple other of my men got what we needed and moved outside to set the trap.

The two dead guys were, well, dead, to be exact. Other than that, I had nothing to report except the dead were not enemy; they were from Chechnya, and they had comms and night vision devices as well as some military gear.

EOD looked at me after we turned them over. "These boys be trained, Ridge Boss, and they are the probes. We are in for some more of this, for sure." I replied, "Yup. Trident 2 Zero, this is Bravo Zulu. I have two EKIAs here. Foreign fighters from Chechnya, I suspect, wearing military issued gear with comms and night vision. Recommend getting some overhead eyes."

"Roger," he replied, and that was that.

The four of us proceeded to lay the claymore field and hide Bangalores in the branches, while some rounds cracked over our heads. Nike and Texas immediately responded, sending someone else to that place the Islamic people think there are some number of virgins waiting. Never figured out why the religious leaders put that into their silly book. I surely wouldn't want to spend eternity with any number of young virgins. Could you imagine the eternal drama of that? Better to stay alive and spend the next forty-one years with a woman who knows which part is for what, and what works, for God's sake.

The next part of the day was more of the same. Each position engaged in random battles as the enemy probed us and formulated their battle plan. Nike and I had a sit down later in the day, talking about the inevitable fight.

"Dude, those hilltops over there, and there, and there are prime real estate, Chief," Nike pointed out. "I would be up there just watching: seeing where people were dying and how we moved, and where those infidel Americans were shooting from," he said.

"Our only salvation is air and that damned mortar tube," I told him.

As the day wound down, the sinking feeling wound up. We had about an hour and a half before the sun would set. Most of us were in the courtyard eating and watching our dog, Turbo, take his anger out on a pillow. I was so damned hot I had taken my body armor off and put it inside the room where I napped hours earlier. I was sitting on the ground, legs crossed, rummaging through the last bit of my MREs. All of a sudden my skin crawled and the hairs on the back of my neck literally stood erect and tall. Now, that sensation is nothing to laugh at. I looked up to the hill 700 yards away and stared at what looked like several red bees flying right at me. As they arched across the sky, it dawned on me to duck—you know, like in the movie *The Matrix* when Reeves bent backward, and the slow-moving bullets went over him. Well, that is just what occurred. Everything really did feel like slow motion. I arched backward. The tracer rounds from the hilltop, from a Russian-made Maug or PKM, hit the wall right where I was and tracked around the inside of the compound wall. I looked around and saw the men diving for cover, then found myself jumping through a window into my "nappy room" while nine RPGs informed us all we had been sloppy and overconfident.

The sound of the explosions was deafening. Dust flew everywhere. I somehow put on my body armor and SCAR H without even knowing it. I cleared my head and put on my comms headset and helmet, frantically trying to make comms and listen in. I recall saying, "Oh my God!" out loud. After five attempts, I became convinced—I mean really clear in my dumb brain—I was the only one still alive. Another volley of rounds hit the wall outside, and off in the distance, I could hear other battles raging. For the first and only time in my life, I said to myself, "I am dead." My legs buckled and I lay there looking up into nothingness.

For a time I couldn't move. Then my Internal Dialogue shifted from something dead to something new entirely. I heard Stacy say to me, 'Do not fear dying. It makes you weak.'

So, in my thoughts, I formed a new dialogue, *I ain't dying without killing as many of them as I can. I would rather my wife and kids read I was dead on top of a pile of enemies, than have them find out I was taken prisoner.*

The prisoner thing wasn't gonna work for me, anyway. I had failed out of SERE (Survive Escape Resist Evade) training because I can't take someone smacking me in the face. When they did that in SERE, I warned the instructor: if he did that again, I would knock him out. Well, he did it again. As I stood over his unconscious body, the other instructors said, "Well, you can leave now. You've failed." As I gained resolve in that second by reflecting on how capture was simply not going to work for me, I turned toward the window in time to see Texas fall from the roof above.

I really have to honestly say it sucks to see your men fall limply off a twelve-foot-high roof. I rushed to the open door and was met by a hail of those damned red bees again. I quickly moved to the window, and due to the angle of the hill above the window, I had to move inside the window frame. My head was kind of exposed, so as I tried to get my cross hairs on that hill, a round hit the window frame an inch from my face, spraying dirt into my eye. I went down, grabbing my eye, thinking for sure it had been taken out. What a pleasant surprise to find it still there. I moved back to the window and held up a pot I'd found in the room, and BANG. One single shot hit the center of the pot.

I am a sniper—have been since 1998—and I smiled because I knew I was up against a worthy shooter. Seven hundred yards is a tough shot. He had missed once, but now he knew the distance and wind, and he thinks he's got me. I grabbed some blankets and pulled them over me. I laid on the floor with my body covered and moved forward slowly, in the shadows. I knew he would not be able to detect movement inside the shadows. I inched forward, constantly looking through my scope, until I could view the hill. I knew the distance and had already dialed 721 yards into the scope. I talked to myself, *Calm down, Thom. Where would you be shooting from? He has to see me perfectly, but be hidden from the hilltop SEAL element. He is smart, so where would I be? Work it out.* I concentrated on those words and worked the terrain with my scope. Then, I saw a flash. "Well, shit, there he is," I said out loud.

I could see the weapons barrel, so I concentrated on relaxing my eyes to let the image clear. Then I saw his back and head and right arm. I took a breath and closed my eyes. Then, all the training at sniper school and all those rounds over the years kicked in. I opened my eye to look at the wind. I could see it moving from left to right at about three miles per hour. The mirage was kicking. I closed my eyes and took another breath. With them still closed, I released the safety. As I opened them, I adjusted my aim to compensate for the wind and released my breath slowly.

Suddenly, I thought of my kids and my wife, and I think of that connection, far away . . . so far away, when I was not this man covered in dust, bullets flying everywhere, my men struggling with their own lives. I blinked, looking at the sniper looking at my window not knowing, and I said, "Do your best, fuck-head. Try to kill me, because here it comes, buddy."

I remember the last things in me: my wife, so sexy; my sons, so strong; my daughter, so everything. I slide the last inch forward, where I would be exposed for a split second, then I squeezed.

Time froze. *Dammit, if you're death, come on. If you are all the things I have done badly come to claim me, then bring it. If you are the blackness of the Shea Clan, then so be it. I know my bullet is gonna kill you—why is it going so fucking slow? At least I died killing you, so your kind will never kill my family or my men.*

Then I saw blood splash the rock behind his head, and all of a sudden my right eye is in pain, and I hear a smack on the ground. I rolled away from the window and grabbed my face. *Oh, shit,* I recall thinking. I recall just holding my eye, afraid to bring my hand down. I didn't have any pain outside the initial shock I felt. Then I thought, *Lying here not shooting, while my men are fighting for their lives, is sorta selfish.* So I rolled over to my hands and knees and pulled my hand away. "Holy shit, no blood," I laughed to myself.

I looked down on the ground where I had taken the shot and saw a round embedded in the ground where my head had been. He had me dead to rights but was too slow—what a chump.

I smiled, bent down, and twisted the bullet out of the ground, then dropped it in my pocket. I recall thinking it would make a great necklace for Stacy. The things you say to yourself in combat are funny. Funnier still is when you believe in yourself too much in combat.

Kids, the shift for me—what this whole book is trying to capture—was right then. That was my Adamantine moment. I was Unbreakable because of the connection with my men, my weapon, the air, the whole bloody fucking mess my Internal Dialogue had given me access to. My Internal Dialogue had given me access to things—all things—to living or dying, to my men, to me.

At that point, I moved to grab Texas, who I thought was dead. But we ran into each other at the door, and, God, I think we hugged each other.

"Dude, where is Nike," I yelled.

"Chief, they are everywhere—from right outside the door to the bottom of the hill 600 yards away. We are fucked," said Texas. He smiled, but I knew he wasn't happy.

"Son, where is your gun?" I asked.

"Oh, they shot the shit out of it, so I left it there and jumped off," he replied.

"OK, where is Nike?" I asked again.

"He jumped off the other side. Hell, I don't know where he is."

I said, "OK, come with me. Here is an M4, but it has only one magazine, so make it count. You and I are going to run across that courtyard through the maze of bullets to see who is alive."

"Oh, Chief? Your radio is off or something. They are trying to make comms with you," Texas added.

Texas moved over and looked at my radio. "Oh," he said, "what . . . did you turn the channel to the music channel or something?" I felt like an idiot, but his joke made me laugh.

On my count, one, two, three, we broke from the cover of the room and rounds were immediately hitting all around us. I was sure both of us were hit. I fell twice but couldn't recall tripping. We dove into the room where the rest of the platoon was, and when I looked up, I was shocked.

All of their guns were pointed right at us. Then they all simultaneously said, "Shit, we are fucked. We can't get out of this room. We are pinned down!"

"OK, shut the fuck up," I said tersely. "We are going to kill as many as we can. Here are my two grenades and my 40 mm bandolier. You two get everyone's grenades and put them in a bag, then meet us at the mortar tube." I pointed to others in succession, saying, "You two get all the 40 mm you can find and all the tubes and meet up at the mortar. Go now. Who has a machine gun? OK, you get in a position to look at the front gate. Every minute, shoot through the gate until you are out of rounds, dead, or I tell you to stop. No one gets in that front gate, you got it? Go now."

Nike and EOD burst into the room. I grabbed them, saying the three of us were going to the mortar and shooting every fucking round we had. "Let's get some."

We moved together, tucked up next to the wall, and found the mortar tube and rounds. As Nike and EOD prepped the tube, the rest of the men consolidated and threw grenades over the wall, shooting 40 mm over the wall toward where Nike and Texas said the enemy were. I called up to the C2 element that we had a full head count and were pinned down, so we were engaging with mortars. Clear altitude and direction. I am not waiting. I heard, "Roger, out."

For the next eternity, we threw grenades, launched 40 and 60 mms, and shot the piss out of the front gate. As I unraveled the last tape on the mortar shell and pulled the pin, I heard C2 say, "Bird checking on, hold the mortars. But I gave the last one to Nike and said to send it.

Finally I called C2, saying, "Winchester on 60 and 40 mike, mike; Winchester on grenades and 7.62 link. Need resupply if anyone can support."

Then I turned my channel to the air net and heard the call sign of a B-1 bomber. Snowman said, "Gents, B-1 checking on, get out the cameras."

I looked around the courtyard into the tired, swollen eyes of the most courageous men on earth. Saw the smiles creep in, saw the future lives and families they would have, and sat down with my back against the wall, saying to myself, *Stacy, I am coming home!*

The B-1 bomber was the most beautiful plane I have ever seen. Any soldier or sailor who has ever been in a pickle like that would tell you the same thing. We watched him drop his entire payload on every enemy who had worked his way to the hilltops. Two thousand-pound bombs dropping 500 yards away are called danger close, and, wow, the shock wave is spectacular. After a bit he called himself Winchester and headed out. By then darkness was setting in, and the mother of all combat planes was eagerly checking on . . . C-130. Love it: don't leave home without that plane, let me tell you.

During the next hour, the men rebuilt the various fighting positions, and ate and drank, saying, "Wow, that was close!" often to each other. The snipers built the position one sandbag higher, even though the roof was begging to fall with the new weight.

I called over to Nike, but he stopped me mid-sentence, "Fuck off, Chief. I would rather fall through the ceiling than take a round." I smiled . . . "So would I."

We leaders met in the compound adjacent to mine and had an interesting discussion. Each of us had our points to make. Our original mission was to stay for two days and clear the other side of the valley. Under that plan, my exhausted men would now leave our compound and patrol over to a series of twelve buildings, rummaging and/or fighting our way through whatever mess we found. Then, we would come back after the night of fun and have no sleep to face a day in an inferior position.

My vote was countered with, "What are you, a pussy? Are you afraid?"

"Well, if you fuckers want to fight from a position where we just got our ass handed to us, then you are fools. We have nothing to gain here. Get those helos in to pick us up, or I can bet you one of your men will surely die," I replied.

"Well, the bosses sitting there back at camp said, 'Good job; kill more enemy,' and they ain't sending a helo until tomorrow night. We are stuck. Best get your platoon together and get the clearance done."

I felt a surging anger like I have never known. Yet, I knew this wasn't anyone's fault. I knew, even then, war is fought by brave men, for reasons that truly didn't matter to anyone, especially back home. We sick men, who eagerly go to hell to piss on the devil, only need permission.

Walking back to the compound, I merely said to myself, "Fuck it, let's go pick another fight. The men will be bored if we just sit here and try to make sense of hell."

I gathered the men of Bravo and put out the word and timeline. While they organized themselves and looked at maps, I sat down and finally had some food and Gatorade. Nothing like hot orange, piss-tasting Gatorade to bring out the flavors of hell.

When we departed the compound, we walked among the dead foreign fighters right outside the front gate. Then we passed the blown apart remains of the other thirty-two foreign fighters we had ripped apart with grenades, 40 mm, and 60 mm mortars. Damn, they had made a great attempt at getting in. "Sorry, gents," I said to myself. "The victory only goes to the ones who win. That is the way of war."

The rest of the night's clearance was basically clearing a ghost town. We only found two old men, who were too tired and old to run away. However, we found out the head enemy lived in the middle of the wooded area about 200 yards from our location . . . in a fortress, the translator said.

I always wanted to see a fortress. I told my LT, "Let's let him lead us there."

With that, we set out on what truly looked like a wild goose chase. We circled back the way we came, through a maze of walls and irrigation ditches, then finally found a thirty-foot high building with no apparent entrance. After walking around the building what seemed like four times, we finally did find a way in. A new truck was inside this nice place. We all laughed at the truck because, at least at night, no apparent road was leading to the building. So we did what any SEAL would do. We popped the tires, cut the fuel lines, and cut the electrical systems.

The next day was slower, with the snipers only killing seven enemy fighters who had tried to climb up the hills near where I had killed the enemy sniper.

Finally, the flight out was truly the biggest sigh of relief I had ever had. Once we were miles away from the fighting area, I closed my eyes and thought of my family again. Stacy, I knew I was no longer afraid of dying. I don't know when or where I will die, but the fear of dying left me for good over the last two days.

When we arrived back in our platoon compound, the operation's center support crew had food and drink set out for us and were all wide-eyed with praise. They had watched most of the fighting on video feed and counted the enemy dead. And while I don't wish that vision on my children, it made me want to tell them something very important: Kids, I can only hope that if you ever see a Navy SEAL or a Special Ops soldier that you acknowledge him in some way. Because you know what he is . . . and what he does for you.

ADAMANTINE LESSON NINE

Never give up

As you digest Section Nine, when you pick your path in life, you will have times when you mentally, physically, and emotionally hit exhaustion. There is no way around hitting it, and there is no way out of this rite of passage. I can safely say you will clearly hit it when you are committed to whatever you are doing. You might be the best at your profession, or just progressing your way up. Yet, you will hit this wall.

I can tell you that my experience has shown me 1,000 ways to not pass through to the other side of exhaustion in the pursuit of greatness. You will undoubtedly be able to find your own poor examples of how to fail. The solution, like all the ones I have shown you, doesn't lie without. The solution lies *within* you. Don't run and don't hide from the pain, the fear, or the exhaustion.

Recognize you have created this path for yourself, and you *need* to be there. Those around you, too, *need* to be there as well. If you run and hide, they will, too. Or they will be forced to go without you. The loss of you may be enough to kill the whole effort. You count. As Stacy put it, "Do not fear dying. It only makes you weak."

We have an underlying Internal Dialogue, a way of being during hard times that brings about perseverance and lack of fear unlike all others I have ever known. I call this a language of "Committed Unattachment." In this language and way of being, you are fully committed to your goal and unattached to your emotions, pains, the whims of others, or even the occasional failure. Distractions don't throw you off, rather, don't throw off your Internal Dialogue. Mastering Internal Dialogue *is* your Unbreakable Life.

SECTION TEN

CLARITY

"Given enough time, any man may master the physical. With enough knowledge, any man may become wise. It is the true warrior who can master both . . . and surpass the result."
—Tien T'ai

"Your work is to discover your work and then with all your heart to give yourself to it."
—Buddha

Life seemed lighter for the next two days. We all got into our routines, whatever they were for each man, and continued to eat, rest, work out, and test our weapons. This totally insane ease of living we had acquired over the past three months can only be appreciated by those warriors who have faced this sort of hell. As I sit here and write to my kids my reasons for living, I reflect on stories I have read about adventurers like Lewis and Clark, or Shackleton, or, even, Columbus. They, too, must have faced horrible environmental conditions, faced the exhausting ups-and-downs of close encounters with death, and, finally, faced the morning when they woke up with no end in sight.

We now faced that exact state of being . . . "Shit, we are only half way." I have read very little about Columbus or Lewis and Clark, but Shackleton's voyage sits next to me on my combat desk. As I was thumbing through, somewhere around the middle, he noted the condition of "No end in sight," and clearly addressed it in a way that reshaped the ultimate outcome of the entire expedition. He simply found a way to focus both his men and himself on each other—away from the conditions, away from thinking about what had happened and what could possibly happen. I am inspired by that thought.

The rest of the book tells some truly incredible tales that aren't physically achievable, then or today. Yet, mentally, the depth of courage, character, and perseverance needed to just get through the day is unfathomable. Hell, I like it more because my men and I are accomplishing and performing inside that same margin—that space where there is no end in sight, the future is unclear.

In an effort to be in this very moment, paying no attention to what has happened or what may happen in the future, I simply got up, walked outside with my rifle, and headed to the range. Along the way I gathered up my platoon and had them load bullets, and as a fun treat, we packed the cooler full of Dr. Pepper and Gatorade. Making the best of this situation truly meant luxury, and Dr. Pepper is like champagne.

Yet, as we wrapped up living in the moment and all sat drinking our "champagne," our boss's truck came tearing down the range road. I looked at Nike and said, "Now, this cannot be good!"

"Ridge Boss, we have a rescue mission. One of the SFA teams is pinned down and have several dudes wounded and several dead," LT told me, with a sort of out-of-place smile.

I got moving. "Nike, pack up and head back. LT and I are going to ride back in his truck and begin planning this mission. I want to see the entire platoon in thirty minutes in the planning tent." Nike received my communication with a shrug and a smile.

While LT and I rode, we discussed what had been previously relayed to him regarding the SF Team and the time line we had to effect a rescue mission. What was clear, even in the brief tactical discussion, was the terrible, mountainous terrain and short amount of time we had to coordinate.

"Boss, all we need is clearance to go, and the amount of time we will be on location."

"Our men truly need nothing else but to know those two things . . . where and how long," I said as a matter of principle.

Once back at camp the immediate intelligence brief described the location and the truth about the Team's disposition. The mission was designated highest priority, and all other missions were put on hold until the

SF Team was rescued. High-level priority makes planning as easy as falling off a rolling log into water. We had our air assets. We had our weapons and gear ready. We had three hours to plan our insertion point and extraction point. I chose to set our time in the target area at forty-eight hours. No one likes to be in the field longer than that.

With the intel package in my hand, I walked over to the planning tent and, within fifteen minutes, had described where we were to insert, how long we were to stay, and where the SF Team was relative to our mountaintop position. I left the men to plan the various elements and special gear and guns we would require to support the team. As I withdrew from the tent, I looked up at the starry night and said, "Shackleton, you are one smart dude. Focus only on the men and the connection to each other."

"Nike, stand here with me for a second," I suggested to him as the rest of the guys walked away. "This is frowned upon during all these silly military leadership courses we all have to attend, but I want to tell you something." I paused for a moment, knowing my pause would make him look up at me. "I have now seen you survive the worst conditions without receiving even a scratch. The platoon sees it as well. You will not die in combat, that is clear. We will be inserting on the ridgeline above the SF Team. I want to you get your sniper thing on again. I doubt we will even take a single round into our position, but I personally intend to use my sniper weapon to hold the enemy at bay. Make sure all the men get that this is going to be a sniper's wet dream."

"Ridge Boss, I appreciate the praise. I would say the same for you. I have no idea how those ten rounds went through your clothing and didn't hit your skin," Nike said as he reached back to his green notebook. "Let's make a wager, then: all this sexy talk and praise is for women. Spartans don't talk this way. The longest kill shot wins the platoon money pool," he said confidently.

"So, what is the pool up to now?" I asked, eyebrow cocked.

"I am not going to tell you the details. That would be illegal," he said as he walked away.

Watching Nike walk back into the tent, I smiled. At the last moment, he turned and saluted with his middle finger. It would be a long night for the men of Bravo platoon, a longer night for the men of that SF Team, and an even longer day tomorrow for the enemy, who would be fighting for their lives.

I walked back to my combat room and slid the curtain shut. I was no longer nervous about going into combat. My lack of nervousness somewhat made me wonder if this was a normal feeling of combat maturity, or me just being jaded by my constant dealings with death. The reason really doesn't matter, because this is what I do and who I am. At some point in the collective lives of my children, I know they will create this sort of condition for themselves. What you say about yourself and what you actually do are the same thing.

For me, I truly enjoy the "everything" about this situation. I love the men. I am a SEAL. My wife loves who I am and what I do. Please let me offer this quote to my kids before I go to battle, again:"We are Sparta."

Queen Gorgo: Spartan!

King Leonidas: Yes, my lady?

Queen Gorgo: Come back with your shield, or on it.

King Leonidas: Yes, my lady.

" . . . tonight we dine in hell."

—From the movie *300*

My combat uniform went on smoothly for the first time. My body armor fit like a glove. My MK17 felt like an extension of my eyes and arms. I loaded each round into my magazines and felt their balance and weight. Everything felt good. My two grenades were solidly affixed to my gear. Even the radio headset seemed to work. I doubted it would work later, but at the moment it felt great. Finally, I lifted my MK13 off the rack and checked the action and attachments. My backpack was loaded with food, water, and extra bullets. Time to go to war.

As I walked out of my combat room, I turned and took off my wedding ring, placing it once again on my computer. The ring would be there when I came back. Hell was no place for Stacy. When I looked up above my computer, I saw the printed quote Stacy had said to me so many months ago:

> *Thom, I need you to come back to us. Do not fear dying. It makes you weak.*

No longer was the wait on the airfield filled with the tensions usually surging through my body prior to all the missions we had been on during the first half of the deployment. I was, however, more uniquely aware of the rest of the platoon. We had all pre-positioned ourselves in the different "sticks" we needed to be in to load the helos. I was always in the first stick, which normally meant the first bird to land and the first bird to receive fire from the enemy. Even that, however, seemed old and trite and of no concern.

My men in stick one were all stretched out on the ground with their helmets off, their heads resting on them. With body armor on, it is difficult to lay down and rest your head, so the only solution is to take off that damned brain bucket and use it for a pillow. I lay with my helmet pillow, listening to the various communications being conducted through my headset. Only our LT stood, attempting to look around and coordinate the ever-resistant cat herd conducting the pre-liftoff nap. I had learned long ago that making these men play military was senseless. I am sure always being the first one to drop my gear and lay down didn't help. Yet, as I looked at LT, I thought to myself, *Good luck, brother.*

In the distance, the whining of the engine turbines brought us all back from thinking of some sexy women or wives to getting ready to load the helos and fly into some new hellish place. I do not know what it was like for the other men, but this pre-flight time was, for me, filled with running through the operation in my head—getting a clear picture in my mind of how the men would step off the helo, where they would go, and what we would do if we were attacked right there on insert. Running through whatever scenario my mind wanted to play with had been disturbing when I was a new chief. Earlier I had attempted to force my mind to focus on the plan. But after experience showed me no plan ever survived initial contact with the enemy, I abandoned that silly way and let the thoughts roll on their own. As I got more comfortable, I realized bits and pieces of the wandering thoughts actually came to fruition. Those brief glimpses allowed me to react faster, because I would recognize them later:

> Kids, I share this idea not as a way to help you all make better choices, but as a way to allow your mind to be at ease with any upcoming event you may have.
>
> The mind is a clearly misunderstood tool. Treat it like an unbridled English Setter . . . it has to be allowed to run freely on

its own in order to be effective. Focus comes only in that instant when you need it.

The movement of the helos toward our position brought us all to our feet and we began walking toward the pickup point. Following the load plan, I was always last to get on once the head count was perfect. Once on the ramp and walking up, the helo gunner would hand me the radio cable so I could hook in and listen to all the related communications that would be passed between the pilots. The motherfuckers talk so fast I could never follow every detail, yet when they saw enemy on target or they were getting shot at, I would at least get a sense of how many enemy and from what direction they were once off the helo. Knowing those two pieces saved our asses, I was listening in like it was rap music, and I hate rap music.

In the air I had "Tommy nap time," with part of me thinking of Stacy and another part listening to pilot rap music. The flight time was going to be close to an hour, because the stupid SF had driven, yes driven, deep into the mountains and had somehow decided to drive through a narrow pass. The map had shown four mountains rising up out of the valley, from 8,000 feet at the valley floor to 9,500 feet where we were going to land. The height would give us a tactical advantage to be sure, but to get there we had to land on a knife's edge, with only the ramp of the helo touching the ground. We would only have a twelve foot by twelve foot area to off load twenty-two SEALs. "It is what it is," was all we could say to each other when I briefed the men.

The pilots ensured we understood that the longer we took to get off, the more drift the helo would have. If we took too long, someone was going to step off into a 500-foot drop. My personal plan was to get off first and immediately get on my hands and knees to crawl forward only ten feet or until I saw or felt the cliff edge. In reality that's not the way it went.

As the one-minute-out call came from Nike, I woke up and disconnected from the helo comms while the ramp was lowering. As I watched, the ramp suddenly stopped halfway instead of fully lowering. Then, suddenly, someone yelled, "Go," and the surge from behind pushed me to my hands and knees while I was still on the helo. So I crawled, with my rucksack on my back and Nike stepping on my fingers, to the edge of the ramp. Once there I saw only six feet of flat ground for twenty-two SEALs and the inability to stop the surge behind me. Somehow I fell out and everyone decided to use me as a stool to ease the strain on their drop from the ramp. I was on my belly waiting for the jump on Thom to stop. Finally the crushing stopped, but somehow I was being pulled toward the edge by both Nike and Jake. In only a couple of seconds, I realized what was actually going on. They both were slipping toward the cliff, and their legs were dangling off the edge, so they were using me to hoist themselves back up. Problem was, I wasn't anchored to anything, either, so all three of us were getting pulled toward the edge. Finally, EOD jumped on my back, and we waited for the helo to lift off.

At least we weren't going over the edge. Then the comedy really began. Within a split second, I felt EOD jump off my back; suddenly, and he was lying next to me, face up. I looked at him puzzled, because his arms and legs were up like he was a turtle on its back. For a second, I thought we were falling down the mountain in freefall. Then I felt the sudden oppressive weight of something push down on my rucksack and my body pressed into the ground. My night vision goggles snapped off, and my helmet got twisted. More accurately, my helmet began to twist my head and neck. Then the weight was gone, and the helo downwash kicked up dust and rocks.

"What the fuck just happened?" I yelled at EOD.

"Jesus God, the helo drifted backward over all of us," he yelled back.

"Damn, let's get the guys up from the ledge and see who we lost," I yelled again to EOD.

I got a sick feeling because I had lost my night vision somewhere. I couldn't see any of my men due to the dust out and darkness. Doing anything other than crawling around would be incredibly stupid, because if I were to stand up, the next step would surely be a long one.

As I searched around, I immediately felt three others doing the same thing. At this point, everything was quiet again, the dust had settled, and the visibility had improved somewhat. EOD was on my right side working toward the cliff edge, when he asked, "Chief, did you lose your goggles?" He handed me the damned things, and I put them up to my eyes, truly surprised they worked. With the aid of the goggles, I immediately saw what looked like everyone on their hands and knees. Texas was being pulled up from the edge by Ground Launch, and both were laughing.

"Everyone stop," I said into my radio. "I want a head count right now."

"Fire Team One is up."

"Fire Team Two, up."

"Fire Team Three, up."

"Fire Team Four is up, but one of us is down the ledge about fifteen feet."

I looked over to KM, who was standing on the edge of the cliff looking down. EOD, Nike, and I walked over and looked over.

"Are you alright down there?" I yelled, trying not to laugh.

"Yes," Salty replied. "But I seemed to have dropped my grenade and am afraid to pick it up."

"Chief, I got this. Just get the men moving toward the sniper positions. We will catch up, or you will hear a big boom. Best if we don't all sit here and watch," EOD said with a laugh and a smile. "If the pin was pulled, it most likely would have gone off. I am just going to stress him out a bit longer. Salty, don't move. I am coming down to you."

The whole situation was morbidly funny. One part of me was still just happy I had not been crushed by the helo losing altitude and then sliding backward over my entire platoon; the other part of me was laughing at EOD wanting to play a joke on Salty, who was clearly in distress, worrying his grenade was going to blow up underneath him if he moved. With every step I anticipated an explosion, but I also felt better about getting away from the edge. Truly funny in a morbid way.

After a bit, EOD and Salty joined the movement along the ridge as we looked for the best vantage point to both see the SF Team and prevent the enemy from moving in on them and us. Damn, we were high up to be sure. No enemy would be able to easily climb the cliffs leading to our ridgeline, and no hilltops were higher than our position within two kilometers. We just had to be able to shoot accurately 700 meters to 2,000 meters. A sniper's wet dream.

At the first point, we realized we would have to dig deep into the rocks, dirt, and gravel to provide the sniper element protection and a comfortable place to rest and hang out. Yet, as we all looked at the ground, a deep, disgusting sigh came out of everyone simultaneously.

"Jeeesssuuuus, this is truly going to suck, digging into this rock and making sandbags," Snowman and All Around said.

"What did you think it was going to be up here on a cliff?" I asked, rather pissed off anyone would complain.

"Well, honestly, I had hoped for cool grass and a Jacuzzi," Snowman said in a provocative tone.

"How about you dig a nice hole and we all piss on you when you get in," Salty answered Snowman. Salty always came to work and hates hearing others complain.

"Alright," I stepped in. "Fun is over: squad two, dig; squad one, let's find you a spot."

Squad one and I broke away and walked along the ridge closer to the SF Team and deeper into the all rock sections. We literally walked along a knife-edge six-foot-wide path, with 100-foot drops on both sides; safe from the enemy, but dangerous even to walk.

We had two hours of darkness remaining. Although we were at 10,000 feet altitude and the temperature was now 70 degrees, I knew the temperature would rise well above 100 degrees during the day, and we would be fighting the heat and dehydration all day long. I was really looking forward to hot Gatorade.

The various rock chimneys and depressions did, however, lend themselves well to sniper positions and shade for the men. So I left squad one with the task of keeping eyes on the SF Team and to watch for enemy men moving in on them. The walk back up the ridge toward squad two was much harder. The altitude was clearly noticeable, and I knew the men digging would be exhausted already.

Once on top of the hill, I saw LT sitting alone and took that as a sign to go over and have a chat.

"LT, I see no easy way for the enemy to approach these positions, or even reach up here with their AK-47s. Even the RPGs will have a tough time. Once Echo platoon gets into position, I will plot their grids and ensure we have 360-degree coverage, but the original plan for positions looks rather good, don't you think?" I asked, flopping down next to him on a jagged rock that went right into my butt cheek.

"I agree. I have made radio comms with the SF Team and am waiting for an update on their status," LT said, in his always business-like way.

I reached into my pocket and withdrew my can of Copenhagen, offering him a dip. He always refused with a disgusted look, which, of course, made me want to offer more frequently throughout the day.

As I sat, I realized I was no longer stressed about being in hell. The pain in my feet and back had not flared at all. The stars even seemed brighter. I kicked back and listened to LT talk to the top players on the ground and back at base. Looking up at the billions of stars I could see through my night vision is always stunning. I was where I wanted to be. My family was safe from this stupid conflict between Islam and Christianity, and we were about to get busy.

Squad two was working like a chain gang, trying to dig deep and fill sandbags, so I decided to pick up one of the positions in order to allow the snipers time to set up their positions and weapons, and get into the mindset of watching and shooting versus digging and being pissed off. However, after an hour of digging, filling, and lifting sandbags, I was wet from head to toe, and tired. All the same, the Bravo welcome mat was out, and we were ready for guests.

Right at dawn we heard enemy AK-47 firing going on down in the valley near the SF Team and, within minutes, I heard the distinct sounds of Nike and Jake shooting multiple .300 Winchester Magnum rounds. Then silence. I turned to watch All Around scanning the target area for the enemy. After a bit he relaxed, his head came off the gun, and he returned to writing something in his notepad. How funny watching these men at this stage in their combat maturity—relaxed, yet very keen about what was going on.

Then the big waiting game and oppressive sun and heat happened. Two hours went by with nothing but locals moving around the target area, doing farming work or carrying water, seemingly oblivious anything was going on. Truly amazing, these men.

At noon, I decided to relieve the snipers and let them get some rest from working and watching. I felt good getting behind the .300 Winchester Magnum again. I could see the entire valley floor, and the scene reminded me of hunting elk in Aspen, Colorado. I began to methodically check all the people moving around. I spent a lot of time watching their movements and seeing if they were hiding stuff or possibly using radios to talk to the real enemy who was clearly in the area. After an hour of scanning, I noticed a window with a barrel sticking out of it. At 1,200 yards determining if the thing was a barrel or the handle of a rake was extremely difficult. I was not sure, so I watched and watched and watched. Every so often it would withdraw into the window, then poke back out.

I played this watching game for an entire hour. My right eye felt like it was being pulled through the other side of the scope by a vacuum. Then, finally, the enemy guy in the building must have completed his prayers and decided to shoot at the SF Team. Either he was retarded, or didn't think we could shoot that far. I checked the wind and the down angle several times, then dialed in my firing solution one last time. I waited for the right presentation to shoot.

The poor enemy soldier didn't get the return fire from the SF Team he had prayed for, so he decided to move into the middle of the next door-frame. As he lifted the AK-47 once again, I fired. The recoil of the rifle knocked the gun somewhat out of position. After sliding the bolt back and forth to load a new round, I took another minute to pick up the exact doorframe among all the other doors down in the valley. Finally, I found the man again, who was now lying on the ground with a big pool of blood seeping through his man-dress. The gun lay alongside his body, and he was trying to crawl backward while pulling the weapon along with him. So I fired again. Once I reloaded and found the correct door, all I could see were his feet on the threshold of the door; his body was back in the shadows of the room.

I watched for a bit, then All Around said to me, "Chief, where are you looking? Let me see if I can help."

"No need. He is done. You can have the position back; my work is done here," I said as I watched two unarmed women pull the enemy's body back into the room.

"You suck, you know that, Chief?" All Around said as I stood up and looked at him.

"Oh, you been talking to my wife, haven't you?" I smiled.

I crawled out of position to allow All Around to fill it. Everyone had been watching with either binos or their own gun-mounted scopes. We heard responses from the other homes, and I use the term homes very loosely, because the buildings looked like mud huts from up where we were. Four men with AK-47s and PKMs had run away, and were moving in and out of alleyways and darting into huts. We were tracking their movement the best we could with hand-held scopes, when without being asked, Snowman called up an Apache wing to look at our target area. Hell, I didn't even know they were close enough to see.

Yet, as he worked his magic, they had eyes on, and although, the enemy was now 2,000 meters away, I said, "Don't engage . . .

> LT, let's let this play out. I assume they are going to get reinforcements, and have no idea we have birds up above. At the risk of getting those SF bubbas hit harder, I suggest we let them bring their extended family," I said, imagining they would feel safe and bring all sorts of bigger long-range weapons.

> "Too easy, Chief. We have a B1 and two Apaches, and this is what we are here to do, isn't it?" he retorted rather matter-of-factly, as if he had already designed this to play out his way.

> "Snowman, I don't think this will be fast, though. How much fuel time do they have?" I asked, wanting to make sure if this did play out, we didn't find ourselves with no support at all.

> "Around an hour and a half, give or take," Snowman replied.

The temperature now was 120 degrees, and we were feeling the effects. The wait would completely suck. I did what any good leader would do. I laid down under the small bit of shade we had and closed my eyes. Normally, I only dreamed of Stacy and the kids while I was in the middle of combat, but now no dreams came—just sleep. I was thankful.

After an hour, the birds called in they were going to return to base and refuel. We were alone, yet the heat of the day may have served us, because no enemy returned. So we waited and waited. Periodically, from Echo platoon's direction, we heard firing, and the occasional update across the radio told the story of random enemy with AKs trying to get close to the SF bubbas. And we waited.

An hour before twilight, the family of enemy, with much better firepower, crossed a stream in a nice, pretty, single file line about 3,000 meters away. Well out of our range to engage with our weapons. But, the poor bastards were immediately spotted by the two Apaches we now had back on station. Snowman worked his magic like a snake slowly coiling around his prey. He talked the helos on, seductively allowing the enemy to feel secure. Yet, the enemy had decided to take a position in a hut with women. So we waited. I suggested we hit the ground in front of the hut with rockets, well out of any collateral damage range, and make the enemy run out to a place where there were no women and children.

LT agreed, and we flushed them out.

The next thirty minutes were like a wild-goose chase. The eight new enemy guys ran out and split up. We decided to follow the ones carrying the PKMs and RPGs. They were fast, but ultimately, made a mistake. The four of them went into an underground hole, or cave of some kind. Once they were locked down in one spot, Snowman and the Apache pilots worked out a surprise for them. Right at last light one of them stepped out of the opening holding his RPG and a set of binos, and for a minute, we were looking at him and he was looking at us. Then, a big, bright light and massive explosion engulfed the cave entrance and the poor guy. Since there was no wind, the cloud lasted fifteen minutes. Finally, the Apache pilot confirmed a positive hit and no collateral damage, well, at least not to anything other than the front and back of the cave.

The rest of the night was spent on the methodical extraction of the SF Team. We waited our turn for pickup and joked and chatted about what had happened and what we were going to do the next few days. The strain of combat had either made us all completely crazy, or the men had literally decided if it was time to die, so be it. In the meantime, we all took advantage of each opportunity to enjoy what we had.

As I was waiting for the helo that night, I wondered if I would be able to keep the ease and zest for life once I was back home. Part of me wished I could continue to be and feel this way forever, yet another part wanted to simply leave it and get back to a life where I could raise my children. As the helo landed, and dust and rocks flew in my face, I wanted to never leave, because I felt life with family and a boring job would be a more ruthless hell.

ADAMANTINE LESSON TEN

The Crossroad of Language

At some point in your life, early or very late, you may come to a place where the constant pounding of stress and the continued effort to succeed dramatically changes something in you. A crossroads of sorts. On one hand, you will use your Internal Dialogue to reshape your composure and help adjust to the never-ending in-your-face events of life. If you are on this Internal Dialogue success path, suddenly the dialogue will become your actions, so it will not be so loud in your head.

On the other hand, if you are not mastering your Internal Dialogue, if you are allowing the environment to shape your words, then your own weak Internal Dialogue will be so loud you will have to succumb to what it says to you. Either way, the Internal Dialogue you have runs the show. Maybe this is when and why so many soldiers in war, and so many post-trauma people, fall apart.

I want you to know the difference between the two paths. The latter path is one where you have no idea you even have an Internal Dialogue shaping your actions. Here the environment, rather than you, shapes your Internal Dialogue. That becomes overwhelming and you do what it tells you to. Environmental relationship pressures may shape you to truly believe this person is not the right one for you. Or, since this person you are in a relationship with cheats, your unmastered Internal Dialogue tells you that is the final straw, and you listen and quit.

The other path is quite different altogether. This mastered path of Internal Dialogue is truly what reshapes battles from complete loss to victory in a split second. On this path, and when you are using Internal Dialogue to shape your actions and the actions of others, the environment around you, or maybe it is the perspective you then have of the environment around you, gets transformed. I suggest this is where true peace is. Not in the absence of pain, or strife, or loss, or combat, or death, but in the ability to *be* in the moment, and not be somewhere else.

PART FOUR

YOUR LIFE

SECTION ELEVEN

Now

"We don't do our past or our future, so I only value this moment. I think always on This, and I am happy. I am only living Right Now."
—Thom Shea, Afghanistan 2009.

I haven't taken the time to write for several days. We have recently been working on the flight plans to return home. As exciting as that seemed at first, it is now proving to be more emotionally draining than actually exhilarating. Everyone clearly wants to get out of this hell, but we are somewhat concerned with emotionally letting go, than physically making a mistake on the next mission. The end is in sight, yet this is the most dangerous time.

As I write this, we are planning the next few missions, which will also be what we call the "turn over" missions, with SEAL Team One. I am sharing this insight with you so you, too, become very conscious of when you either start a new job or turn over a project to someone new, you need to keep two facts in mind. The first one is when you are at the top of your game, telling others what you have learned and showing them how to be successful can be quite difficult. The second point is the people coming in are always more eager than experienced. Be realistic in your goals, and tone down your efforts.

The whole process reminds me of my teaching my sons how to play football. Each play, each drill seems so clear to me, but watching my sons not even understand how to grab the football makes for some frustrating times. I think this process will be the same: tons of frustration and many harsh words will be exchanged.

With that in mind, we have two missions we will be taking the new SEAL Team One folks on that will serve to open their eyes to the reality of what we face here and also provide them with the leadership they will need to ease them into our hell . . . their hell.

The first target we are developing for the leadership turn over is a very complicated mission. Today, we were watching the target area on video and noticed the enemy is connecting wires each night all around the target area.

Nike laughs while watching it, saying, "Well, at least we know where the mines are. This will be a piece of cake."

"Sure, it does. How about we all just take wire cutters, then?" EOD wasn't smiling because he knew this was going to be complicated not only for him, but also for us trying to find them at night and avoiding stepping on the mines in order to find them.

For the next few days, we watched the target and enemy do the same thing each night and morning:

As I watched, I kept saying, "They are lulling me to sleep. It looks too easy. I suggest we take the inner ring of buildings and just wait for daylight. Let's bring an entire SF Team with their trainees to take the outer ring so that while we clear the market in daylight, the enemy doesn't surround us."

"Yeah, that would be my suggestion, and we need to make sure the SEAL Team One gents don't lead any of this." LT reaffirmed my thoughts of complication mixed with zeal.

Finally, the day came when SEAL Team One's leadership had arrived. That very morning, part of Echo platoon had left for home, and the rest of us had cleaned the barracks and gotten some space set aside for the many boxes Team One would bring. We were all rather excited to welcome the new guys to the hell that we had created. I had decided to walk across the street to meet the oncoming men, while some of my men went to pick up the boxes of war.

When the shuttle bus door opened and I walked inside to give them their first welcome, I was awestruck at the wide eyes. They were looking at me as if they didn't know who I was. After talking a bit, I sat down, and one of my close friends from SEAL Team One leaned over and said, "Damn, you look like you lost twenty pounds and grew five years older." I said, "Bro, if you only knew."

We immediately got them settled into their rooms and oriented the new warriors to the armory. Eventually, we went to the chow hall to eat. I sat down with the two new platoon chiefs, and we were chatting about unrelated shit, when I finally stopped and said, "Gents, this place is a firefight every time you go out. We have been hit on insert while on the helos, we have fought our way for miles to the target area, and we have been in five-day fire fights. It is no joke and not worth trying something new, nor unduly risking your men."

"Yeah, we have been reading your after-action reports. Have you all really been using 60 mm mortars?" my buddy asked, like that was an odd thing to put into an after-action.

"Are you kidding me? We have shot over 100 rounds! We have shot 81 mm rockets, used Bangalore torpedoes, set up claymore fields, and shot over 5,000 .50 cal machine gun rounds. On our third mission, we 'Winchestered' two B-1 bombers. The deal is to survive at **all** costs," I said without blinking.

"Today, we are going to take you all out so that you can sight in all your weapons. Then tonight, we have a warning order for the first mission, which will begin three nights from tonight. I need to know after the warning order—no bullshit, ok?—if you think your men can handle this mission. Don't be a gung-ho idiot and say, "Yes." I can tell you eight mines have already been located on target, and the enemy has guys moving on target all the time."

"Well, we didn't come here to play poker," my buddy said while he laughed.

The next few days were spent settling in and planning the details with SEAL Team One. We had a full-blown rehearsal with all involved, and as I looked at the gear SEAL Team One was carrying, I tried not to laugh. I suppose we looked like that when we first got here. The men were carrying ten magazines of bullets. Their gear looked damn heavy and bulky, and I knew if I said anything, it wouldn't go over too well. So I did a stupid thing and kept my mouth shut. I regret not saying anything.

The day of the first turn over mission with SEAL Team One finally came. We all had our final meeting on the flow of events and order of battle. The men from SEAL Team One were excited, and I have to admit that if you were an outsider looking in, you would not note any difference. We were all used to stress and don't even call stress, stress any more. Stress is just the pain in the ass that happens prior to actually starting anything.

Due to the isolation of the target and the immediate need for the helos to fly back and pick up the SF elements, we had decided to land close to the targets. I hated landing close. Close always meant chaos, mixed with dust and urgency. Someone always makes a minor mistake during those three tactical issues. Hell, I was thinking I may even misstep and trip on a fucking mine.

As we loaded the helos, however, the reality of combat came surging back, and all the greyness of thought went away. The sound of the comms checks, helos engines, and the smells of it all tend to wake the distant call of being a warrior back to the surface. I am no longer clear what it calls up in new men waiting for their first firefight, and honestly, at the time, I could have cared less. It was time to fight, and I liked fighting.

Upon landing, we were immediately supposed to move south 200 yards to the tip of the village and secure those few buildings so that we could have a foothold in the area in case the devil found out we were in his back yard. But, again, you can wipe your ass with the paper that the original plan was written on. The helos kicked up so much dust that none of us could see two feet in front of us. Without a lick of wind that night, the dust just hung there. One of the helos had decided to land 500 yards east in an area we told them not to land because intelligence had said it was mined.

"LT, for fuck's sake did that helo land over there in that mine field?" I remarked rather pissed off.

"Nothing we can do about it now. Linking up will take too long. Just move out. If we don't hear an explosion, then we know that mission is to continue," he said with his always business-like attitude he had with me. I always thought his joking with others while always straight and to the point with me was funny.

"Nike, do you have your bearings yet?" I asked.

"Um, yeah, but a twelve-foot-high wall is right in front of me that none of us saw on the map or overhead images. And, the fucking thing has no corners," he said in his always pissed-off way.

"We don't have time. Just get two ladders up, and we can climb up and over while this dust cloud is here."

The climbing over the wall took a bit more time than expected, but eventually we moved away from the wall and out of the cloud right into the first buildings. The men did what they normally do with precision and speed. Within ten minutes, the three buildings were clear. As I stood outside listening to the reports and waiting for all the troops to link up with me, even the lost crew that landed in the mine field, I noticed no one reported any people found on target . . . none. Five people were cooking and eating just two hours ago. I recall saying to myself with a jaded attitude, 'Oh, boy: here we go!'

The next step in the mission was to linkup. Echo platoon and SEAL Team One would move to the west side of the target area, and myself and parts of Bravo would take over the initial buildings of the target, then wait until daylight to clear through the mined streets. Well, that was the plan. Funny how shit doesn't work out so well.

Once we separated, I took part of my crew to the east side and cleared the first structure, putting some snipers on the roof. As I was walking behind the building, our dog, Turbo, came over to me and sat down. I looked down and recalled the dog handler telling me if the dog sits down, it is because he smells explosives. I immediately called out to my dog handler and EOD:

"Hey, why the fuck is Turbo sitting between my legs?"

EOD and the handler turned and looked at me and said together, "Chief, don't move."

"Don't worry, I am not going to move a muscle!"

EOD moved over to me waiving his wand, and as he got right up next to me, he said, "Yep, that is a pressure plate right between your legs. Jesus you are the luckiest man I have ever known. Just hold on while I cut these wires."

"You have got to be kidding me. What if it blows up?"

"If it does, then it won't matter because we will both be dead. That is the thing I like most about defusing bombs. If I fuck up, then I won't feel this slipped disc in my back any more."

"Well, that is a good point. I have to admit, that is a great point."

After a bit, EOD defused the pressure plate from wherever it was. I took a step backward and became uniquely aware of every single bit of ground around me. I noticed the rocks, pebbles, sand, ridges—everything. Turbo was called back, and he walked away wagging his tail, then got a treat from the dog handler. I moved back to the corner of the building and watched EOD trace the wires toward the bomb. He looked up and said it was an old tank round packed with homemade explosives.

He finally stood up, stretched, yawned, and walked over to me.

"Thom, that motherfucker had your name on it. I think you need to buy a lotto ticket."

I laughed and said, "No, I need to name my next kid after you."

Obviously, we were not going to move any further during the dark time. I heard over the radio the SF guys were landing on their part of the target. I climbed up the ladder to look at how my snipers were positioned and see how the other crews were progressing. I had the intent to tell everyone we had marked our first pressure plate, but when I looked around, I saw several chem-lights EOD was told to use to mark known plates so that others wouldn't inadvertently walk over them. I recall thinking to myself, *Why in the hell is a line of chem-lights going up a hill we were not going to clear during the night hours?*

The next hour would be the oddest in my life. As you read through this, please get that things happen, and you must rise to the occasion; you must keep a level head; and you must fight the screaming Internal Dialogue that is telling you to panic and run.

I reached up to hit the button that would allow me to talk to the guys moving up the hill. The very second I touched the button, a huge bright light accompanied by an incredibly fucking loud explosion happened right up on the hill where no one was supposed to be. A moment of silence followed after the audible explosion. At that kind of moment, you don't dare move, as you are waiting to see if any rounds are being shot at you.

As we all waited, Nike looked back at me and said,

"Chief, I hate turn over missions."

After the pause, one of the men from Echo called over the radio that he needed immediate medevac. That was all that was said. That was all that needed to be said. After twenty years of being in wars all over this crazy planet, all a warrior needs to know is "what" happened, "where" is it, and "how" long do I need to be there. This particular situation met the "what" happened thing. I knew "where" the bloody SEAL was. And I didn't want to be here any longer...the "how."

Luckily, one of the helos had just dropped off the SF guys and was only five minutes away. Our comms expert called him back and gave him the map location where we were going to clear a landing spot. What he didn't tell the helo pilot is that four of my guys ran across an uncleared mine field to clear another minefield so that the helo could land. I don't think the helo pilot would have landed had he known the truth.

Thank God the minefield was unmanned and not one the enemy was then going to shoot our asses off as we went to rescue the downed SEAL Team One guy. Yes, not three days in hell, and a new guy had already gotten severely wounded. However, the rescue went down without a hitch. Other than the fact that the mine had gone low order, which means it didn't fully blow up, we experienced little danger. The helo landed, and Dan Gnossen and Echo platoon's corpsman got on to fly immediately to a hospital.

The rest of the clearance went on as if nothing had ever happened. We found hundreds of pounds of explosives, drugs, and more drugs. We did what we do best. We burned all the bad stuff and waited for the enemy to come see what all the smoke was. Then the craziest thing happened: some poor enemy car must not have gotten the word that the Americans were around and decided to drive a car loaded with guns and drugs into the south side of town, where they then decided to shoot at us, not knowing they were fully surrounded. Poor fellas.

The remainder of the day was the usual suspects. Enemy soldiers would probe our position, shoot at us, and we would accurately shoot at them. Trying to explain the goings on of war is surreal for me. I have seen so much war, it truly seems normal to say, "I shot two guys and my snipers shot nine others. Then we hiked out into the desert and waited for the helos to pick us up."

Once back, we all headed over to see Dan. He had lost both his legs from above the knees. He was still alive and rather in good spirits. We awarded him a Bronze Star for Valor that morning. He had shown some sick bravery in the middle of losing his legs, he truly had. The EOD guy had crawled across Dan's bloody body to cut the wires to the other bomb that had not blown up but needed to be defused so that it, too, wouldn't go off. Now that was some sick brave shit. They all had gotten rocked, but they kept their heads.

I walked back to my room knowing Stacy, as the ombudsman, would have known about the injury. My not calling would worry her more. When I opened my computer and typed in, hello, I am waiting. Stacy immediately connected on cam and said:

"Oh, shit I thought it was you. The skipper called me two nights ago and said a SEAL in your location was seriously wounded then hung up. I have had the worst day thinking it was you. So, I know you can't say anything, but how are you and your men?"

"Well, it is now official. Turn over missions are stupid. We should just have the leaders come here and show them around base, then we leave. Dan got his legs blown off in the first hour, of the first night, of the first mission. I am tired now, for sure. I need not ask how exhausted you are. I only have two more weeks, and I am out of here."

"Thom, listen to me. As much as waiting on pins and needles to find out if you or one of your men were injured sucked, I do not ever want you to let your guard down. I am sure coming home is on your mind, but you still have work to do. You and I have talked about many things over the years, and one thing has been a constant theme. You told me before we got married that if we were going to make this relationship work and not fall prey to the things that cause divorces, we both have to create each moment like no other moments before had happened, and not think of any future moments. You are meant to be there. Fight until you are on the plane headed home.

Thom, I need you to come back to us. Do not fear dying. It makes you weak.

"Stacy, I am tired. I really don't give a shit anymore. Everything here just pisses me off. We need to leave here and drop a nuke bomb. These people don't care about democracy. Our leaders are kidding themselves. We don't even have a victory plan. And for God's sake, all the local people the SF are training, and now we have to train, want to shoot us in the back," I replied from the deepest place of 'I don't care' possible.

"Yeah, well get over your shit fast! Remember all of this is a game. Either you play with it, or it plays with you. I personally say you should play the role of a Spartan and go to war—not some pussy who dreams of something stupid and believes that life could be different. Do you have another mission?" Stacy said so matter-of-factly I didn't even know she asked a question. "Thom, do you have another mission planned?"

"Yes, we do," I said sorta under my breath.

"Alright, so do you remember when you told me when you were a boy how fun it was to hunt all day? You would hunt rain or shine because you loved just to track a deer, even if you didn't get to shoot it," Stacy said as if she was calling to something in me that was hidden.

"Yeah, I miss hunting," I breathed back to her.

"Well, tell me about your hunt in Colorado, that elk hunt where you hiked up that mountain, even though you had a fever and were coughing. Why did you do that?" She suggestively was laying down the rules for the fight to get me back.

"Oh, that one. I parked my car and climbed up to 12,000 feet and finally shot the Imperial elk at 500 yards with my 30-06. I then spent the next three days climbing up and down to get the meat, antlers, and hide out," I said as I recalled the feeling of fun and enjoyment of hunting flooding my mind.

"Now is the time for you to just say to yourself that hunting is fun and go hunt some more. You have nothing to do but hunt," she said in a playful way.

"Damn, I hate when you do this. Can't a man complain about any-thing around you?" I asked, knowing she was spot on.

"I love that you are a hunter and enjoy being a SEAL. It is OK that you are there."

As I turned off the computer, I jumped into my Tempur-Pedic bed and lay dreaming of that elk hunt and the hundreds of deer hunts during my youth. Hunting had been a way to get away from all the shitty things about being young, like having to follow rules, fit in, and do whatever someone else wanted. Hunting an animal for hours, following its tracks, and trying to think what the animal was doing made me feel totally at peace with the world. I even recalled finally aiming at a buck I had hunted for twenty hours, and as I looked through my scope and watched him breathe and move his muscles, I had decided to let him go.

As I drifted off to sleep, I recalled the playfulness that was supposed to be life. Life was supposed to be fun and playful no matter the conditions. The only way to overcome conditions was to create fun through just saying I enjoy doing what I was doing.

The next day, I woke up refreshed and walked over to the intel shop to pick up a mission that would be exactly what the doctor ordered. One final hunt.

I do not recall any of the details of the planning or the next few days, but I do recall we decided to take a mission where we would fly in right at daylight using some Russian MI17 helos. The flight in was impressive just flying ten feet off the ground at 120 miles per hour with no seatbelts. My legs were hanging out the back, and I decided I wasn't going to die here. The hunt was on!

We landed just fifty yards from our target building and sprinted like our hair was on fire. Within two minutes, we had the compound cleared and were setting up our sniper positions. Within forty-five minutes, I had shot an enemy soldier who was aiming at us. His buddy had run away, and I was tracking his movement along a wall about 280 yards away. I imagined he was thinking he could sprint from the cover of the wall and go the thirty yards without being shot. As he broke from cover, I saw he had a grenade launcher and could see his muscles rippling. I led the bullet about three mils in front of him and squeezed. He fell and dropped the launcher. I watched. I watched the blood flow into the dirt. Then I watched the wall from where he had come and waited. Bullets were flying over my head from one of his buddies, so I ducked down and waited. His buddy would try to save the launcher I was sure. They rarely care about their buddies, but they do care about those launchers. After twenty minutes of waiting, I eased up over the small wall and put my cross hairs on it . . . and waited some more. I saw him carrying a bush in front of him, slowly moving himself and the bush toward the grenade launcher. I held off and let him try. He was patient. I don't think I would have tried that move. I had to give him credit for trying. The moment he picked up the launcher, I shot him in the space right in front of his ear. He wouldn't have felt it nor heard it. He most certainly wouldn't be launching that grenade! He wouldn't be taking a single American life either.

I watched him for another three minutes and decided to try to shoot the launcher itself. After ten attempts, I finally hit it mid-tube, and it broke into pieces.

Later that day, I watched a van drop off armed enemy soldiers. They were long shots, so I missed the first five. Finally, on the sixth shot, the man in black with a machine gun dropped in his tracks. I felt like a hunter again.

Toward the end of the day, we lost all communications with the base and with the helos that were supposed to come pick us up. However, our plan had specified if we lost communications, they were to pick us up fifteen minutes before dark. Around thirty minutes before dark, we were still in a firefight, but clearly the helo was coming to get us. At the fifteen minute mark, we dropped everything we were doing and ran as we heard the helo fly in. It landed 100 yards from our position in the middle of a field. That sprint was not fun. Enemy rounds were hitting everywhere. Once on the helo, we flew straight toward the enemy. Nike and Jake were shooting out the back of the helo as we passed over the enemy.

The elation of flying away from the last combat target of my career as a SEAL was exciting. I survived hell. I brought all my men through hell without a scratch.

ADAMANTINE LESSON ELEVEN

Living in this moment

You do not have to go to war to face death. However, you should not run from death. Death is the most inevitable thing of life.

I would ask you to get in touch with what your Internal Dialogue is saying about death, about your fear of death, and your fear about living. Internal Dialogue is really the whole point of each of the exercises. Like the man said in the movie *Tommy Boy*, "You don't have to stick your head up a bull's ass to look at the steaks. Just take the butcher's word for it." Do not fear death. It makes you weak.

SECTION TWELVE

FUTURE

"The best teacher is not the one who knows most,
but the one who is most capable of reducing knowledge
to that simple compound of the obvious and wonderful."
—H.L. Mencken

"When a young person, even a gifted one, grows up without proximate liv-
ing examples of what she may aspire to become—whether lawyer, scientist,
artist, or leader, in any realm—her goal remains abstract. Such models as
appear in books or on the news, however inspiring or revered, are ulti-
mately too remote to be real, let alone influential. But a role model in the
flesh provides more than inspiration; his or her very existence is confirma-
tion of possibilities one may have every reason to doubt, saying,
'Yes, someone like me can do this.'"
—Sonia Sotomayor

As we landed from our last combat engagement, the pilot and helo had endured far more than we had thought. Bullet holes rimmed the cockpit window and traced throughout the frame. The rest of the platoon walked back to the buses, and I stayed to talk with the pilots.

"Jesus, guys, sorry for the bullet holes in the bird," I said.

"Forget it. That was the funniest thing we had ever seen. You all running through the bullets right into the back. Those small bullets will never bring down a helo like ours," one of the pilots said without even looking up at me.

Once on the bus to take us back to our compound for our debriefing, I saw all the smiles and felt the sense of "oh my God it is over" in the men's demeanor. As I stood in front looking back, I noticed Nike's eyes were tearing up. Once the bus pulled away, he stood up, hugged me, and said, "I owe you everything."

I replied, "I don't have the words."

The rest of the night was the standard dinner, debrief, and weapons cleaning. Since we were all elated to be done, the whole barracks and armory rattled with music and guys talking about the day of killing and what they would do when they got home and had time with their wives and girlfriends. I doubt if they would actually do some of the things that were mentioned, but I do love the fact that they were ready to go home.

For me, I had similar thoughts of finally being with Stacy, but my thoughts were also holding Chance, Autumn, and Garrett: of being at their ball games, taking them to lacrosse and cross-country matches, and seeing the fruit of my combat labors come to life.

Unbelievable! We made it! It is over!

The weight of a lifetime finally came crashing down on me as I headed back to my combat room. I suppose the room was no longer a combat room at this point . . . maybe just a place to safely sleep and to finally let go of the pressure of having to keep my men alive. I will be coming home to my family very soon.

I climbed up into my Tempur-Pedic bed, the tears of frustration and finality leaked out of my blood-shot eyes as they closed.

In my dream, I stood in the falls of Louisa Lake. Captain Pat was sitting on the rock ledge above me, smiling. His hand, which had had three of the fingers blown off in combat in World War II, rubbed his hip, which had come out of its socket in a helicopter crash in Vietnam.

"Thom, you were never alone," he said without looking up at me. "I was not the only one with you. Never forget that although your wife helped you, another critical player got you through this hell. Do you know who that is?" Pat asked, staring right through me.

"Yes."

I awoke several hours later, not having moved a muscle. Except for the drool on my pillow, the only thing that changed in the room was the fact the men and I were no longer preparing for the next mission. Although I had the urge and the five months of routine coursing through my system, I no longer desired to kill the enemy. My system had already moved on.

That is the way of things for warriors in war. When it is over, it is over. When the Internal Dialogue shifts to something new, so does the body, the mind, and the emotions. Too bad, too few soldiers understand that key point. Maybe if they did, Post Traumatic Stress Disorder (PTSD) would not have such a grip on so many. Although you may hear about and read about soldiers who can't let it go or warriors who, once back home, have nightmares about combat and killing, I personally couldn't care less about what had happened or what would happen with the next platoon. As I have pointed out in each chapter regarding mastering your Internal Dialogue, mine was clear and concise: "I am alive. Bravo platoon is alive. We did our part. Time to move on and do something else."

As I stretched my legs and climbed down, the dream of Captain Pat flooded back in. I had not realized the importance of having a mentor. Jerry and Tammy Barber had been that for me and Stacy throughout this journey through hell.

ADAMANTINE LESSON TWELVE

Your contribution to others for them

Stacy, Autumn, Garrett, and Chance, this lesson of performance is cap-stoned with *being* a contribution and being contributed to. Some will call it Mentoring. I actually do not. The whole meaning of mentor has been destroyed by our military leaders, who have not seen war, in hopes to sound smart and profound. It has become a descriptor of actions one might take to connect and lead men and show them the proper way.

My task for you all is to discover that thing in you that is a contribution to those around you and to find that which is in you that will be contributed to. Without those two distinctions to that language you have learned to use inside your Internal Dialogue, the level at which you can and will perform will plateau rather quickly.

The first step in this final task is to be up to something greater than what you think is possible. In reflection of my life, the past six months can be an example for you to not just swing for the fence, but to swing for the parking lot outside the stadium! *Be* big, *be* brave in the face of everything that will get in your way, *Be* humble when someone comes forward and encourages you, and fail gracefully. Those three states of *being* are worth contributing to by those who seek someone like you.

I failed every single (first attempt) at performing beyond what I dreamed possible. I failed out of the United States Military Academy, then finally graduated from Ball State on the Dean's List. I hit rock bottom during four separate attempts to make it through SEAL training and finally graduated number two in Class 207. Finally, when I took on adventure racing, I did not complete the first five races.

I swung for the parking lot, got knocked down or sideways, got back up and staked myself out and asked for help, and swung again. I want you to access that form of living, when your Internal Dialogue you have shaped into a mighty force drives your actions.

Do not fear dying. Fear makes you weak.
I **am** coming back to you, my loves.

SECTION THIRTEEN

Past

"Some birds are not meant to be caged, that's all. Their feathers are too bright, their songs too sweet and wild. Therefore, you let them go, otherwise, when you open the cage to feed them, they somehow fly out past you. Part of you knows imprisoning them in the first place was wrong, so you rejoice at their freedom. The place where you live is that much more drab and empty with their departure."
—Stephen King, *Rita Hayworth* and *Shawshank Redemption: A Story from Different Seasons*

Three years have passed since I dared open up all my rantings and thoughts that I had tried to share with you during my deployment into hell, not that I have dreams of all the combat and stresses from my experiences. I can still feel the elation of combat and still feel the closeness I once shared with my men. The urgency of sharing my life with you has diminished, though.

I suppose that is the way of things for warriors and human beings all over the planet. Each day in hell was so intense and lacking of my family, all I had wanted to do then was share it all. However, now that I am back home with my family, I get to feel their warmth; I get to talk with them about their day; and I get to lay next them all at night, finally getting to kiss them all as they drift to sleep.

"You are safe, and I am here to protect you."

The days of hell are long past now. We have all moved on to our lives, to other lives. The exploits and success of the 2009 deployment for TU Trident and Bravo platoon are now legend in the SEAL Teams. New tactics for combat were developed due to many of the "things" we faced and overcame. Many weapons were created in response to what we needed to kill more enemy . . . that is what war is all about for the US military, in general, and the SEAL Teams in particular. It is all about training to kill the enemy and not getting killed. Too bad that truth gets miscommunicated, and bad politics back home make the truth wrong in some way. Ironically, the safe condition we create back home by killing the enemy in his own country denies and then reinforces the silly idea that "since I feel safe here, no bad guys are out there." Let me tell you this: bad men are indeed out there wanting to do harm to you in ways you cannot dream of. Yet, powerful men who know the truth of safety, freedom, and liberty will never BE safe. We will never be free and never truly have the condition of liberty without one key element—the willingness and national embrace of training men and women to passionately eradicate those entities who would take it all from us. The US is the last best hope for the development of mankind and liberty.

Social welfare and reform without earning it is like giving all of liberty and prosperity away. Earn the things that you want and appreciate the things you have earned. Never give up your safety and ability to protect yourself to anyone . . . especially politicians.

Some of the men from Bravo are currently back fighting in hell, living the shit all over again. Several have gotten out and are seeking higher forms of education, and some of us are training SEALs to go back to hell and survive. Yet, we are all changed from our time together into hell.

My point man, Nike, will forever hold a special spot in my soul. He could not be killed by the enemy. Bullets would miss him as if God himself had deemed him worthy of eternal life. He laughed when the enemy shot at him as if he knew they would miss. Nike never ran from a fight, and actually ran toward the sound of gunfire as if those drum beats were magnets pulling him. I recall one operation in the mountains of hell, where he and I were in a sniper position taking a heavy volume of fire from enemy machine guns. Nike and I were bathed in the light of slayers that night. We both emptied our twenty-round magazines three times, when Nike looked over at me. As I looked over at him, rounds screamed between us, and he rolled to face me, saying, "Damn. I swallowed my Copenhagen on that one. Could you pass me your can please? I cannot hope to continue without another dip." As I reached to find my can, he said, "Hurry, dammit. My gun simply refuses to fire until I get that dip!" I laughed and slid him the can, and he slowly opened it, pushing a pinch into his lip. At that, he stood up, shouldered his rifle, and shot the last two enemy as they were turning the corner thirty-five yards from us. As he looked down at me, he said, "You can get up now; we are done here."

We buried Nike last month. He died on vacation in Bali, of all places.

I have moved on as well. No way am I going to Bali, I can assure you of that fact. I learned one thing that sticks with me still and drives everything I do, "Search out the thing that is in everyone . . . the thing that is unbreakable, or what we have called Adamantine and nurture it. Feed it and teach others to get access to it. This will make all the difference, as nothing else truly matters.

Recently, Stacy and I have decided to dig up all the old emails and my scattered writings I had either written on paper or on my computer so I could begin to read many of the lessons. I do have to admit that compiling each lesson and recalling all the stressful situations has proven to be tough.

> As you read this final section, I want you to understand that your father brought back all his men from hell so that they, too, could have a family and live in this sacred land of the American Experiment of Liberty. Also, know that in spite of the fact that your father has looked death in the face and often times was very quick to yell and not seem to listen well, that I deeply love each of you.

The last week in hell was the most emotionally stressful time for us all. Echo platoon members had already flown out of country and back to the States, while we of Bravo platoon had four airlift flights cancel on us. SEAL Team One had completely taken over our rooms, and we all were living like lost cats waiting for our flight. The shift in tempo was dramatic, and sitting around watching the warriors from SEAL Team One train and plan missions without us was like watching another man kiss our collective wives.

However, our flight finally came, and the sight of hell passing under the plane as we took off was surreal. It looked so benign, even the mountains reminded me of some really great mountain biking trips I had taken while doing adventure races. Yet, I knew somewhere down there some American was fighting for his life and risking everything for someone else.

I only lasted about two hours during the flight until my heart rate slowed so much I couldn't keep my eyes open. For God's sake, I hope my children don't inherit my slow heart rate of forty beats per minute when I am at rest, because yawning during a hot date or in school may not serve them well.

We arrived in Germany for a three day scheduled delay to adjust ourselves from the immediate stresses of combat to the patience needed to be a father, or husband, or as the leaders put it, a better adjusted citizen. For me, I simply wanted to sleep, eat sushi, drink wine, and maybe get a massage.

The days actually went by rather quickly. The food was perfect, and the massage was exactly what the doctor ordered. We all had to complete some silly stress paperwork so that some psych doctor could publish some doctoral paper on how hell stresses the human mind and body. He wasn't there and his distant point won't teach or relay anything of value.

I took four hot baths a day. For some strange reason, the hot water was better than any drug or therapy I could have gone through. I came to find out every man of Bravo did the same thing as I did: eat, sleep, take hot baths, and sleep and eat and take more hot baths.

Finally, we all took commercial flights back home and that was that. No more war. No more hell. I would never lead my platoon again in combat. I am still sad about that.

Thank you for coming and picking me up at the airport. Seeing you four waving and crying because "daddy is home" was the greatest gift a warrior can ever receive. Warriors are hard wired for hell, and that hard wiring is constructed by the hands of his wife and family. You make me who I am, and seeing you all made hell totally go away.

Autumn, thank you for learning the lyrics to Peter Gabriel's song, "In Your Eyes." I am not sorry I cried as you sang it to me. I know as you get older, you will read this book and become the woman you *need* to *be*.

Garrett, hugging you and feeling your arms wrap around my

neck will forever be the reason I survived hell . . . to feel the desperate need of a son for his father. Read these lessons and become the man you were born to BE.

Chance. Your name says everything. You are Stacy's and my chance to be a family. You were my chance to be a dad, and you are your own chance to be a man. In you lives all the strength, passion, aggression, and love I have in my life. These lessons will serve you well.

Stacy, lying next to you that first night in bed, feeling your perfect body and kissing your lips, was totally worth all the time I risked my life in hell—to get back to you. Each word written was because of you. Each life I took was to come home to you. Every moment away was another moment I had with you in my heart, making me strong and making us stronger.

After leaving SEAL Team Seven, I took over the West Coast SEAL Sniper Program and had to apply every lesson I talked about in this book. Teaching new snipers to do impossible things with both their rifles and their own Internal Dialogues was now my responsibility, which was no easy task, let me tell you that. SEALs are the most skeptical humans on the planet, and if shit you say doesn't make them better, they simply tell you to "go to hell." Since I had already been in hell, no one told me to go back, well at least to my face. What the students did do was shoot impossible shots as they learned to sneak up on us like the predators they truly were.

As I conclude this final section and wait for the day I retire, I work my final job in the SEAL Teams. I work in combat research and development. Although the job is intriguing and I do get to help develop all the next generation night vision, lasers, scopes, and weapons, I long for the bullets whizzing by my head. Not a day goes by that I don't look at all the new men going through training and wish I were covered in saltwater and sand, and out of breath. Not a day goes by that I don't see the platoons going through training and dream of taking another group deploying to hell.

I was asked recently by my boss why I was retiring and giving up becoming a SEAL Team Command master chief. My answer must have caught him off guard:

"The time has come for me to let go and create another life. I led men in combat; I taught men to become SEALs; I trained SEALs to become snipers; and I developed two new scopes and a laser range finder. It is time, don't you think? I have no regrets. I need to get out of the way and let the new guys have the helm."

"Good point, Thom."

I have led a violent, aggressive life. Every SEAL does. I was never the best SEAL, nor was I the fastest, strongest, or meanest (I know my kids think I am the meanest). I am laughing as I write this because as I look back at my career and my deployments, I have to admit I made more mistakes than I had successes. I just never made the same mistake twice, and I never made a mistake when life and death were on the line. I suppose I was lucky in that regard. Many SEALs were far better than I at most of the things that make SEALs good.

I have seen more death than I care to remember. Many of my friends have been killed in combat, and some have died doing other things. I have also put many of our nation's enemies in the ground or in prison. Oddly, the killing doesn't affect me as much as the death of my friends. I was present when we laid Mike Monsoor into the ground. He had jumped on a grenade in Ramadi and saved many of his platoon mates. He had been a student of mine when I was an instructor in BUD/S training. We all took off our tridents and nailed them all into his coffin that day. I have lost track of the number of SEAL funerals I attended. Yet, the final one I will ever attend was Nike's, my point man and lead sniper from Bravo platoon. Since he is dead now, I will tell you this: his real name is Mike Tatham. He was my buddy, and he saved my life countless times. I will not go to another funeral. I want to live long enough so that none of my friends have to go to my funeral, and I don't want to be buried in the ground. Please take my ashes to Louisa Falls in Canada.

I ain't dead yet, though. Until that time actually happens, I want to spend all of my energies helping my children grow and teaching them all to live the Adamantine Life that I have described in this book, *Unbreakable*.

I would like to recapture the thirteen lessons and tell you all why they are so important.

An Adamantine Life, or an Unbreakable Life, really means understanding the human performance. You already are performing perfectly. It already exists and has evolved, adapted, evolved, and will continue to do so, and that is the way we all function.

The Human performance has a basic structure to it. Each one will be very easily recognized. Let me lay them out for you in no particular order, although some order of value and precedence may exist. After twenty-five years of honing and mastering each one, I can say definitely that the order we put them in makes no difference.

I like to use the image of the five inverted pyramids. An inverted pyramid visually represents how a small thought or idea grows from something that did not exist at all to something later that actually exists, has a big base, and affects more than the originator.

I want you to imagine the five inverted pyramids of human performance. One will be identified as mastering of the Body. Another will be mastering of Intellect. The third will be mastering of Spirituality, and yet another is the mastery of Wealth. And finally, the mastery of Relationships. I am sure we could debate on the names and categories, yet in any and every human endeavor regarding performance, these five pyramids become the universal components. Now I want you to imagine the five pyramids are in a circle and an invisible string is connecting each pyramid to a center point, or perhaps a web.

Take a second and look briefly at how you personally grope with mastering these five pyramids. Take, for instance, your body. Notice the way it looks, what it feels like, how it performs, or doesn't perform in some cases. I just want you to notice that. Run through that same brief noticing with the other four pyramids. With Wealth, notice what you invest in, how you spend your money, how much money you have saved up, and notice your debt. Just notice it. Notice as well your level of spiritual mastery in whatever religion you hold for yourself. Notice then the current situation we find ourselves in with becoming masters of intellectual achievements. Notice many others whom either you know or have heard about, who have attained some very serious high levels of intellect informally. Finally, identify where you are regarding relationships, which can be teams you are on, groups you participate in, and even romantic relationships.

I want you to notice you are at various levels. I ask you simply notice you have some degree of mastery in each and that those around you have other degrees of mastery.

Now I want to tell you a story of human performance. In the world of Navy SEALs, we constantly seek very high levels of performance in each category. Maybe not wealth in the aspect of becoming rich, but to a certain degree, we handle, develop and control money and material and have mastered some aspect of wealth. The actual mastery of making money and having material wealth is only one part of mastering wealth.

Yet in the other three prominent pyramids we are recognized as masters. And for the sake of this discussion, we have sought to constantly improve on relationship, physical, and intellectual abilities and performance and have achieved some very serious high levels. Right now as you read this, I can tell you that somewhere on this planet, SEALS are pushing the boundaries of those three pyramids well beyond what you would even think possible. I have seen SEALS band together as a team and overcome the most hellish conditions simply because of their mastery of relationships. I have witnessed SEALs physically achieve impossible feats because of the constant pushing of his own physical boundaries. And as you can guess, I have witnessed SEALs use their intellect and smarts to create and recall things that far surpass normal human ability.

Finally, for the sake of this conversation on the human performance in an Adamantine life, I will merely say men and women across the globe are clearly masters of spirituality—from the Yogis and the Buddhist monks, to the Catholic priests and the preachers. Many others have attained spirituality in a cave all by themselves.

We have a six-month course for our own SEAL growth called Basic Underwater Demolitions School. This is our entry point for discovering what it takes to push beyond our previous limitations and produce extraordinary results. This brings me to the point of my initial tale. We have a very high attrition rate. We only graduate 15 percent. I want to share with you the broader discussion of why that is the case and how what we have found actually will have an immediate effect on you, your own life, and your performance no matter what you are up to.

In the attempt to discover the answer, we looked at improving the gear we use to get the jobs done in an efficient and productive way. We bought better shoes and chaffing guard, because your performance is dramatically affected when your legs, feet, and armpits are bleeding from chaffing.

We spent monies improving the teaching ability of the instructors and enhanced the curriculum. We bought high quality tables, chairs, computers, and screens. Our staff and facilities are now state of the art, as is our equipment.

Our latest effort was to screen our applicants more thoroughly to weed out the ones we thought would not make it prior to starting. We also spent millions on a pre-training workout program that we thought would make the men physically harder and more resistant to injury.

We implemented all these reasonable improvements that MIT, top business schools, and human performance labs had recommended.

What we found in our effort to make SEALs better was that this invisible string between the five pyramids was actually where every level of human performance starts and stops. I want you to notice that your Internal Dialogue is already and always working before, during, and after everything you do.

So, here is what we found:

None of the "stuff" we did, bought, or paid for made any significant difference to the attrition rate. We all were dumbfounded. This is also what most corporations do. This is what we all do; I think, don't you? We spend all of our efforts trying to adjust the outside world or influences in the hope that our personal performance, and maybe our lives, improve.

It's sort of analogous to buying a better car, clothes, and getting on another diet or workout routine. We must realize our own Internal Dialogue didn't shift, so the same results continue to happen again, again, and again.

Mastering the five pyramids of human performance and grasping your Internal Dialogue actually bridges the gap between who you were to your goals. That bridge will make all the difference. Ultimately, the only thing that makes any significant difference is what we all actually DO— our results and our performance. The only way to alter our performance is to expose and then master our Internal Dialogue.

I began to look at each SEAL's Internal Dialogue—what he was saying to himself about himself or his environment, whether he quit or succeeded. The biggest point is that they all had an Internal Dialogue. Your Internal Dialogue is running twenty-four hours a day, can you believe it?

Take a second now, stop, and either close your eyes or keep them open: I want you to get the first taste of your Internal Dialogue. Ready . . . go.

First notice if you are saying anything to yourself. Notice that you may even say, "No, I don't have an Internal Dialogue." Well, that is still an Internal Dialogue.

Here is what I found: Internal Dialogue runs the show—It *runs the show*. You dress the way you do because of it. You go to school because of it. You stay up late studying because of it; well, some of you do. And those who don't, don't because of it. And you didn't even know it was there!

More importantly, you didn't think you had any control over it. Let me tell you, you do; it is yours, and it is actually the only thing you do have control of in this life. And, it controls everything.

I want you to go back and remember you have these five pyramids of the human performance in your Unbreakable Life. In the beginning, you took notice of your body, wealth, intellect, spirituality, and relationships. That noticing is the surface of your Internal Dialogue. The manifestation of that is how you look, your grades, your boyfriend, your religion, and how much money you have either in your pocket or in someone else's.

In the process of moving through Adamantine Lesson One, you will have pushed through the most subtle human performance test known to man. The experience is not to get in shape, although it is a great by-product to be sure. The lesson is to get you truly in touch with your Internal Dialogue. Without knowing you had one in the first place, you will have experienced how subversive and counterproductive self-talk is. Internal Dialogue is not self-talk. Self-talk is what is on the surface to protect you from exposing your Internal Dialogue. My first gift to you is *keeping your word* by mastering your Internal Dialogue.

In Adamantine Lesson Two, I wanted you to encounter fear. Fear is nothing more than an Internal Dialogue that stops you from acting. The second gift of an Unbreakable Life is *owning fear* and adjusting your Internal Dialogue to take action.

With Adamantine Lesson Three, you master the body, your physical abilities. I wanted you to experience true exhaustion, pain, and maybe being sick in the effort. In facing exhaustion, pain, and sickness, you may have had to start over in order to meet the goal. I want you to experience what your Internal Dialogue was and said about it all, and what you did when your Internal Dialogue was yelling at you to stop. The third gift of an Unbreakable Life is to have experienced *being broken, rebuilding, and doing it again*, reshaping your Internal Dialogue to do it until it is complete no matter the cost to your body.

While in Adamantine Lesson Four, you will master not only relationships, but you will also notice and feel what your Internal Dialogue has to say about it all. A distinct difference exists between urgent attraction that comes on you like a freight train and the relationship you create using your Internal Dialogue. Relationships need to be created anew every second of every day for the rest of your life. If you don't create it using Internal Dialogue, it dies. The pivotal point in the path of an Unbreakable Life is to *create love* using your Internal Dialogue.

Adamantine Lesson Five is my discussion about *mastering spirituality*. Hope and faith are not spirituality. As you looked into and experienced those words and when they are used, you will have noticed how desperately not in action you were when you used them. If your Internal Dialogue is not mastered in some way prior to Adamantine Lesson Five, you will have gotten disillusioned. I suggest spiritual people do not use hope and faith because true spiritual people don't need faith—they know. They will not have hope because they are relentlessly pursuing their convictions. An Adamantine life is Unbreakable because mastering your own Internal Dialogue and reshaping it away from hope and faith enables you to know and relentlessly act on that connection to a divine power.

Tackling Adamantine Lesson Six may have felt absurd. Yet, your *point of view* regarding everything is shaped by you, and you alone. And that reshaping only comes from mastering your Internal Dialogue. Your performance in everything is relative to your points of view. That point of view can, and will, change, and so must your Internal Dialogue. Battles are immediately shifted as your point of view shifts. Don't let the environment dictate your point of view; instead, shape your point of view with the masterful stroke of your Internal Dialogue. You will have an Unbreakable Life.

Adamantine Lesson Seven is partly a relationship idea, yet mastering *connecting your efforts to the efforts of others* is key to the human performance. While working with others, you will have noticed how you affect them, and them, you. That connection effect is filtered through your Internal Dialogue and theirs. If you notice another's effort is not working, don't look to change them. Instead, look to reshape your Internal Dialogue preventing you from connecting to them. This is a great gift, but I have to admit, it is fucking hard as hell. I have to work on it all the time. I suck at it, to be honest, and I know it is all in my own Internal Dialogue, not in their actions. Because my actions come from my Internal Dialogue.

The *Mentors and Masters* Adamantine Lesson may come early or later in life. You will not notice it until you have mastered your Internal Dialogue. Once you master it, you will see everyone around you is very willing to help. It took me forty-four years. OK, I am a slow learner.

Adamantine Lesson Nine for me comes easy. My Internal Dialogue is always to never give up. It is the loudest thing in my head. I thought for the longest time I was born with it. Yet, as I have learned how Internal Dialogue really works, I know that is a crutch to think you are born with something. In reality, you shape and evolve. However, learn to listen to your own Internal Dialogue and learn to be relentless. The ninth gift of an Unbreakable Life is to tell yourself to *NEVER give up. Never.*

Adamantine Lesson Ten is *a game*, and by the time you get to mastering your Internal Dialogue, you will be ready for this game. Most people are terribly affected by their environments—weather, people, and everything external to them. We all are, yet cold is cold. Cold is neither bad nor good. What most people don't realize is they are giving meaning to their environment, thus living a life that is totally shaped by their outside world. Here is how you will know you have mastered your own Internal Dialogue: when it is raining outside and you're tired and want to stay inside because you hate the cold and hate being wet, I want you to say to yourself, "God I so love the rain; it makes me feel energetic, and I love the way the coldness seeps into my bones. I feel so alive." Then, go out and take action on that new Internal Dialogue.

Adamantine Lesson Eleven is a tough nut to crack, so to speak. It is *encountering death*. It is seeing what death does to your Internal Dialogue, yet not letting it shape it in any lasting way. Death will scream for a lasting Internal Dialogue. You will have to master not death itself, but master your Internal Dialogue *about* death. Allow yourself to pass through both the sadness and the anger, and the way it makes you perform. At the end, see death merely as a passing, then move on. It is not calloused, nor unfeeling. One of the greatest gifts is to feel and to move on. Holding on is a disease of the weak mind.

Adamantine Lesson Twelve is something for later in life, I think. *Being a contribution and being contributed to* are two distinctly different actions that have two very unique Internal Dialogues. I have personally had the hardest time with others contributing anything to me. Rather, my Internal Dialogue here is very hard for me to get a grip on and reshape. Praise in the form of a contribution screams loudly in my ears, when I say to myself, "I did nothing to deserve this praise. I was merely keeping myself from dying and keeping my teammates alive." When I received the Silver Star and the Bronze Star for stuff I did in "hell," I struggled. When Jerry and Tammy put on the SEAL Gala in South Carolina because they wanted to contribute to the SEAL Teams and to Bravo platoon, I felt awkward. I am working on this, and I pray my family can help me work on it, too.

Finally, Adamantine Lesson Thirteen is the masterful stroke of genius. I recognize I have yet to talk about this particular one until now.

ADAMANTINE LESSON THIRTEEN

Moving on in the midst of hanging on

The past and all the things that happened to you, and even the past of others, is only carried forward in Internal Dialogue. It only lives there. Deal with it when it comes up and affects your and other people's actions. But, recognize it as an impostor. You are not your past achievements or failings, nor are other people. Clean that shit up fast and create an Internal Dialogue that gives you access to this moment. Remember, each moment is always being shaped and reshaped by Internal Dialogue. Be cautious, because if you are not shaping this moment, someone else may be.

An Adamantine, Unbreakable Life sounds like: I AM . . . fill in the blank, and hold on for the ride of your life. It is your life, you know!

Acknowledgements

Writing down the thoughts of war and love and family in a meaningful way is equally as hard as making it through BUD/S and combat. The experience is real, is frustrating, and is time consuming. I literally quit 100 times and got back up and started over due to the support and advice and love from a great many people.

This whole project started out like most successful things over a beer with a friend at a shooting resort called The Site in Chicago. Jerry Barber and I had talked about writing a "collective efforts" of the things we had learned in our lives. Without Jerry there would never have been the deep NEED to go back and share. Oddly enough the first effort started out with the title of *Spartan Wife*. I leave that for Stacy to write.

Without Stacy *Unbreakable* would have broken and died and quite simply never even started. In Stacy's Internal Dialogue *Unbreakable* was born. Autumn, Garrett, and Chance did not even know what I was doing because the writing of *Unbreakable* happened at night, and in the daytime watching them live, I was inspired once again to continue.

My close friend Bret Anderson read a section and connected me to my publisher, Larry Carpenter at Carpenter's Son Publishing, and my editor, Lorraine Bossé-Smith. They either took pity on me or "got it" and converted a manuscript written in crayon and blood. I don't know how they made sense of it all with every other word being a curse word.

There is an old saying, "if you build it, he will come." Well that saying is not true in any sense of any word. No one came—there was no market, no platform, nothing—until Meg McAllister read the edited book and literally risked her perfect reputation on *Unbreakable*.

To my close friends: John Arnold, who demands authenticity; Doug Kim, who was hard to convince; and finally, Stecker, who, like me, is insatiable.

Finally, to every Navy SEAL that ever was, is, or will be; and to Bravo platoon and SEAL Team Seven.

You all are Unbreakable.